The Heart of the Gospel

Princeton Theological Monograph Series

K. C. Hanson, Charles M. Collier, and D. Christopher Spinks,
Series Editors

Recent volumes in the series:

Philip Ruge-Jones
*Cross in Tensions: Luther's Theology of the Cross
as Theologico-social Critique*

Charles Bellinger
The Trinitarian Self: The Key to the Puzzle of Violence

Michael S. Hogue
*The Tangled Bank: Toward an Ecotheological Ethics
of Responsible Participation*

Linden J. DeBie
*Speculative Theology and Common-Sense Religion: Mercersburg
and the Conservative Roots of American Religion*

Kevin Twain Lowery
Salvaging Wesley's Agenda: A New Paradigm for Wesleyan Virtue Ethics

Steven B. Sherman
*Revitalizing Theological Epistemology: Holistic Evangelical Approaches
to the Knowledge of God*

Ronald F. Satta
The Sacred Text: Biblical Authority in Nineteenth-Century America

Christian T. Collins Winn
*"Jesus is Victor!": The Significance of the Blumhardts
for the Theology of Karl Barth*

The Heart of the Gospel

A. B. Simpson, the Fourfold Gospel,
and Late Nineteenth-Century Evangelical Theology

BERNIE A. VAN DE WALLE

☞PICKWICK *Publications* · Eugene, Oregon

THE HEART OF THE GOSPEL
A. B. Simpson, the Fourfold Gospel, and Late Nineteenth-Century Evangelical
Theology

Princeton Theological Monograph Series 106

Pickwick Publications
A Division of Wipf and Stock Publishers
199 W. 8th Ave., Suite 3
Eugene, OR 97401

www.wipfandstock.com

ISBN 13: 978-1-4982-5147-1

Cataloging-in-Publication data:

Van De Walle, Bernie A.
    The heart of the gospel : A. B. Simpson, the fourfold gospel, and late
    nineteenth-century evangelical theology / Bernie A. Van De Walle; Foreword
    by Donald W. Dayton.

    xviii + 210 p. ; 23 cm. — Includes bibliographical references.

    Princeton Theological Monograph Series 106

    ISBN 13: 978-1-4982-5147-1

    1. Simpson, A. B. (Albert B.). 2. Christian and Missionary Alliance—
History. 3. Christian and Missionary Alliance—Doctrines. 4. Pentecostalism—
History. 5. Dayton, Donald W. I. Title. II. Series.

BX6700.Z8 S57 2009

Manufactured in the U.S.A.

For Colleen, Dave, and Ken

Contents

Foreword

It was a pleasure to get to know Bernie Van De Walle when he condescended to come down from Canada for his doctoral studies at Drew University (Madison, New Jersey). It was an honor for me to chair his dissertation committee. I remember fondly a trip to New York to visit the Times Square site of the "Gospel Tabernacle" (founded by A. B. Simpson and the fountainhead of the Christian and Missionary Alliance) and the shock to Bernie to discover that it is now John's Pizza, and that the church balcony is now a full bar. We also visited, merely two blocks away, the church (now the Westside Theatre—then presenting *The Vagina Monologues*!) served by the key figure of the Social Gospel movement, Walter Rauschenbusch. Among other things, we pondered seriously whether Simpson's church had at the time the more vital and complex social ministry. It is now again an honor (perhaps a "second blessing"—in the language of the Holiness Movement that plays an important role in this book) to be asked to introduce his work in published form. This I am delighted to do.

Since his doctoral work, Bernie has become a colleague and friend. We see each other in various academic and church meetings. If you know Bernie, you probably know of his strange hobby of visiting the graves of the famous, particularly the religious famous. When we meet, he has a list of graves to visit. On the East Coast (especially Brooklyn) we tracked down the graves of several figures of the Holiness Movement, including ones that play a role in this book. On the West Coast we have visited the graves of several Holiness and Pentecostal figures—and also such Hollywood icons as Rudolph Valentino, Cecil B. DeMille, George Reeves of *Superman* fame, as well as others that do not play a role in this book. In the process we have made some interesting discoveries. Few seem to be aware of the fact that Charles Fuller, founder of Fuller Theological Seminary, is buried in a plot that ironically carries the number 666. At this news one Fuller faculty member threw his hands in the air and exclaimed that this might require a rethinking of his eschatology!

This book is an exposition of the theology of A. B. Simpson in terms of the "fourfold gospel" he preached and made famous far beyond the bounds of the Christian and Missionary Alliance. As such, it is the most useful exposition of his theology that I know. Bernie achieves this by a careful comparison and contrast with others figures and peers of the period (A. J. Gordon, William Boardman, A. T. Pierson, R. A. Torrey, et al.). This method allows Bernie to make clear both the distinctive elements of Simpson's thought and permits us to see the continuities with his contemporaries in the late nineteenth century who emphasized the same four themes: Salvation, Sanctification, Physical Healing, and the Return of Christ. Bernie shows that Simpson's thought is a distillation and epitome of late nineteenth-century "evangelical" preaching and an excellent window into that world. Simpson is a somewhat neglected and understudied figure. In bringing this material to the fore, Bernie has served us well.

Furthermore I am convinced that his study has revolutionary implications for the study of modern "evangelicalism." The word "evangelical" is so imprecise that I have on occasion called for a moratorium on its use so that we would be forced to think more clearly about such matters by developing alternative terminologies. For some, as in the Evangelical Lutheran Church of America, "evangelical" refers to classical Protestantism (especially Luther, in German *Evangelisch*). Others, as in the recent five-volume history with InterVarsity Press, root "evangelicalism" in the eighteenth-century "Evangelical Revival"—so that historian Mark Noll of that project now says that "evangelicalism" did not exist before that century. More recently, in the mid twentieth century, a party of fundamentalists revived the word and called themselves "neo-evangelicals," though they soon dropped the prefix (Germans have appropriated the English to speak of these folk as *Evangelikalen* to distinguish them from classical Protestants or the later "Pietists" or advocates in the nineteenth century of the theology of the awakening movements). More recently, for the last quarter century, the word has taken on ideological connotations, especially in the media, where the New Religious Right has contributed to a usage that emphasizes a conservative political agenda. These are quite different phenomena that deserve to be distinguished; and intellectual confusions abound when this is not done.

One of the most significant of these confusions is the tendency to interpret the longer history of "evangelicalism" though the lens of the "fundamentalist/modernist controversy" of the 1920s, utilizing a "conservative/liberal" paradigm or spectrum of analysis. This confusion is multiplied often by the use of the conflicts in the Presbyterian Church that were focused in the split of Princeton Seminary and the formation of Westminster Seminary and the Orthodox Presbyterian Church. This way of reading the history has gradually, over the last few decades, unraveled for me—so much so that I have largely abandoned it and have been forced to develop alternative perspectives. I have been shaped more by the categories of the Methodist tradition, which was the most influential Protestant tradition in nineteenth-century North America. In that context one ponders the formation of the Holiness Movement and Pentecostalism as the paradigmatic subcultures to understand modern "evangelicalism," and notices that the vast majority of the denominational members of the National Association of Evangelicals (NAE) are drawn from these traditions.

Rather than using the Presbyterian categories to interpret the history of Methodism, I am more and more inclined to use the categories of Methodism to interpret Presbyterianism and the emergence of the modern "evangelical" subculture. I mean this quite seriously. The Presbyterian approach focuses on the 1920s, privileges the Orthodox Presbyterian Church (OPC) as the paradigmatic "evangelical" denomination, and elevates Professor J. Gresham Machen of Princeton and Westminster as the key figure. The Methodist reading of Presbyterian history directs attention to the late nineteenth century when Canadian Presbyterian A. B. Simpson, under the influence of a variety of Holiness currents, was led to the founding of "parachurch" movements that have coalesced into the Christian and Missionary Alliance (C&MA). I think that anyone with even the slightest acquaintance with modern "evangelicalism" would agree that the C&MA is much more central than the OPC to that stream of "evangelicalism" that finds expression in the NAE and parallel institutions.

If there is any truth in this historiographical reorientation, then the study of A. B. Simpson and the C&MA becomes the key to unlock many puzzles of the contemporary American scene. And if so, Bernie's study of Simpson gains an importance that transcends any denominational limitations that it might otherwise appear to have. As a faithful son of the C&MA now teaching theology and denominational heritage at Ambrose University College in Canada, Bernie takes primary interest is in a careful exposition of Simpson's thought. But he is not unaware of the wider implications of his work. Simpson's articulation of the "fourfold gospel," and Bernie's expounding of it, are extraordinarily useful for wider questions.

The first point, Jesus, Our Savior, reminds us that modern "evangelicalism" stands in the line of "modern revivalism." Its history and character should be told as a chapter in the history of modern revivalism that begins with the "evangelical revival" and traces though the line of such evangelists as Charles Grandison Finney, D. L. Moody, Billy Sunday, and in our own time Billy Graham. This is the line in which A. B. Simpson stood—a fact that regularly gets suppressed in the dominant Presbyterian (and fundamentalist/modernist) reading.

This point gains confirmation from an unusual source. Daryl Hart, who reflects the Westminster theological culture where he served on the faculty after writing a doctoral dissertation on J. Gresham Machen before a stint as director of the Institute for the Study of American Evangelicals (ISAE) at Wheaton College, increasingly sharply distinguishes these two movements. His book *Deconstructing Evangelicalism* is essentially a critique of the revivalist stream in favor of the "reformed confessionalism" that he and Westminster Seminary advocate. In other recent books, he has turned his attention to the interpretation and advocacy of "conservative Presbyterianism." These tensions surface, but are not given the attention they deserve, in George Marsden's history of Fuller Seminary, *Reforming Fundamentalism*, a study in the emergence of "neo-evangelicalism." Fuller was birthed out of the "Old Fashioned Revival Hour," the radio ministry of founder Charles Fuller. Is the history of Fuller a chapter in the history or revivalism a chapter in the history of Presbyterian orthodoxy—or the story of institution born in the former but over time gravitating toward the latter?

Bernie cites Horace Bushnell's classic book *Christian Nurture*. This book is often described as the fountainhead of American "liberal" theology. It is more precisely described as an attack on revivalism with its pressure on all to the crisis experience of being "born again" as Christians. Bushnell argued instead that children should be raised in the faith so that they would never know themselves not being Christian. Charles Hodge, that great defender of Presbyterian orthodoxy at Princeton for half a century, welcomed at least this major point of Bushnell, arguing that it was essentially that of "old-school Presbyterians," who on the basis of infant baptism and their "covenantal" understanding of the Christian life, took a similar position. This point helps one understand why Hodge's successor at Princeton, Benjamin B. Warfield, would often take on A. B. Simpson as a major object of his polemics in his essays against *Perfectionism and Counterfeit Miracles*.

Warfield's polemics bring us to the second point of the "four-fold gospel:" Jesus, Our Sanctifier. If one takes John Wesley as the paradigmatic figure of the "evangelical revival," this movement tended to take sanctification, rather than justification (as in the case of Luther) as the organizing principle of theology. Or, one may speak of a shift from "forensic" or courtroom metaphors (being declared righteous) to biological metaphors (regeneration or being "born again"). Methodism bequeathed to the nineteenth century a struggle over the nature of this "sanctification." In America this produced a great variety of "higher life" teachings that called Christians to a profounder expression of the Christian life. A radical wing of the Holiness Movement looked forward to a "second blessing" in which the sinful nature would be eradicated. Pentecostals would transform this into a second experience of the "baptism of the Holy Spirit." The revivalist tradition from Finney to Graham carried these themes in a more moderate form that expected a "suppression" of the sinful nature that would find expression in the "victorious Christian life." (Even Bill Bright's neo-evangelical student movement, Campus Crusade for Christ, passed out two pamphlets, one on conversion and another on being "filled with the Holy Spirit.") It is in this culture that we must interpret A. B. Simpson, who had, as Bernie suggests, one foot in the "Holiness" side and one foot in the more moderate forms of the revivalist tradition.

This theme pervades modern "evangelicalism" and comes close to being defining of the subculture. One might say that "evangelicals," historically at least, have been the sort of people who read devotionally such books as Hannah Whitall Smith's *The Christian's Secret of a Happy Life*, Lettie Cowman's *Stream in the Desert*, or (with President George Bush!) Oswald Chambers' *My Utmost for His Highest*. These are the sort of books that one is likely to receive as premiums after contributions to ministries as diverse as "fundamentalist" Jerry Falwell and "charismatic Baptist" Pat Robertson. And again, figures of this sort are those that would loom large in the polemics of B. B. Warfield—along with A. B. Simpson.

The third theme of "divine" healing or "faith healing" (of which Simpson was the major advocate in the late nineteenth century) was perhaps less universally emphasized. This teaching had European roots in late Pietism but was first sharply articulated by Holiness Episcopalian Charles Cullis, the teacher of Simpson. In some circles this theme has been suppressed—so that some C&MA pastors I have known are shocked to discover Simpson's reputation in this area and his early radical polemics against the use of medical "means." But the theme is present not only in many wings of the Holiness Movement, but almost universally in Pentecostal and Charismatic circles—and again becomes much more useful in defining the boundaries of modern "evangelical-ism" than many other proposals.

This doctrine is also another useful reminder of the extent to which "evangelicalism" is better understood as "protest" against classical Protestantism than its perpetuation, as in the case of "reformed ortho-doxy." And again, we should remind ourselves of the polemics of the Princeton theologians against these teachings so much at the core of Simpson's understanding of the gospel.

The final theme of the "four-fold gospel" is Jesus, Our "Coming King"—the emphasis on the return of Christ that dominates most forms of "evangelicalism." Again, the motif is almost universal and much more defining than other proposals such as the view of Scripture. "Evangelicalism" is the sort of movement that cannot be understood apart from questions of eschatology and millennialism—from its politi-cal support of Israel to its fascination with the Left Behind novels of our own time. Simpson's articulation is a useful reminder of the centrality of this issue.

Interestingly, this theme has been suppressed in much contempo-rary "evangelical" historiography. In 1970 Earnest Sandeen published his University of Chicago dissertation as *Roots of Fundamentalism*. This was a product of his struggle to understand theologically what he had expe-rienced as an undergraduate at neo-evangelical icon Wheaton College. He expounded this experience in terms of the history of the rise in the nineteenth century of dispensational premillennialism, which then required the near-dictation theory of biblical inspiration being defended at Princeton. "Neo-evangelical" historiography has not been as receptive to this perspective as has that of "continuing fundamentalists."

As I have worked my way through the sources, I have become increasingly an advocate of the work of Sandeen. I am now convinced that the fundamentalist/modernist controversy was in many ways essentially a struggle over the worldview of dispensationalism. This cannot be argued in detail here, but a few indications might be useful. Nearly every issue of the conflict is illuminated by eschatology. Early attacks on the "ecumenical movement" (such as the InterChurch World Movement) were motivated by the conviction that it was "postmillennial" in tendency because it tried to raise money to rebuild the infrastructure of Europe after the bombing of World War I. The curricula of the Bible Schools (Simpson's Nyack College was an early archetype of these schools), in their abbreviated form and rejection of the disciplines of the "liberal arts," reflect this world view (postmillennial evangelists founded universities and liberal arts colleges like Oberlin and early Wheaton). Even the anti-evolution campaigns are to great extent dependent, as in W. B. Riley's *Daniel vs. Darwin*, on an eschatology of "decline" (required also by modern creationists). Such illustrations could be multiplied, but the point is that "evangelicalism" must be interpreted in light of eschatology—and A. B. Simpson's formulation makes it difficult to do otherwise.

Bernie points out the extent to which this fourfold pattern dominates what have become the major centers of modern "evangelicalism"— from those in the wake of the work of A. J. Gordon in Boston through R. A. Torrey at Chicago's Moody Bible Institute and elsewhere. Bernie could have emphasized the extension of this orientation to Southern California as Torrey moved west to the Bible Institute of Los Angeles (now Biola University). The pattern appears in the Pentecostal version of the Foursquare Gospel of Aimee Semple McPherson, reflected in most forms of Pentecostalism. I remember a paper of Joel Carpenter, then-director of the ISAE at Wheaton College, that expounded the late nineteenth-century missionary culture in terms of the revivalist call to conversion, the search for the "higher Christian life," and the expectation of the imminence of the return of Christ. I have also been fascinated with the Doug Frank's book *Less than Conquerors*, which attempts to describe the culture of early twentieth-century "evangelicalism. The book is essentially a critique (under the influence of such figures as Jacques Ellul) of the Evangelical Free Church tradition in which he was reared. In part because he has less apologetic interest in defending the tradition, he can be "franker" about its character, and centers his critique on the culture of revivalism, the victorious Christian life tradition.

I have also found Simpson's formulation of the "four-fold" gospel for the interpretation of "evangelicalism" in other cultures. Korean Christianity, for example, reveals the deep impress of these themes. The two sizeable Holiness denominations take the "four-fold" gospel as normative (one university has named its four major buildings after the four motif). Korean Pentecostalism has in some cases revised the "four-square" pattern but still reveals that it is struggling with this paradigm. The surprise for me was to find the fourfold pattern also in Korean Presbyterianism. I was teaching in a Pentecostal university and would ask, as we considered each theme, if the Presbyterians in Korea were revivalist, taught a second experience of being filled with the Spirit, held healing services in their churches, and were basically dispensationalist in orientation. At each point I received an affirmative answer and was encouraged by this experience to later teach a seminar on Korean Christianity at Drew University that used the "four-fold gospel" as a general hermeneutic.

It is for such reasons that I welcome Bernie's study of Simpson in its published form. I commend it to you not only as a very useful study of A. B. Simpson and his context, but also because I believe that it provides useful clues for the interpretation of broader "evangelical" currents.

—Donald W. Dayton
Pasadena, California
May 2008

Acknowledgements

A WORK OF THIS TYPE IS NEVER COMPLETED ON ONE'S OWN. I WOULD like to thank the faculty, staff, administration, and Board of Ambrose University College and Seminary, who have provided me with the time and resources to pursue and complete this project. In particular, I would like to thank Sandy Ayer, Co-director of the Archibald-Thomson Library and his former archival assistant, Carol Petkau, for the invaluable help they gave me in delving the depths of the Archibald-Thomson Special Collections.

Further thanks go to my dear friends Dr. Andy Reimer and Barry Holtslander (and in later stages, Sandy Ayer), who, to varying degrees, gave helpful advice and assistance in the writing and editing process. I am also grateful to my teaching assistants over the past few years, Charity Quick, Tara Robertson, Ben Platz, and Chris Smith, who helped this project along in numerous ways. Rev. A. Barry Bruce and the people of Heritage Alliance Church in Regina, Saskatchewan are to be commended for having provided me a quiet and private place to concentrate and work. My mentors, Drs. Balmer, Dayton, Irvin, and Oden, true to the gentlemen scholars they are, have always been both gracious and helpful.

My parents, Raymond and Nellie Van De Walle, modeled those characteristics which are needed to undertake this kind of project: the value of hard work, tenacity, honor, and family. My wife's parents, Albert and Jean Lutzer, were also a constant source of support. Finally, I must express my gratitude to my wife, Colleen, and my sons, Dave and Ken, for the many personal sacrifices that they have made in order to allow me to pursue the completion of this project. I will always be in their debt and they will always be the best of my treasures.

The Legacy of Albert Benjamin Simpson

ALBERT BENJAMIN SIMPSON WAS BORN IN CAVENDISH, PRINCE EDWARD
Island, in December 1843, to staunch Scottish Presbyterian parents. As a
result of a series of traumatic personal events, including grave illness, he
dedicated his life to ministry and to the pursuit of holiness early in life. In
October 1861, young Albert enrolled at Knox College at the University
of Toronto, the leading seminary of Canadian Presbyterianism,[1] with
the blessing of his family but without their financial support. Simpson
excelled at his studies, winning prizes for papers defending the historic Calvinism of the denomination. Upon graduation in 1865, he
began his service as the pastor of Canada's second-largest Presbyterian
church, Knox Church in Hamilton, Ontario. During his ministry there,
church attendance more than doubled "from 297 to 646."[2] Simpson left
Hamilton in 1874 to become the minister of a large Presbyterian church
in Louisville, Kentucky, where he saw "the same gratifying results he
had known in Hamilton."[3] In 1879 he moved to the bustling and rapidly
expanding metropolis of New York City to take up what would be his
last Presbyterian charge. It was in New York City that Simpson would
achieve his greatest success, but it would not come as a Presbyterian
minister. Indeed, he left the Presbyterian Church in 1881, having come
to doubt the very doctrines that he had so staunchly and ably defended

---

1. In *The Evangelical Movement*, Mark Ellingsen mentions that Simpson received
his seminary training in Princeton, even though all of Simpson's biographies give
lengthy accounts of his student days at Knox, about which a fair amount is known.
In the same work, Ellingsen incorrectly gives 1844 as the year of Simpson's birth
(Ellingsen, *Evangelical Movement*, 142).

2. Niklaus et al., *All for Jesus*, 30.

3. Ibid., 33.

while a student. He went on to found a movement that would become his corporate legacy—The Christian and Missionary Alliance.[4]

Denominational Founder

Simpson never intended to start a new denomination: the C&MA simply came into being as the practical institutional outworking of his newfound convictions. He began, in fact, by establishing two fraternal parachurch organizations: the Christian Alliance, to support and encourage the "Deeper Christian Life"; and the Evangelical Missionary Alliance, to promote the evangelization of the world.[5] He believed that any move to denominationalism or sectarianism would short-circuit the very purpose of these Alliances, as is evident from the following extract from one of his editorials.

> One of the greatest dangers in the Alliance movement is to isolate ourselves from the great currents of Christian thought and life among the churches by getting into exclusive circles and trying to build up a petty work which scarcely differs in its spirit from a sectarian movement. While in many cases a local work requires to be organized and maintained as a mission or an independent church, let us always be careful to avoid the mistake of representing this as an Alliance church or antagonizing other churches or pastors. God has called us in this work to an interdenominational mission and has a message through us for all his people.[6]

The very name "Alliance" gives an indication of the nature of the organizations Simpson sought to develop. He did not try to found another denomination or to steal away people from existing churches. Rather he simply wanted to bring together Christians "of whatsoever evangelical name"[7] who were longing to experience the Christian life more deeply. This fraternal union that would become the C&MA was to supplement, not replace, the work of legitimate evangelical churches. He sought to found "not an ecclesiastical body, but a fraternal body of believers, in

---

4. Henceforth and popularly called either the Alliance or the C&MA.

5 In 1897, ten years after their original inception, these two would come together to form what is now known as the Christian and Missionary Alliance.

6. Simpson, "Editorial," 8 February 1913, 289.

7. Christian and Missionary Alliance, *Annual Report* (1912), 39.

cordial harmony with Christians of every name."[8] He did not despise denominations but felt that they were not meeting all of the church's needs. "There is no antagonism whatever in the Alliance to any of the evangelical churches," he insisted, "but a desire to help them in every proper way, and to promote the interests of Christ's kingdom in connection with every proper Christian organization and work."[9] Simpson always conceived of the Alliance as a partner and not a competitor with the denominations in the fulfilling of the Great Commission.

> The two societies which were afterwards merged into The Christian and Missionary Alliance were organized at Old Orchard, Maine, in the summer of 1887, for the purpose of uniting in Christian fellowship and testimony, in a purely fraternal alliance, the large number of consecrated Christians in the various evangelical churches, who believe in the Lord Jesus as Saviour, Sanctifier, Healer and coming Lord, and also of uniting their efforts in the special aggressive work of word-wide evangelization.[10]

For this reason, under the leadership of Simpson, the Alliances never sought to become denominations in their own right.

Simpson's own vision was not that the denominations would be left behind by the popularity and "righteousness" of the Alliances, but that through the invigorating influence of the Alliances, the ministry

8. Christian Alliance, *Christian Alliance Yearbook* (1888), 48.

9. Simpson, *Story of the Christian and Missionary Alliance*, 6.

10. In later years, the attitude and goals remained the same. "The objects sought by this Society include the following:

> 1. To promote unity of faith in the Lord Jesus in His fullness, earnest effort for the conversion of souls, and the deepening of the spiritual life of Christians everywhere, by means of teaching and testimony in the power of the Holy Spirit, without reference to ecclesiastical uniformity, but in cordial sympathy with all evangelical Christians or organizations.

> 2. That Christians in a given locality, in sympathy with the truths for which the Alliance stands, but of different church affiliations, may be afforded fellowship with one another and with the larger association of kindred believers, without affecting their denominational relations, may be stimulated as loyal witnesses to Jesus Christ and His fullness, and may have a common channel for voluntary cooperation in world-wide full gospel efforts. (Christian and Missionary Alliance, *Annual Report* [1912], 39–40).

of the denominations themselves would flourish. Simpson describes this anticipated animating influence as "the most significant feature of the . . . work," for it stimulates "faith in God and earnest aggressive work for our fellowmen among other Christian organizations as well as individuals."[11]

In order to foster this ecumenical and cooperative spirit, the regulations for membership in the first group—the Christian Alliance—were quite open. One needed only to hold to the evangelical essentials[12] and the "Fourfold Gospel" as taught by Simpson and the Alliance.[13] Both

11. Originally a paper read at the Quarter Centennial of the Gospel Tabernacle Church, New York, Feb. 11, 1907. Simpson, "Story of Providence," 164.

12. While issues of activity and piety may have played a role in defining what it meant to be evangelical, in defining themselves as evangelicals, Simpson, the Christian Alliance, and the Evangelical (International) Missionary Alliance did so primarily on doctrinal grounds. This can be seen in their reply to the question "Is the Christian Alliance an Evangelical Body?" In answering in the affirmative, they compared themselves doctrinally with the Evangelical Alliance. The doctrinal stance of the Evangelical Alliance, founded in London in 1846, and of the Evangelical Alliance in the United States, founded in 1867, was seen by Simpson and his lieutenants as the prototype of what it meant to be truly evangelical. The founding doctrinal statement of the Evangelical Alliance asserted such teachings as the inspiration and authority of Scriptures, the Trinitarian nature of God, the Incarnation, the Atonement, the immortality of the human soul, and eternal reward or punishment. These and other doctrinal assertions, the C&MA took as its own. In defining its own doctrinal stance, the Evangelical (International) Missionary Alliance declared, "[We] believe in God the Father, God the Son, and God the Holy Ghost, in the verbal inspiration of the Holy Scriptures as originally given, in the vicarious atonement of the Lord Jesus Christ, in the eternal salvation of all who believe in Him, and the everlasting punishment of all who reject Him." The only thing that they believed distinguished them from the Evangelical Alliance was their special emphasis on the Fourfold Gospel, and they did not feel that these distinctive teachings were in conflict with evangelical theology. Simpson, "Is the Christian Alliance an Evangelical Body?" 274. For more on the doctrinal views of the early Evangelical Alliance, see Randall and Hilborn, One Body in Christ, 358–59. For an investigation of the Evangelical Alliance's impact in America see Jordan, Evangelical Alliance for the United States of America, 1847–1900.

13. Doctrinally, the Alliance was "founded on the especial basis of the Fourfold Gospel. . . . In other respects, and with reference to all other doctrines not expressed in the Fourfold Gospel, its attitude is strictly evangelical, holding most firmly to the verbal inspiration of the Holy Scriptures, the doctrine of the Trinity, the atoning sacrifice of the Lord Jesus Christ, and the necessity of the regenerating and sanctifying work of the Holy Ghost" (Simpson, Story of the Christian and Missionary Alliance, 6). Still Simpson and the Alliance were sufficiently open to other views to allow members to fudge on the premillennial aspect of the Fourfold Gospel (Coming King). On this aspect, members had only to be "willing to give [premillennialism] their candid and prayerful consideration" (Christian Alliance, Christian Alliance Yearbook [1888], 50).

the early leadership of the Alliance and those invited to speak at its Tabernacle, conventions, and classes reflect the ecumenical diversity for which Simpson hoped. Many of Simpson's closest confidants within the Alliance did not share his Presbyterian background, nor did he insist that they must. Frederic Farr, who served as Dean of the Missionary Training Institute and as a member of the Board of Managers, was an ordained Baptist minister; William MacArthur, one of Simpson's closest friends and partners was also a Baptist; William Fenton, the inaugural vice president of the Evangelical Missionary Alliance, had Brethren ties; Albert Funk, a Mennonite minister, was the first secretary of the Alliance's Foreign Department and also became superintendent of the Institute; George Pardington, the Alliance's first professional theologian, received his degree from Drew Theological School (a Methodist institution), was the son of a Methodist minister, and was a Methodist minister himself for a time; Henry Wilson, an Episcopal priest, was especially close to Simpson, and the two would often participate together in services, with Simpson preaching and Wilson serving the Eucharist; finally, Paul Rader, who succeeded Simpson as president, was the son of a Methodist minister and he himself served for awhile as a Congregationalist minister.[14]

The guest speakers who supplied Alliance pulpits also reflected this denominational diversity. They represented a "Who's Who" of late nineteenth-century evangelicalism and included such luminaries as H. Gratton Guinness, J. Hudson Taylor, F. B. Meyer, Andrew Murray, C. I. Scofield, A. J. Gordon, A. T. Pierson, and George F. Pentecost. Although none of them ever made the Alliance his primary home, they shared the passion and priorities of Simpson and the Alliance. Simpson, in turn, spoke at many of their meetings.

The second group—the Evangelical Missionary Alliance—also sought to "be universal," to have "catholic and unsectarian" character and spirit, "and . . . to unite Christians of all evangelical denominations" in the promulgation of the gospel.[15] Given its ecumenical outlook, the Evangelical Missionary Alliance also tried to draw resources and support from wherever they might suitably come. Moreover, it sent eligible

14. Niklaus et al., *All for Jesus*, 257–76.
15. Simpson, "New Missionary Alliance," 365.

missionaries "without regard to their denominational preferences."[16] These missionaries were not to import their own denominational prejudices and "bigotries" into the fields they served. The only ecclesiastical regulations that the Alliance professed to enforce were those that were "in harmony with [broader] evangelical truth."[17] Simpson regarded denominational prejudices and hostilities as a blemish upon the church and not as required essentials for new, naïve, and innocent congregations. Rather he and his colleagues felt that

> the undenominational principle is the most satisfactory and adjustable by far in heathen lands, and surely most in accordance with the highest principles of Christianity. The devoted churchman cannot wish to fasten on the simple minds of people the old bigotries of our unfortunate divisions, and the tendency in all missionary lands is to union and primitive catholicity and simplicity.[18]

Other advantages to operating in this ecumenical framework included the ability to liberate funds for missionary support and to pool resources. By appealing to donors outside its own immediate circle, the Alliance felt that it was able to bring in more money than it could if it were its own denomination. It found validation for its approach to fundraising in England, where

> The financial results of such [undenominational] societies have been found most satisfactory. . . . There within the past few years a great number of undenominational missionary agencies have sprung up. But they in no sense weakened the old societies, but only stimulated and strengthened them, while they have reached new constituencies and called forth new treasures for God's work. The result is that the average missionary contribution of English Christians are [sic] more than double those of their wealthier brethren in America. There are millions of dollars in this land awaiting the touch of God's consecrating fire, and the church has not even begun to learn the meaning of the necessity of consecrated giving.[19]

16. Ibid., 365.
17. Ibid.
18. Ibid., 367.
19. Ibid.

Simpson and the Alliance did not wish to compete with other missionary agencies for either workers or resources, for God had already given the supply, and they had only to get their hands on it. This confidence predisposed the Evangelical Missionary Alliance to welcome "the co-operation of such evangelical denominations and groups of churches or Christians, not identified with it in corporate relations, as may be disposed to send their missionaries under its Board and contribute their missionary offerings through its Treasurer."[20] Early Alliance missionary effort was an ecumenical effort.

Despite its nonsectarian ethos, the C&MA could not avoid becoming a denomination. The very success of its evangelistic efforts left it with large numbers of new converts whose only church homes were local Alliance "branches."[21] To care for them properly, the fledgling organization had to organize its branches into churches and eventually to recognize itself as a denomination and to reorganize itself as such.[22] The C&MA continues to grow steadily in the United States, Canada, and abroad and now claims more than sixteen thousand individual congregations and 4.5 million members and adherents in more than eighty countries worldwide.[23]

Missionary Statesman

A. B. Simpson was not only the founder and leader of a denomination; he was also one of the leading missionary statesmen of his day. The nineteenth century has been described as "the great century" in the history of missionary activity. The Protestant missionary enterprise grew in numbers and breadth. It was "the age of the most extensive geographic spread of Christianity,"[24] And no inhabited continent was

20. Christian and Missionary Alliance, *Annual Report* (1912), 41.

21. The earliest C&MA congregations were called branches, not churches. It was all part of Simpson's intent not to found a new and separate denomination but to provide a place for like-minded individuals to come to focus on the deeper spiritual life and missions and to return to their home churches and spread this message there.

22. It was not until 1974 that the C&MA officially considered itself a denomination, though for years before "the movement [Simpson] had founded was . . . a denomination in everything but name" (Niklaus et al., *All for Jesus*, 229).

23. Christian and Missionary Alliance in Canada, "Statistics." http://cmalliance.ca/statisticsp88.php.

24. Latourette, *Great Century*, 1.

immune from this spiritual annexation. According to Kenneth Scott Latourette, the foremost historian of missions, "Never before in the history of the Christian church had such a concerted, organized, herculean effort been made to take the gospel to the ends of the earth."[25] This unprecedented expansion

> was due in part to the work of many Western Protestant mission societies representing the Evangelical Awakening. Of decisive importance in this rapid advancement were the mission efforts of Protestants working on their own initiative, both locally and outside of their own [ecclesiastical] communities. Protestant mission work in the nineteenth century may be characterized as "ecumenical": There were increasing contacts and common agreements, first on the mission fields and then at the level of the sending bodies.[26]

Parachurch mission agencies and evangelical "alliances" sprang up everywhere during this era. In contrast to their denominational contemporaries, these youthful organizations, with their almost nonexistent bureaucracies, were highly mobile and adapted quickly to the many new and diverse fields into which missionaries were flooding. Their missionaries could go where they wished, go when they wished, and do what they wished. Without the input of these eager and energetic new missionary bodies, "the great century" could not have been so great.

Denominational missions and, to an even greater extent, parachurch "faith missions" enabled American revivalist Protestantism to move into areas of the world that, in its eyes, had never before seen "the light of the Gospel." In their intense zeal these missionary sending agencies aimed at nothing less than the total and immediate saturation of the globe with their brand of the Christian message. This missionary enthusiasm was spurred on by the afterglow of the Evangelical Awakening and the attendant emphases on personal conversion, devout regenerate life, social concern, and witness to the saving love of God in Christ.[27]

No less motivating were the varied millennial visions that were sometimes accompanied by vivid pictures of the torments of hell that

---

25. Kane, *Understanding Christian Missions*, 150.

26. Wind, "Protestant Missionary Movement," 237.

27. Ibid.

surely awaited the unreached and, therefore, unrepentant "heathen."[28] Earlier in the century, noted revivalist and postmillennialist Charles G. Finney had declared that if the churches would whole-heartedly accept their duty the world could be evangelized in as little as three years.[29] Finney's optimism was shared by a particular segment of the premillennial camp who believed that it was the timing of God, and their responsibility, in one great sweep, to evangelize the whole world. Indeed, if they were faithful, the task could be completed not only within their lifetime but within ten years. The urgency of this evangelistic task and the perceived possibility of ushering in the millennium through its speedy completion, determined this group's philosophy of missions:

> Prodded by images of hundreds of millions of lost souls and by the premillennial belief that time was short before Christ's return, the founders of independent missions decided that direct and widespread evangelization was the highest priority and that all else that missions customarily did should come second.[30]

These missions were in the soul-saving business and would not be distracted by endeavors of less importance.

Many of the scores of new mission agencies that sprang up during the late nineteenth century were driven by the visionary passion of their charismatic leaders. Many of the most notable of these leaders had never been and never would become missionaries themselves. A prime example was A. T. Pierson, a Philadelphia pastor who has been called "the greatest of the missionary advocates of the century."[31] Pierson and his fellows believed that missionary concern could and should be felt by both those who went abroad and those who stayed at home. Those who did not go could actively participate in the missionary enterprise by commissioning those who did, by praying for them, and by supplying their financial means.[32]

Simpson summed up this philosophy of missions in the phrase "If you cannot go, you can send,"[33] and he resolved to labor "just the same as

---

28. Tucker, *From Jerusalem to Irian Jaya*, 290.
29. McLoughlin, *Revivals, Awakenings, and Reform*, 130.
30. Carpenter, "Propagating the Faith Once Delivered," 98.
31. Robert, "Arthur Tappan Pierson," vii.
32. Simpson, *Missionary Messages*, 65–66.
33. Simpson, *Coming One*, 227.

if [he] were permitted to go among them."[34] If a Christian neither went nor sent, he or she would have to answer to God for this neglect at the final judgment.[35] Simpson did not confine his involvement in the missionary enterprise to the financial and spiritual support of individual missionaries, however. He also tirelessly promoted missions by keeping the urgency of the task before those who were already convinced of it, and by proclaiming it to those who were not yet aware of it. He became "an advocate for the lost before the conscience of North America."[36] One admiring biographer went so far as to say that the organization that Simpson founded would grow to be "one of the greatest missionary agencies of modern times."[37]

The whole of Simpson's background contributed to his missionary zeal and, to some extent, he had always been interested in foreign missions. The seed of interest had been planted before his birth through his mother's constant prayer that this child would be set aside for the service of God, "whether minister or missionary."[38] He was too young to remember his own baptism, when Presbyterian missionary John Geddie, the great "Apostle to the Islands," had dedicated him to God. His mother, however, never let him forget the fact or the circumstances surrounding it. Throughout his life he felt, or imagined he felt, Geddie's holy hand upon his brow, and his knowledge of it remained with him as a charge and a benediction.[39] His father had also been a warm friend of the missionary cause, and young Albert had from his early years heard missions talked about around the dinner table. He also began to read about missions, and his sister recalled that "When Albert was about nine years of age, he read the life of Rev. John Williams, the martyr missionary

---

34. A. B. Simpson in a sermon "The Macedonian Call," as quoted in Thompson, *Life of A. B. Simpson*, 120.

35. Simpson, *Missionary Messages*, 16.

36. Turnbull, "Introduction," 1.

37. This missionary imperative often became particularized as a mandate to bring the Gospel to a particular ethnic group, region, or nation. Indeed, a large number of independent "faith missions" bore names reflective of such focused passions: Africa Inland Mission, Sudan Interior Mission, and, perhaps the most famous of all, J. Hudson Taylor's China Inland Mission (see Tozer, *Wingspread*, 63).

38. Niklaus et al., *All for Jesus*, 20.

39. Tozer, *Wingspread*, 61.

of Erromanga, and was so impressed with it that he devoted himself to the work of the Lord, and he never swerved from his determination."[40]

Simpson's passion for missions did not exhibit itself to any extent in his early ministry. It was not until his Louisville pastorate that it began to manifest itself to any degree.[41] This resurgence of interest began as a result of an arresting sermon on missionary responsibility that he had heard at a Deeper Life conference in Watkins Glen, New York, in 1878. On his return trip to Louisville, he stayed over near Chicago with some friends, and it was here that he experienced his own "Macedonian call," a dream in which he saw a large mass of unsaved people wringing their hands in torment and calling upon him to save them. Though Simpson was ready to sail to the mission field on the basis of this vision, his wife assured him that she and their children did not share his sense of call. He took the thinly veiled threat to heart and sought to fulfill his missionary longings in other ways.

Nevertheless from this event forward, Simpson felt himself fully invested in the missionary enterprise. It became for him not an optional, extracurricular work of the church but rather, in the words of Alliance theologian and historian Samuel Stoesz, "part of the church's normal life and Spirit-filled function,"[42] and a vital sign of the church's overall health and its understanding and commitment to the gospel. The true church is a missionary church and, consequently, the true Christian, in some fashion, must be a missionary Christian. This conviction led Simpson to give up his pastorate in Louisville and to accept an invitation to a new charge in New York City.

The move to New York made sense for one who wished to be involved in the missionary endeavor but was unable to go abroad himself. New York was one of the busiest ports in the world, and it was the chief point of entry for new immigrants. Simpson wanted to be there to meet these newcomers, and the Gospel Tabernacle that he founded was originally intended to appeal to the poor, the disenfranchised, and the downtrodden. In a sense, with people from the far reaches of the globe arriving at New York, the world—the mission field—was coming to Simpson. Yet New York was also the ideal base for a missionary-sending

40. Thompson, *Life of A. B. Simpson*, 118–19.

41. McKaig, "Educational Philosophy of A. B. Simpson," 15.

42. Stoesz, *Understanding My Church*, 187.

agency, for just as the ships came from the "ends of the earth," so too they returned. Besides, New York was both a travel and a financial center, and so it would be able to supply all the resources that a missionary agency would need.

It must be restated that Simpson did not envisage his Christian and Missionary Alliance as an alternative or a competitor to existing denominational mission agencies. He sought, rather, to supplement their efforts by dispatching his missionary associates only to areas where no other mission was active. He encouraged the members of the Alliance to support the Alliance's independent missionaries only if their home churches did not support a mission sending agency. In the words of the Constitution of the Evangelical Missionary Alliance (1887), the aim and object of the Alliance was "to carry the Gospel 'to all nations,' with special reference to the needs of the destitute and unoccupied fields of the heathen world."[43]

This desire not to rob from existing evangelical mission agencies included not only an avoidance of the areas in which others were already ministering, but also a refusal to compete for the resources with which they were ministering. For the most part, the established denominational agencies sent missionaries who were already trained and experienced clerics. In the tradition of the American entrepreneurial spirit, Simpson and his faith-mission colleagues chose to rely on unconventional missionaries. Simpson talked regularly about reaching "God's neglected people" with "God's neglected resources"—women and laity. Indeed, the faith missions often attracted and, indeed, targeted those who had been overlooked by or "felt neglected by more bureaucratic structures."[44] They also shortened the interval between the moment of recruitment and the time of deployment by waiving vocational ministry experience as a prerequisite for missionary service and by providing their workers with minimal training. However, this use of "God's neglected resources," was no more haphazard than was the targeting of unreached fields. In fact, the very constitution of the Evangelical Missionary Alliance called for it.

> a) The work of laymen is one of God's chosen instrumentalities in this age. The urgency is so great that there is not always time

43. "Constitution of the Evangelical Missionary Alliance (1887)," 40.

44. Robert, "Crisis of Missions," 31.

for long technical preparation. The qualities especially needed are plain, practical energy and adaptation and entire consecration, and these are not found exclusively or always in the highest degree in professional ministers. We do not disparage the ministry, but God is calling His Church to use all her resources and agencies.

b) The ministry of woman is another prominent token of our time, both in the home and foreign field, and we believe He desires to emphasize it and utilize it still more. The foreign mission needs 100,000 women today, and place for everyone. At the mid-May Conference, the other day, 1,000 were called for North Africa alone, and this would only give one woman to every 10,000 heathen women and children in the field.[45]

This strategy helped make the Christian and Missionary Alliance, in the words of one missiologist "[the] most significant faith mission . . . in North America."[46]

Popular Publisher

Simpson's missionary concern can also be seen in the string of missionary periodicals that he began to publish even before he broke with the Presbyterian Church and founded the C&MA. They served as yet another creative outlet for his passion to promote missions among those who shared his vision but could not themselves serve as missionaries. Indeed, a magazine could do more for the missionary cause than preaching and teaching, for its potential audience would be far greater and far more diverse than any single congregation—and especially if it did not limit itself to a standard theological defense of the cause of missions. Simpson dreamt bigger than that. This magazine would be unlike anything else that had ever appeared before. He wanted to capture his readers' imaginations and transport them to the very fields that the church was reaching. And his venture would break new journalistic ground, for contemporary "missionary literature was so dull and uninteresting that nobody ever thought of reading it except as a duty he owed the cause to which he belonged."[47] His revolutionary periodical would include "a digest of missionary news, full of reports of work

45. "Constitution of the Evangelical Missionary Alliance (1887)," 41.

46. Robert, *Occupy Until I Come*, 186.

47. Simpson, "Missionary Wings," 315.

accomplished, interesting descriptions of conditions among the heathen, a challenge to the churches, and a call."[48]

The Gospel in All Lands appeared for the first time in February 1880, to general acclaim, and became the standard that subsequent missionary periodicals would emulate. Part of its appeal stemmed from Simpson's use of the latest technology in the preparation and presentation of the magazine. He illustrated it "with the newest type [of] woodcuts and . . . engravings made from . . . photographs taken on the trail."[49]

Simpson's pioneering effort was "the first illustrated missionary magazine in North America,"[50] and it was soon copied by others. Even scholars thought highly of his efforts, as A. E. Thompson, Simpson biographer, makes clear:

> Dr. Harlan P. Beach, professor of Missions in Yale University, showed his respect for Simpson's publishing efforts when he said: "Do not forget to mention as one of his great achievements the institution of a pictorial review. Dr. Simpson was the first to make the missionary story beautiful and attractive."[51]

The burden of producing such a magazine twice a month, however, proved to be more than Simpson's chronically frail constitution could bear. He could not sustain the demands of both his regular ministry and the editing of a periodical of this size and quality. So, in 1881, Simpson turned over the editorship of *The Gospel in All Lands* to Methodist publisher Eugene R. Smith. He still longed to edit a missionary periodical, however, and so in January 1882 he brought out the first issue of *The Word, the Work, and the World*. It would eventually become the official organ of the Alliance, and it has been published continuously, under a variety of titles, ever since.

The Alliance's institutional constitutions, minutes, and proceedings were regularly published in *The Word, the Work, and the World* and its successors.[52] The Missionary Institute that Simpson would later

48. Tozer, *Wingspread*, 65–66.

49. Ibid., 66.

50. Nienkirchen, *A. B. Simpson*, 22.

51. Thompson, *Life of A. B. Simpson*, 122.

52. For example, the initial constitutions of the Christian Alliance and the Evangelical Missionary Alliance appeared in *The Word, the Work, and the World* in the August/September 1887 issue. To this day, the C&MA, in accordance with its own

found used it to report institutional news, to promote its programs, and to recruit students. Simpson remained the editor for many years, wrote many of the 'anonymous' articles that were published in it, and used it to promote his own views as well as those of the Alliance. It was Simpson's printed voice to the world, and the control that he exercised as editor over the content of each issue should not be underestimated. *Living Truths*, a monthly periodical that appeared from 1902 to 1907, served a different purpose. It was published anonymously by Simpson and the C&MA and was provided as a tool for "Fourfold Gospel Christians to use with their church friends" who would not otherwise be interested in Deeper Life themes.[53]

Simpson once declared that "the printing press has been as widely used in the Alliance work as any other agency,"[54] and this was not only true of periodicals. The denominational press printed over one hundred separate books by Simpson, most of which were simply compilations of Simpson sermons on a common theme. For the most part, these books were released as colporteur editions to make them more easily available and affordable to the general public. While the majority of texts were by Simpson, the denominational press published titles by others sympathetic to C&MA themes. Simpson was also a prolific poet and hymn writer, and many of his poems and hymns found their way into Alliance hymnals. Until its demise in 2006, C&MA's publishing house, Christian Publications, was founded in 1883 and published works by Simpson, A. W. Tozer, other Alliance figures, and Alliance writers sympathetic to the Alliance cause.

Work at Nyack

Simpson and his colleagues believed that the missionaries that they would commission required at least minimal training. To meet this need, Simpson developed a training center, and thereby became one of the pioneers of the Bible institute movement. Present-day Nyack College and Alliance Theological Seminary trace their roots back to the Missionary Training College, which formally opened on October

bylaws, uses the *Alliance Life*, the current incarnation, to make official announcements to its constituency.

53. Niklaus et al., *All for Jesus*, 100–101.

54. Simpson, "Story of Providence," 36.

1, 1883, on Eighth Avenue in New York City.[55] Simpson founded the
school to provide a place "where godly and consecrated young men
and women can be prepared to go forth as laborers into the neglected
fields."[56]

The training provided both practical and academic opportunities.
Simpson initially wanted to keep both the college and the housing for
its students in the heart of the city to provide "ample opportunity for
actual Mission work in the wide field afforded by a great city"[57] and to
work in concert with the established activities of the Gospel Tabernacle.
The curriculum included courses in Bible, church history, English, and
apologetics. Lecturers who taught regularly at the Institute included
such renowned figures as A. J. Gordon, A. T. Pierson, and George F.
Pentecost.[58]

In the minds of most members and adherents of the C&MA, the
name "Nyack" conjures up a picture of the college of the same name that
has remained the center of Alliance clerical training for over one hundred years. The extent of the early Alliance's attachment to the one-time
country village, however, is much broader than this. Indeed, despite
popular Alliance opinion to the contrary, the Alliance did not found
Nyack, neither was the Alliance the first evangelical body to base its
work there. The Alliance arrived in Nyack in 1897, three years after "the
Christian Herald opened Montlawn, its summer home for tenement
children."[59] The *Herald's* decision to establish the camp in this Edenic
rural setting was the result of a worldview that was based "on a slum-
ridden urban society's increasing idolization of the out-of-doors."[60] The
Alliance established its own operations at Nyack on the basis of similar
idealistic reasoning. Simpson, too, coveted the supposed benefits of the
rural lifestyle, and at first did not simply want to relocate the Institute

55. Niklaus et al., *All for Jesus*, 59. Nyack College claims its inception dating back to
1882 "based on documentation dating back to the late 1890's," which probably counts as
part of its heritage Simpson's less formal training of workers in the Gospel Tabernacle.
Though not the first of the nineteenth-century Bible schools, of all the existing institutions, Nyack College is the oldest. (Niklaus et al., *All for Jesus*, 283 n. 24).

56. Ibid., 58.

57. Ibid., 59.

58. Ibid.

59. Magnuson, *Salvation in the Slums*, 62–63.

60. Ibid., 62.

but to found an entire Christian community along the lines of Old Orchard, Ocean Grove, and Keswick, all of which had become centers of significant religious movements. The ministry of Simpson's exalted dreams required not just a building but the sort of autonomous community that only a place like Nyack could hope to provide.

Simpson did not try to hide the fact that he hoped to attract hundreds of full-time Christian residents to Nyack. To this end, he and a few other investors formed the Nyack Heights Land and Improvement Company, purchased a large tract of property, subdivided it, and offered the lots for "development for residential purposes and institutional work."[61] The residential aspect of the plan failed miserably, and Simpson assumed all financial losses from his own resources.

The Alliance relocated the Missionary Training Institute to Nyack for financial reasons as well. By 1897 the Institute had outgrown its New York City facilities and found itself forced to turn away prospective students that it would normally have accepted. Then, as now, New York City property was extremely expensive. To build a suitable building in the city would have cost the Alliance more than six times what it cost to erect a comparable structure in Nyack. The construction of the new buildings ended up being the only part of Simpson's grand plan to be realized.

Nyack College currently has an enrollment of over one thousand students, but the educational enterprise of the C&MA has also spread beyond Nyack to include five colleges and five graduate schools in the United States and Canada.[62] Moreover, since the development of indigenous leadership remains one of the priorities of Alliance missions, most fields offer some kind of theological education. As of 31 December 2005, 121 C&MA theological schools with over 7,500 students were in operation.[63]

61. Pardington, *Twenty-five Wonderful Years*, 40.

62. These other schools include Alliance Theological Seminary in Nyack, NY; Crown College and Crown Graduate School, in St. Bonifacius, MN; Simpson College and Graduate School in Redding, CA. Ambrose University College and Seminary, in Calgary, AB, Canada, is a joint effort between the Christian and Missionary Alliance in Canada and the Church of the Nazarene, Canada. Toccoa Falls College and Graduate School in Toccoa Falls, GA, while an independent institution, is an associate college of the C&MA.

63. Christian and Missionary Alliance in Canada, "Statistics," http://cmalliance.ca/statisticsp88.php.

Influential Teacher and Preacher

Simpson's broadest and most lasting influence lies in his role as a teacher and preacher. Though the establishment of the denomination, the publications, the worldwide missionary movement, and the schools are all noteworthy and have their place within Simpson's legacy, all these to a greater or lesser extent are only products of Simpson's larger vision and message. It was this vision that spawned these institutions as tools for both the initial implementation and the anticipated realization of the larger vision that Simpson held. The influence of Simpson and his vision, then as now, is greater than the C&MA and its various ministries. Due to Simpson's extensive preaching, teaching, print, and convention ministries, the "reality is that Simpson's wingspread extends far beyond the Christian and Missionary Alliance and the institutions it has spawned."[64] The teaching and preaching ministry of Simpson, and the vision of which he spoke, did not remain locked up within the Alliance alone, but traces of it are found on the larger evangelical landscape. The Alliance is where Simpson's impact is most forcefully felt, but his vision moved others as well and they, too, have a place within Simpson's legacy.

Simpson's views exerted an especially strong influence on Pentecostalism, the fastest-growing and most influential church movement of the twentieth century, and on Assemblies of God,[65] ("the largest, strongest, and most affluent white Pentecostal denomination"[66]) in particular. One Pentecostal historian has been so bold as to call Simpson "one of the towering figures in modern Church history,"[67] to whom they "owe a great debt."[68] Pentecostal historians and theologians attest to Simpson's pervasive influence on Pentecostal churches. Indeed, his "theology, spirituality, ministry, and polity became an inspiration to many in the Pentecostal movement."[69] Carl Brumback lists seven different ways in which Pentecostalism is directly indebted to Simpson and

---

64. Kinlaw, "Foreword," xi.

65. Nienkirchen, *A. B. Simpson*, 41.

66. *Dictionary of Christianity in America*, s.v. "Assemblies of God," 23.

67. Brumback, *Suddenly*, 94.

68. Ibid.

69. *Dictionary of Pentecostal and Charismatic Movements*, s.v. "Simpson, Albert Benjamin," 786.

the C&MA.[70] Assemblies of God historian Edith Blumhofer has much to say about the breadth of Simpson's influence on Pentecostalism,[71] and David W. Faupel, whose own heritage is the "New Order of the Latter Rain" movement, mentions Simpson as one of the "prominent Holiness leaders of the late nineteenth century" upon whom the "early Pentecostals drew heavily."[72] William Menzies identifies Simpson and the C&MA as the "single most important influence from the Keswick world that came upon the embryonic Pentecostal revival."[73]

These appreciative observations have their roots "in the past percep-tions of Pentecostal pioneers who had firsthand exposure to [Simpson's movement]. An examination of the sources reveals the appreciative attitude of several prominent early personalities toward the contribu-tion made by Simpson . . . to their spiritual journeys."[74] Charles Fox Parham, who some consider the father of the Pentecostal movement, not only visited Nyack but was also exposed to the ministry of Simpson. Indeed, much of Parham's own teaching was directly modeled on that of Simpson. Articles by Simpson regularly appeared in Parham's peri-odical, *Apostolic Faith*.[75] Parham's most famous student, Agnes Ozman, who was reputedly the first person in the modern era whose baptism in the Spirit was evidenced by speaking in tongues, had studied under Simpson and his associates at the "Christian Mission Alliance [*sic*] Bible School"[76] before she began attending Parham's school in Topeka, Kansas. D. Wesley Myland, a protégé of Simpson, and a former Alliance pastor

70. These debts are 1) doctrines borrowed from Alliance, particularly sanctifica-tion and healing; 2) the hymns of Simpson; 3) the writings of Simpson, George P. Pardington, and A. W. Tozer; 4) Alliance terminology (e.g., "Gospel Tabernacle," "full gospel"); 5) polity borrowed by Assemblies of God; 6) the worldwide missionary vision; and 7) numerous leaders trained by Alliance (Brumback, *Suddenly*, 94).

71. "Men and women whose spiritual pilgrimage had led them to Christian and Missionary Alliance branches around the country would make vital contribution to American Pentecostalism, and Simpson's books, hymns, and missionary vision in-formed Pentecostal spirituality for decades" (Blumhofer, *Restoring the Faith*, 78).

72. Faupel, "American Pentecostal Movement," 91.

73 Menzies, "Non-Wesleyan Origins of the Pentecostal Movement," 87.

74 Nienkirchen, *A. B. Simpson*, 29.

75. Goff, *Fields White Unto Harvest*, 54. One of Parham's students, James Goss, later insisted that Parham's theology was directly dependent upon the fourfold scheme of Simpson, especially with respect to sanctification and healing (Nienkirchen, *A. B. Simpson*, 30).

76. LaBerge, *What Hath God Wrought*, 23.

and teacher, became one of the founding educators of Pentecostalism and was partly responsible for developing the fuller Pentecostal understanding of the highly influential "Latter Rain" theology. Simpson's impact on Pentecostal leaders was not limited to the United States alone. A. H. Argue, the founding pastor of Calvary Temple in Winnipeg, Manitoba, and one of the fathers of Canadian Pentecostalism, attributes his own interest in the movement to an experience of physical healing through Simpson's ministry.[77] W. W. Simpson (no relation), a pioneer Pentecostal missionary, imbibed much of his missiological fervor from Simpson while a student at Nyack, though the two disagreed over the role of tongues in the missionary enterprise.[78]

Also noteworthy in the same connection is the fact that many of the first Pentecostal churches and many of the first converts to Pentecostalism had once been associated with the C&MA. So great was the Pentecostal revival within the Alliance that many thought that Pentecostalism itself was nothing more than a split within the Alliance.[79] Indeed, a good number of Alliance adherents became Pentecostals because they wanted the freedom to experience the baptism of the Holy Spirit with speaking in tongues, and because they had come to espouse the Pentecostal "evidence doctrine." The Alliance did not officially deny the validity of such an experience, but it did not seem to encourage it either. Such losses by the C&MA were "substantial among branch members, official workers, and missionaries."[80]

Though the Pentecostals identify Simpson as a source for their polity, hymnody, and even their missionary zeal,[81] his greatest influence upon them was theological

77. Brumback, *Suddenly*, 85.

78. *Dictionary of Pentecostal and Charismatic Movements*, s.v. "Simpson, William Wallace," 787; Nienkirchen, *A. B. Simpson*, 111–12.

79. Dayton, *Theological Roots*, 176.

80. *Dictionary of Pentecostal and Charismatic Movements*, s.v. "Christian and Missionary Alliance," 164.

81. The testimony of one woman shows the influence of Simpson on the missionary perspective of one particular Pentecostal congregation.

> It was a few years later (in 1911) that father took over the pastorate of the Christian and Missionary Alliance Church in Cleveland, Ohio. Nearly all the members of this church had now received the Baptism of the Holy Spirit, and voted to become the Pentecostal Church of Cleveland, Ohio. The missionary vision inculcated in their

The Christian and Missionary Alliance shared with the apostolic faith movement understandings of Christ, the Holy Spirit, healing, and the second coming, and Simpson had written books and songs that helped popularize practical dimensions of the spirituality these teachings fostered. He had encouraged expectation of spiritual gifts and had anticipated a miraculous end-times enduement of ability to proclaim the gospel in foreign languages.[82]

Of particular theological influence was Simpson's christocentric gestalt (Jesus as Savior, Sanctifier, Healer, and Coming King), a composite that he called the "Fourfold Gospel." Even non-Pentecostal theologian Harvey Cox recognizes this indebtedness, noting that Simpson's Fourfold Gospel continues "to serve as the core of doctrine for millions of pentecostals [*sic*] in several different denominations."[83] Pioneer Pentecostal theologians merely substituted "Baptizer in the Holy Spirit." for "Sanctifier." They did not regard this move as a break with Simpson's theology so much as a necessary step beyond it or the "culmination of it."[84] The extent of Simpson's influence on Pentecostalism is perhaps most clearly seen in the name that the popular Pentecostal figure Aimee Semple McPherson gave to the denomination she founded: the International Church of the Foursquare Gospel.

Like Simpson, "Sister Aimee" claimed that she too received her title in an act of direct inspiration.[85] Her "Foursquare Gospel," that bears a strikingly close resemblance to Simpson's *gestalt*, comprises "Jesus the Savior, Jesus the Baptizer with the Holy Spirit, Jesus the Healer, Jesus the Coming King."[86] One of her biographers claims that it cannot be estab-

hearts through association with Dr. Simpson and the Christian and Missionary Alliance permeated this church and the burden and vision of missions never dimmed through all of Father and Mother Kerr's ministry.

"A Letter from Christine Kerr Pierce to the Author, (September 15, 1959)" (Brumback, *Suddenly*, 80).

82. Blumhofer, *Restoring the Faith*, 77–78.

83. Cox, *Fire from Heaven*, 128.

84. Synan, *In the Latter Days*, 52.

85. McPherson identifies her "illumination" occurring while preaching a message on the vision of Ezekiel in Oakland, California, in July 1922 (McPherson, *Aimee Semple McPherson*, 110–12).

86. McPherson, *Aimee Semple McPherson*, 112.

lished with any degree of certainty that she borrowed her formula from Simpson.[87] More telling, and perhaps more on the mark, is the opinion of Foursquare historian James Bradley who, contrary "to McPherson's own claims to originality, however, contended that McPherson in fact owed a large debt to Simpson."[88] Given the pervasive influence of Simpson's teaching within early Pentecostalism and her own acquaintance with Alliance people (including Simpson's successor as president of the Alliance, Paul Rader), it would seem natural and logical to assume the influence of Simpson rather than deny it.

The Heart of the Gospel

Few if any of A. B. Simpson's numerous and impressive achievements were unique in their day, and Simpson himself was neither a theological anomaly nor a theological innovator. Even that aspect most closely identified with Simpson—the Fourfold Gospel—was peculiar to neither him nor the C&MA. Rather the Fourfold Gospel was simply an encapsulation of the central theological themes of late nineteenth-century evangelicalism. The call to personal salvation lay at the heart of revivalism; the Holiness movement emphasized sanctification; the burgeoning Divine healing movement (of which Simpson may have been *the* key figure) had proponents on both sides of the Atlantic; and interest in premillennial eschatology had been steadily growing since the outbreak of the French Revolution. Moreover, other well-known preachers of the era in the other leading American cities (D. L. Moody of Chicago, A. J. Gordon of Boston, and A. T. Pierson of Philadelphia) all promoted a message remarkably similar to Simpson's, though with different emphases.

Yet the derivative nature of Simpson's theology does not diminish his importance as a leading figure of late nineteenth-century conservative Protestantism. On the contrary, the commonness of Simpson's theological concerns and passions—those that make up his Fourfold Gospel and were adopted, if slightly altered, by Pentecostalism—serve as a microcosm of popular, late nineteenth-century evangelical theology and practice. To understand Simpson's theology is to understand late nineteenth-century American evangelical theology. Simpson's Fourfold

87. Blumhofer, *Aimee Semple McPherson*, 191.
88. Nienkirchen, *A. B. Simpson*, 37.

Gospel was not something peculiar to himself or the C&MA. Rather, in the late nineteenth century, it was the heart of the gospel.

"Himself"

Once it was the blessing,
Now it is the Lord;
Once it was the feeling,
Now it is His Word.
Once His gifts I wanted,
Now the Giver own;
Once I sought for healing,
Now Himself alone.

All in all forever,
Jesus will I sing;
Everything in Jesus,
And Jesus everything.

Once 'twas painful trying,
Now 'tis perfect trust;
Once a half salvation,
Now the uttermost.
Once 'twas ceaseless holding,
Now He holds me fast;
Once 'twas constant drifting,
Now my anchor's cast.

Once 'twas busy planning,
Now 'tis trustful prayer;
Once 'twas anxious caring,
Now He has the care.
Once 'twas what I wanted,
Now what Jesus says;
Once 'twas constant asking,
Now 'tis ceaseless praise.

Once it was my working,
His it hence shall be;
Once I tried to use Him,
Now He uses me.
Once the power I wanted,
Now the Mighty One;
Once for self I labored,
Now for Him alone.

Once I hoped in Jesus,
Now I know He's mine;
Once my lamps were dying,
Now they brightly shine.
Once for death I waited,
Now His coming hail;
And my hopes are anchored,
Safe within the vail.[89]

89. Simpson, "Himself," In *Hymns of the Christian Life*, 248.

Christ, Our Savior

American Revivalism

THE HISTORY OF NINETEENTH-CENTURY AMERICAN PROTESTANT RELIgious life is, largely, the history of the ebb and flow of various religious movements often called "revivals." A revival may be simply defined as an intensified focus on and feeling of religious (primarily Christian) sentiment and activity in a distinct geographical region. Historians of religion often use the most significant of these revivals as points of demarcation in their chronologies of American religious history. This is not to say that revivals were particular either to America or to the nineteenth century, but rather that they shaped that century, as they had no other.

Jonathan Edwards

Many religious phenomena have been called revivals, and though they all bear least a superficial similarity to one another, they are not homogeneous. Perhaps the greatest dissimilarity involves the particular methods that were used in the various revivals. Noted Congregationalist academic, preacher, and early revivalist Jonathan Edwards (1703–1758) believed the revivals of eighteenth-century America to be unexpected, altogether independent, and even "surprising" works of God. For Edwards, revivals are gracious and wholly autonomous works of God through which he brings people near to himself. No human action can stimulate revival. It remains the exclusive work of God. This understanding is not surprising given Edwards's Puritan roots and his lifelong fidelity to traditional Reformed theology. Many of his best-known works directly reject the idea of human agency in the realm of salvation, insisting instead on the impervious sovereignty of God in such matters.[1]

Charles Finney

Edwards's definition of revival, however, would not survive unchallenged, even within historically Reformed movements. The first major nineteenth-century American revivalist, Charles Grandison Finney (1792–1875), was and always remained Reformed by creed and association. Like Edwards, he was a noted preacher, revivalist, and academic. Yet, Finney's view of the nature of revival was very different from that of Edwards, for he championed Arminianism, which Edwards considered a threat against which traditional Reformed soteriology needed to be defended.[2] Edwards emphasized divine agency in revival and salvation, whereas Finney believed that human action was indispensible to both.[3] Finney was not alone in this opinion. In fact, "[f]reedom of choice was basic to nineteenth-century revivalism."[4] Indeed, most revivalists believed that while revival may be sparked by or flow from some miraculous event, revival itself is the result of both human decision and divine action. Revival involves nothing more miraculous than humanity's engaging in the "right use of the [divinely] constituted means."[5] God sovereignly determines the means of revival, but humanity is responsible to implement these divinely ordained means. If the means were rightly implemented, revival would follow.

Although Finney believed that human action is essential to revival, he did not deny the foundational role of God. He simply asserted that God was not the lone agent of revival. God is, rather, revival's indispensable enabler. Just as both humanity and God are both responsible for the growth of a good crop, both are necessary in the successful fruition of revival.[6] Though humanity provides the manual labor, all is for

1. These include but are not limited to such titles as "Careful and Strict Inquiry into the Modern Prevailing Notions of that Freedom of the Will," "God Glorified in Man's Dependence," and, perhaps the best-known work, "Sinners in the Hands of an Angry God."

2. Edwards, *Faithful Narrative*, 13.

3. Finney, *Revivals of Religion*, 4.

4. Thomas, *Revivalism and Cultural Change*, 68.

5. Finney, *Revivals of Religion*, 5.

6. Ibid.

naught if the blessing of God does not accompany it. Humanity's role in revival, therefore, is more than just that of passive and grateful receiver, as Edwards had claimed.

Finney's departure from Edwards on the essential nature of revival would come to affect the whole of the revivalistic tradition to follow. Revival and salvation were no longer understood to be things gratefully but passively experienced. Now revivals were to be sought, planned for, initiated, conducted, and achieved. William G. McLoughlin has described this shift in understanding as the "Arminianized Calvinism [that would come to be] called evangelicalism."[7]

The Revival of 1857–1858

Until just before the Civil War, revivals were usually associated with certain prominent leaders. For example, the First Great Awakening is associated with Jonathan Edwards and George Whitefield, and the Second Great Awakening with Charles Finney and Nathaniel Taylor. The Prayer Revival (or the Lay Revival) of 1857–1858 was different. Although it did not lack for leaders,[8] none had the stature of an Edwards or a Finney. In that sense it was faceless, though it was nonetheless powerful and influential. It was marked by a popular leadership and an ecumenical spirit:[9] church walls could not confine it; ecclesiastical hierarchies could not control it; particular creedal positions could not contain it. The public prayer meetings that distinguished this revival were neither normally held in churches nor necessarily led by clergy. Anyone might lead or participate in these meetings—and they did.[10]

---

7. McLoughlin, *Modern Revivalism*, 13.

8. Timothy Smith identifies Jeremiah C. Lanphier as one of the earliest people to come to prominence in connection with this revival. It may be said that those public figures that emerged from this revival were far more renowned than those who originated it. Smith, *Revivalism and Social Reform*, 63.

9. The heart of this spirit is seen in the common form of the multitude of prayer meetings that constituted this revival. Within fairly loose boundaries, all were permitted to speak, pray, and lead in song with no distinction being made between laity and clergy (See Smith, *Revivalism and Social Reform*, 64).

10. As Katherine Long has noted, this license was not extended with the same liberality to women. Though their presence was strongly felt, their leadership and their active participation was sharply curtailed or marginalized (Long, *Revival of 1857–58*, 92).

The emphasis on evangelism that characterized the Prayer Meeting Revival "blurred denominational lines and diminished the denominational ambitions for aggrandizement."[11] The task at hand, the belief that it could be accomplished, and the fever of spiritual excitement took precedence over denominational or creedal borders. The bond that most closely tied one participant to another was collegiality—the common responsibility for reaching lost souls. Leadership was based on one's perceived gifting in evangelism. This populist emphasis opened the door of Christian ministry to all, regardless of their theological training or affiliation, and paved the way for the rise of countless interdenominational parachurch movements, such as the Christian and Missionary Alliance.[12]

The Nature of Revival

The question may naturally arise, what is the purpose of revival? That is, though revival may be defined as an intensified focus on and feeling of religious (primarily Christian) sentiment and activity in a distinct geographical region, one may still ask: What was the object of revival? Was revival an initiatory event that brought people into the fellowship of the church? Or, Was it something for those already part of the church and designed to stimulate within them a desire for a deeper relationship with God? Was the purpose of a revival to expand or to intensify the role of religion in that particular setting? Simply put, was revival primarily a movement to convert the unbeliever or to mature the devotion of the believer? J. Edwin Orr raises this question in *The Event of the Century: The 1857–1858 Awakening*. He contends that in the 1850s, the term "revival" was used to refer to two different, though related, tasks: the "reviving of the company of believers in a given place," and "the reviving of the Christian faith in a community, or nation, or

---

11. Orr, *Event of the Century*, 276.

12. It would not be long before laity would not only be involved in revival but soon take center stage in leading it, with Dwight L. Moody being the most famous and influential of these lay evangelists. Indeed, both Stan Gundry and James Orr deny that Charles Finney and his colleagues exerted any direct influence on the revivalistic style of Moody. Though it may be argued that the influence of Finney's democratizing emphasis on the human will paved the way for the Revival of 1857–1858, Moody was a product, both spiritually and methodologically, of the revival itself, and not of Finney. Orr, *Event of the Century*, 313; Gundry, *Love Them In*, 77–78.

throughout the Christian world."[13] In contemporary usage, however, the term "revival" has come to mean little more than the mass evangelistic meetings associated with the likes of Billy Graham or Luis Palau. For Orr, this definition betrays the real meaning of the term, which ought to be reserved solely for those movements that bring about the spiritual resuscitation of people who were once already spiritually engaged. The term "evangelism" properly describes the activity of seeking to convert unbelievers.

Keith Hardman defines "revival" as *"the restoration of God's people after a period of indifference and decline."*[14] Yet he does not distinguish between evangelism and personal Christian renewal. Instead, he believes that genuine revival has "two main thrusts: (1) the conversion or salvation of a number of unbelievers, and (2) the reestablishment of biblical truth, so that the church is built up and empowered for the work of God in a lost and dying world."[15] To insist that revivalism emphasize one or the other is to deny the dynamic link that exists between the two. Both are not only legitimate but necessary parts of the larger work of revival.

The widespread popularity of A. B. Simpson, A. J. Gordon, A. T. Pierson, and D. L. Moody was due in no small part to the ecumenical climate fostered by the Revival of 1857–1858. Theologically, they are also heirs of this revival as well. They were all solidly "evangelical" in that they followed the "Arminianized Calvinism" of Finney. They also engaged in a revivalism that sought not only to reestablish biblical faith within the church but to evangelize the unconverted as well. They did not separate the two streams but held them both as equal and necessary aspects of an experience of full salvation.

The Atonement—The Basis of Salvation

To understand a particular Christian soteriology, one must also grasp its theory of the atonement. The atonement—the reconciliation of God and humanity made necessary because of the separating effect of sin—with the ministry of Jesus at the center, makes Christian theology particularly Christian. The opinion of the late nineteenth-century

---

13. Orr, *Event of the Century*, xii.

14. Hardman, *Seasons of Refreshing*, 16 (emphasis original).

15. Ibid.

revivalists was no different. They too believed that the atonement lies at the heart of the Christian message, for without it Christianity would be impotent, if not emasculated. [The hope of the Christian faith does not come from the incarnation alone but from a particular atoning act that Jesus performed while he was incarnate.] Shorn of the atonement, the incarnation, though still of some value, would consist of little more than an ultimately ineffectual, sentimental act.[16]

The Nature of Atonement

Though all Christian traditions confess the reality of the atonement, they have had to resort to a variety of competing theories to try to explain its exact nature. Even within the American revivalist tradition, disagreements arose regarding nature, object, and scope of the atonement.[17] Among the subjects of this study, however, there is virtual unanimity. Atonement became necessary because sin had separated humanity from God. Humanity had broken the divine law of God, and therefore, a penalty had to be paid. That penalty was death.

The revivalists situate the nature of atonement in the concepts of "penalty" and "substitution," or "the taking [of] another's place."[18] This view, often called the penal-substitution theory, declares that on the cross Jesus took humanity's penalty upon himself, freeing humanity from the condemnation of the Mosaic law. The death that Jesus endured on the cross was neither the just consequence of his own actions nor

16. This is not to say that exposition of the doctrine of the atonement was a central theme of the preaching of the revivalists. It was not. Though they believed in a particular theology of the atonement, it was, more often than not, simply implicit in their message. John Mark Hicks has noted that the discussions that did occur "focused on the application of the atonement instead of what the atonement accomplished" (Hicks, "What Did Christ's Sacrifice Accomplish," 1). Not surprisingly, given the ecumenical culture flowing from the Revival of 1857–1858, contemporary discussions of the doctrine centered more on its practical implications than on its nature, a subject that would have proved excessively abstract at best, and downright divisive at worst.

17. During the nineteenth century, a number of theories of the atonement either regained popularity or were developed. Among the more influential of these were Nathaniel Taylor's "moral government" theory, the "moral influence" theory championed by Horace Bushnell, and Augustus Strong's "ethical'" theory. While some would say that there was general agreement on the essentials of the atonement, and that any disagreement was only on nonessentials, David F. Wells rightly points out that "[this] seeming unity . . . was an illusion" (Wells, "Collision of Views," 363–64).

18. MacLean, *Dr. Pierson*, 106.

the regrettable result of a heroic though misunderstood life. The death Jesus suffered on the cross was rather a deliberate act of self-sacrificial substitution. He died in a successful attempt to reconcile God and humanity.[19] Not only did the revivalists regard the very fact of the atonement as being crucial to the potency of the Christian faith, but they also believed just as strongly that it was a substitutionary act that satisfied the penalty of the law of God.[20] If the self-sacrifice of Jesus had not been made on its behalf, humanity remained liable for the consequences of its own sin.

On the cross, Christ took upon himself the just punishment that was to be extracted from humanity. The revivalists did not mince words when it came to these concepts of "penalty" and "substitution." A. J. Gordon, for example, held that Jesus Christ "[took] all the penalties and pains of that law into his own bosom. He [threw] himself athwart the track of justice, and [bore] his own breast to its punishments, that we may be spared from them, through his endurance of them."[21] This act of Christ makes believers "legally or judicially free from the penalty of a violated law."[22] Moody agreed: "[Jesus Christ] has suffered all its penalties, and paid all that the law demands."[23] They are "our sorrows, our griefs, our iniquities, our transgressions, and the chastisement of our peace [that Christ accepted]—there is a substitute for you."[24] Pierson taught that Christ "was counted as sin and . . . was dealt with as sin by God in judgment. That constituted the atonement. He took the place of

19. David Wells identifies this theory as "that of classical Protestant orthodoxy" and identifies Charles Hodge of Princeton Seminary as its preeminent American exponent in the nineteenth century (Wells, "Collision of Views," 365).

20. "You ask me what my hope is; it is that Christ died for my sins, in my stead, in my place, and therefore I can enter into life eternal. Take that doctrine of substitution out of the Bible and my hope is lost" (Moody, "There Is No Difference," 47). "The substitution of an innocent Victim for the sinner is the basis of Justification by Faith" (Pierson, *Believer's Life*, 23).

21. Gordon, *Grace and Glory*, 9.

22. Gordon, *Ministry of the Spirit*, 110.

23. Moody, "There Is No Difference," 47. Shortly after his death, it was said of Moody that "his theology was full of the charm of naïveté. It was rather that of a child than a man. Two words will characterize it—*evangelical* and *conservative*." The greatest emphasis of his preaching may be said to have been laid upon the "blood atonement in the death of Christ, and the immediate salvation of any one who accepted the redeeming merits of his death, by an act of faith" (Goss, *Echoes from the Pulpit and Platform*, 93).

24. Moody, *Glad Tidings*, 293.

sinners, and He took the place of their sin before God."[25] Pierson also put forth this succinct definition of the atonement :

> The root idea of the gospel is that, by the substitution of Christ for the sinner before the law, in a perfect life of obedience and a death of vicarious suffering, the ends of the law and of justice were so answered as that God could judicially acquit the sinner and yet not tarnish the glory of his own perfection.[26]

Given "Christ's vicarious sacrifice,"[27] the penalty of the law was satisfied and no longer loomed over humanity.

There is no doubt that Simpson saw the atonement in the same way. At the heart of his theology,[28] and certainly of his soteriology, was the doctrine of penal substitution.[29] "Christ's sacrifice," Simpson wrote, "stands at the very entrance of all our access to and communion with God."[30] It was on the cross, through the death of Jesus, that "divine provision [was made] for human salvation."[31] The very name "Jesus" meant that this one would make atonement[32] and serve as a "substitution for the guilty."[33] The work of Christ on the cross did not simply serve as an

25. MacLean, *Dr. Pierson*, 90.

26. Pierson, *Vital Union with Christ*, 15.

27. Gordon, *Yet Speaking*, 66.

28. Not only was Simpson's doctrine of salvation built squarely upon this idea of penal substitution, but other aspects of his theology, most especially that of healing, were dependent on this idea as well. These other areas will be examined in subsequent chapters of this work. In 1897, active membership in the newly amalgamated Christian and Missionary Alliance required an unreserved subscription to the "vicarious atonement of the Lord Jesus" (Simpson, "Editorial," *Christian and Missionary Alliance* 12 [March 1897], 252).

29. "The one business of the Son of God was to settle the question of sin" (Simpson, *Evangelistic Addresses*, 24).

30. Simpson, *Christ in the Tabernacle*, 28.

31. Simpson, *Old Faith and the New Gospels*, 77. Though Simpson's construction of a theology of the atonement in this work is minimal, he leaves no question in his readers' minds that he is standing squarely against the "example" theory of Reginald Campbell in *The New Theology*, especially the chapter titled, "The Atonement." See Campbell, *New Theology*, 166.

32. Simpson, *Gospel of Matthew*, 21. The work of Jesus Christ was to "bring [humanity] to God, to make reconciliation or atonement, which literally means, 'at-onement'" (Simpson, *Evangelistic Addresses*, 24).

33. Simpson, *Cross of Christ*, 7.

example, nor was it merely an expression of Christ's love for humanity.[34] Rather, it worked in such a way that God now considers righteous those who were formerly not so. The work of Jesus Christ was "to save us from the penalty of sin," and it was this penalty that "this Babe of Bethlehem came to bear . . . for sinful man."[35] The atonement of Jesus Christ meant that

> Christ came to bear away our sins and bring us back to our Father in forgiveness and acceptance. . . . Christ has come to bring you back to Him and is waiting to right all wrongs between you and heaven, to forgive all your sin through His atonement in your stead and to make you as right with God as if you had never sinned. This is the first step in the salvation of the soul.[36]

The Object of the Atonement

The penal-substitutionary theory holds that the object of the work of atonement was exclusively divine. Over and over again, the revivalists spoke of Jesus Christ as the one who took the place of a sinful humanity to satisfy the penalty prescribed by God's law. Atonement was not aimed at changing humanity's attitude toward God. Rather, it sought to affect the divine disposition. It had as its primary object the satisfaction of the demands of God's law. Any renovation of human character that might result from the death of Christ on the cross was consequential but not primary.

According to A. T. Pierson, what occurred in the atonement was not the intervention of a loving Son, on the one hand, before an entirely wrathful and ferocious Father, on the other.[37] The Godhead is not

34. It was not that Simpson did not see such benefits to humanity in the cross. He considered them, rather, to be ancillary to the main purpose of the cross. Indeed, in a chapter titled "The Kaleidoscope of the Cross" Simpson lists twenty "phases" associated with the cross of which "example" and "a revelation of love" are but two (Simpson, *Cross of Christ*, 1–11).

35. Simpson, *Evangelistic Addresses*, 26.

36. Ibid., 58.

37. Based on his reading of John 3:16, Pierson rejected any theory of the atonement that would see God the Son intervening between sinners and a solely and wholly wrathful God the Father. It is just as much the love of God the Father that instigates the work of the atonement as it is the love of God the Son. It is the very love of the Father that sends the Son (Pierson, *Heart of the Gospel*, 26–27).

conflicted in its attitude toward humanity. The love of both Father and Son initiated and resulted in the sacrifice of the Son. God has always loved humanity. The atonement did not change the mind or heart of God. Indeed, because of their rejection of the law of God, "[t]he alienation has been solely on the side of [humankind]."[38]

Still, it must be clearly understood that humanity was not the object of the atonement. Rather, the statutes of the divine law demanded satisfaction, and so the atonement, though its object remains divine, is a work of the entire Godhead. It is a work of a loving and righteous God being true to both the righteousness of the divine law and his love. In his righteousness, he cannot overlook the breach of his holy law. His love for humanity, however, demands that he satisfy these same requirements himself. Atonement has the divine as both its provision and its object.[39] God initiates this work, and God, or at least the requirements of the law, is the one to whom it is directed.

Simpson agreed that the atonement was a divine work with a divine object, and although he nowhere explicitly states Pierson's point regarding the disposition of the Father in comparison to that of the Son, he does speak about the love of the Father motivating the sending of the Son. The Father did not have to be appeased: it was the penalty of the divine law that had to be satisfied.

The Fuller Language of Atonement

Though the revivalists used primarily the language of penal substitution, their view of the atonement does not correspond exactly to any particular classical theory. Indeed, they appealed to the full spectrum

---

38. Pierson, *Believer's Life*, 46.

39. A. J. Gordon said that only Christ "is great enough for such an interposition. God alone can shield us from God. The eternal Son is the only being that can intercept eternal punishment and ward it off from us" (Gordon, *Grace and Glory*, 9).

James Findlay has tried to assert that Dwight L. Moody subscribed to a "moral-influence" theory of the atonement, whereby the work of Jesus Christ on the cross seeks primarily to alter the attitude of humanity to God, rather than the inclination of God toward humanity (Findlay, *Dwight L. Moody*, 232–34). Stanley Gundry has demonstrated the deficiencies of Findlay's work and contends that he may have misread both Moody and the classical theories on this central doctrine. Moody, Gundry maintains, holds to the idea of penal substitution as do the other revivalists, for he, too, uses the "themes of broken law, consequent punishment, divine wrath, debt, substitution, and satisfaction [that] imply this understanding" (Gundry, *Love Them In*, 103–9, 116).

of scriptural imagery,[40] for as a divine mystery, the atonement exceeds the capacity of human language to describe it. Certainly one metaphor alone, even that of penal substitution, cannot express the depth of meaning of this act of God, so the revivalists used as many as they could, including "ransom," "satisfaction,"[41] and "commercial exchange."[42] Only when one sees the whole picture created by this mosaic of imagery is the revivalists' doctrine of the atonement rightly and completely understood.[43] Nevertheless, the overall thrust and central motif remains that of penal substitution.

Simpson too uses a wide variety of biblical imagery to describe the atonement, although, like the other revivalists, penal substitution remained his central, organizing, and ruling motif. Though Simpson, in his writings, frequently uses the terms "ransom" and "redemption," he never considers Satan or any being other than God to be their object. Indeed, on more than one occasion, he mixes his metaphors, juxtaposing ransom, redemption, satisfaction, and substitution.[44] Penal substitution is so pervasive in Simpson's theology that it ends up informing how he interprets the other aspects of the atonement kaleidoscope.

---

40. "As used by Moody, [the atonement] is essentially a penal concept, though other themes are intermingled" (Gundry, *Love Them In*, 117, 113).

41. In various places Moody gave credence to the ransom theory of the atonement. Nevertheless, he gives the primacy to penal substitution. For him, the blood of Christ is precious "because *it redeems us*. Not only from the hands of the devil, but from the hands of the law. It redeems me from the curse of the law; it brings me out from under the law. The law condemns me, but Christ has satisfied the claims of the law" (Moody, *Best of D. L. Moody*, 15).

42. "But we are not redeemed by such corruptible things [as silver and gold], but by the precious blood of Christ. Redemption means 'buying back;' we had sold ourselves for naught, and Christ redeemed us and bought us back" (Moody, *Sovereign Grace*, 107).

43. "The motif of substitution is relevant to the penalty of condemnation to which man is subject for having broken the law of God. As used by Moody, it is essentially a penal concept, though other themes are mingled." Gundry also points out that Moody uses words such as "deliverance" and "cleansing" to describe the atonement, words that may be understood as relating to a "dramatic *Christus Victor*" theory (Gundry, *Love Them In*, 103–9, 117).

44. Here is one example: "The death of Jesus Christ, . . . was . . . a *ransom* for the guilty and a *satisfaction* to the righteousness of God for the sins of men" (emphasis added; Simpson, *Christ Life*, 17). Note that even in this instance, he does not use the term "ransom" in reference to captivity but to guilt. The context defines exactly what that term denotes—something along the lines of "redemption" or "satisfaction."

Mutual Exchange

Through his work on the cross, Jesus took upon himself the penalty of the law rightfully intended for humanity. Yet through this work, humanity also becomes the object of God's Christ-directed benevolence. On the one hand, Jesus takes those disadvantages that are rightfully and properly humanity's and makes them his own. On the other, the benefits that are rightfully and properly those of Christ alone come to belong to those in whom he dwells by the Holy Spirit. Substitution does not result merely in a one-sided deposit but in a reciprocity—an "exchange."[45] What was once the possession of one becomes the possession of the other, and vice versa.

Assent, faith, and designation do not result in God's blessing humanity.[46] Instead, blessing is the result of the believer's intimate union with Christ, the actual object of God's benevolence. Through profound and mystical union with Christ, the believer receives not only the benefit of a diverted wrath, but also the benefit of God's graciousness toward the Son. This is not based merely on the identification of the believer with Christ. Rather, it is the consequence of Christ's being intimately and mystically joined with the believer in one person. Blessing is not simply imputed to the believer through some wholly objective transaction, but rather is received because of the infusion of Christ in the believer's life. The believer does not simply receive the person of Christ, but as Christ receives the blessing of the Father, so too the believer, as the receptacle of Christ, becomes the receiver of what Christ himself receives.

---

45. "He was counted as sin, and He was dealt with as sin by God in judgment. That constituted the atonement. He took the place of sinners, and He took the place of their sin before God. And now He had righteousness that was infinite, and here is the exchange. Our sin He takes. His righteousness we take. There is a change of place" (MacLean, *Dr. Pierson*, 90). "Through [dwelling in the believer] Christ both gives and takes,—gives the Father's life and blessedness, and takes the believer's death and wretchedness." "Christ possesses every blessing and eternal salvation; they are henceforth the property of the soul. The soul possesses every vice and sin; they become henceforth the property of Christ" (Gordon, *In Christ*, 17).

46. "If [one] would have life it must be by personal union with Jesus Christ" (Pierson, *Heart of the Gospel*, 132). "Salvation does not come by a creed. It comes by . . . Christ" (MacLean, *Dr. Pierson*, 79). "Faith is not only belief—an intellectual process of the apprehension and reception of truth, but it is a trust—a bond of fellowship between Jesus Christ and the believer" (Pierson, *Coming of the Lord*, 73).

Simpson, like the others, did not believe in an objective salvation based simply on divine fiat.[47] Nor is regeneration the infusion of some nameless, faceless, divine energy into the previously dead. The blessedness of the Christian does not come simply through the work of Christ on the cross, but "especially through the person of Christ," who so "unites [the Christian] to Himself" that the Christian "is put into the very position which He Himself occupies."[48] Christ alone, resident in the life of the believer, makes the atonement possible. The power that renews sinful humanity is not simply power but the indwelling of the very person of Jesus Christ. Humanity is regenerated, not by some renovation of its own being, but by the very life of Jesus living in it.

Consequently, for Simpson, salvation is more than just a restoration to some prefall condition, for some degree of human divinization accompanies this indwelling of Christ. His indwelling lifts humanity to a higher nature than it ever could have acquired on its own. Redeemed humanity experiences far more than even unfallen humanity ever did or could. Simpson is clear on this:

> Unfallen man was only a creature made in the image of God, but a little lower than the angels. Redeemed man has been raised above the rank of angels to partake of the very nature of God, to be joint-heir with the Son of God and to share eternally the throne of his Creator and the attributes of the eternal Son, our glorious Head.[49]

> What is the highest Christian life? What is the life that God is trying to reproduce in the lives of His saints? Is it the repair of a wrecked humanity? Is it simply the restoration of Adamic purity? Is it only the bringing back of the human soul to the condition in which it was before the fall? This would be a poor result for such tremendous cost as the death of the Lord Jesus Christ, and what guarantee have we that, if this were accomplished tomorrow, the wreck would not be repeated next day, and the race as lost as ever. No, God has accomplished something very much

---

47. "Life in Him! Not in a book, not in a doctrine, not in an experience, not in a man, but in Jesus Christ is the Source and Channel of God's life, and from Him we get that life" (Simpson, "Friday Meeting Talks," 207). (This extract is from a sermon Simpson preached at the Gospel Tabernacle on 28 September 1900).

48. Simpson, *Fullness of Christ*, 130–31.

49. Simpson, *Evangelistic Addresses*, 14.

higher; nothing less, in fact, than the new creation of a new race, patterned not after the human, but the Divine.[50]

Humanity is so closely united with the divine "Being, . . . that, eternally like his Lord, the redeemed man shall be not only a man, but a man united with God and possessing in the depths of his being the very spirit and nature of the eternal Jehovah."[51] Here too Simpson departs from his theological heritage.[52]

The Extent of the Atonement

Because the problem of sin is universal,[53] and because the condemnation of humanity is also universal,[54] the remedy, the revivalists asserted, must also be universal.[55] They did not subscribe to a doctrine of "limited atonement," according to which the atoning work of Jesus Christ was designed to secure the salvation of only a select few. Rather, they believed atonement to be "unlimited" and its benefits available to all. The atonement owes its universality to Christ's infinite value (that was more than enough to offset the negative account of sin) and to God's intent and design to offer it without restriction.

Moody preached that Jesus "tasted death for every man, and he has made it possible for every man to be saved."[56] He noted that the fact that the gospel invitation is addressed to "whosoever will" implies this universality. "It takes in all; nobody is left out."[57] Pierson, too, asserted the potential universality of the atonement, for in Scripture Christ "is represented as dying for all," and his death was intended to relieve "the weight of a world's sins."[58] The benefits of Christ's atonement are for

50. Simpson, "Highest Christian Life," 101.

51. Simpson, *Evangelistic Addresses*, 15.

52. For a thorough treatment of Simpson on the topic of divinization or *theosis*, see Van De Walle, "How High of a Christian Life?"

53. "God never said that all men were sinners alike, but He did say that all men were alike sinners." "The fact of sin, the fact of guilt, the fact of condemnation, is a universal fact, and there is no difference between them as to the fact of sin, and guilt, and penalty, and wrath" (MacLean, *Dr. Pierson*, 138).

54. Pierson, *Believer's Life*, 22.

55. Gundry, *Love Them In*, 124.

56. Moody, *Best of D. L. Moody*, 15.

57. Moody, *Glad Tidings*, 77.

58. MacLean, *Dr. Pierson*, 266, 270.

all that will take them. They are for "whosoever will" and limited only by "whosoever won't."[59] The universality of the atonement is limited only in appropriation and application. God's design does not limit the atonement.[60]

In line with his Reformed upbringing, Simpson was convinced of the universal condemnation of humanity. All human beings were tainted by sin, and sin prevented their having relationship with God. Because of this universal condemnation, all were also in need of salvation. Whether they were adult or child, man or woman, educated or illiterate, rich or poor, all were suffering under the oppressive burden of damnation and all needed the release that Christ alone could provide.

59. Moody, *Notes from My Bible*, 108. Moody goes on to say, "if you are willing to go to Christ, there is no power on earth can keep you away. Now, these men who say they can't come, just be honest and put in the right word and say you won't come" (Moody, *Glad Tidings*, 83). Moreover there is nothing to hinder this whole audience from coming out on the Lord's side tonight, and confessing Jesus Christ to be their Savior; there is nothing but your will to prevent it" (Moody, *Glad Tidings*, 182).

60. "How wonderful that God should thus have made provision for that generic fall of the whole race in Adam, by the atoning work of Christ; and then for the specific fall of each voluntary transgressor, by faith in the Lord Jesus Christ" (Pierson, *Believer's Life*, 20). Gordon, in particular, used this understanding of the atonement to respond to the idea of a universal atonement, both potentially and actually, based on the universal fatherhood of God. The atonement is potentially universal because of the infinitely valuable death of Christ and not because of creation's natural relationship with its Creator. "[Take] the doctrine of vicarious atonement, which the Son of God reveals as God's method of forgiving sin,—what a scandal it is in the eyes of many who had settled the whole question on the ground of the infinite fatherhood of God" (Gordon, *Grace and Glory*, 8–9). "And God forbid that when the Scriptures have told us plainly that 'as many as received him to them he gave the power to become the sons of God,' we should waste our ministry in trying to persuade men that by the universal fatherhood all are the sons of God, whatever their condition. A single gospel sermon, heard and believed and obeyed, can make the deepest sinner a son of God, a partaker of the divine nature; but a thousand sermons can never makes sons of God of those who, by nature, are the children of wrath, and by their willful, persistent rejection of Christ are choosing that the wrath of God shall be upon them" (Gordon, *Grace and Glory*, 28–29).

A. T. Pierson speaks about the ultimate universal response of humanity to the gospel, but this should not be misread as an endorsement of what might be called classical universalism. Pierson does not say that all people of all times and from all places will respond to the gospel invitation of Christ and be saved. Rather, he is pointing out that at the final consummation of history, not only will all nations be represented in the church, but all will become aware of the rule of Christ, even though some will continue to reject it (Pierson, *God and Missions Today*, 45).

This is the testimony of God's Word from beginning to end. "All have sinned and come short of the glory of God. There is none righteous, no not one." From every age and from every land the testimony of human nature is the same. Man's conscience instinctively testifies to his sin. The burden of sin, the fear of punishment cannot be charmed away by pleasure, poetry, art, or philosophy. It is this that makes life miserable and death terrible, for "the sting of death is sin" and "the wages of sin is death."[61]

Sin, the universal problem, has catastrophic consequences, and the attendant guilt cannot be relieved by anything but the release that comes with Jesus.

In his understanding of God's response to this universal condemnation, however, Simpson had drifted from his theological forebears. He believed not only that the blessings obtained by Christ's work on the cross were infinitely valuable, but that the objects of these blessings were potentially universal. He believed the atonement to be unlimited, first of all because of universal value of Christ's atoning death (and with this, historic Presbyterianism would raise no argument). Jesus is divine and eternal, and so the value of his death is eternal too. The sacrifice and atonement of Christ were "sufficient for all."[62] Second, and more to the point, the advantages of the atonement are universal in that they are potentially available to the same group who sit under the universal condemnation of God. The universal predicament has called out for a universal solution, and God, in Christ, has provided one. Jesus's death on the cross was an act "accessible and available to all"—with the whole of humanity as its potential object. That is, it was, again, for "whosoever will."[63] For Simpson, the gospel was only good news "because of [this] universality." Echoing his peers, he asserted, "Whosoever will may take it and live,"[64] for Jesus Christ "has given to us a salvation that is adequate, adapted, and designed for the whole world."[65]

61. Simpson, *Earnests of the Coming Age*, 47.

62. Simpson, *Christ in the Tabernacle*, 28; Simpson, *Evangelistic Addresses*, 16–17.

63. Simpson, *Missionary Messages*, 57.

64. Simpson, *Fourfold Gospel*, 20.

65. Simpson, *Missionary Messages*, 52.

Decision—The Means of Salvation

Revivalism and the Exercise of the Will

At the heart of late nineteenth-century revivalistic soteriology was a belief in the freedom and ability of the human will. The human will, though no longer in pristine condition, was believed to be neither impotent nor inconsequential in the work of salvation. In contrast to their predecessors, whose Calvinistic soteriology denied that the human will had either the freedom or the ability even to respond to the offer of salvation (let alone to initiate the individual's own way to salvation), the late nineteenth-century revivalists thought that the individual decision of the will in the event of salvation was essential.[66] The earlier brand of Calvinism, represented in America by Jonathan Edwards, and later by the Princeton theologians Charles Hodge and B. B. Warfield, staunchly defended the unqualified sovereignty of God in all matters. In their view, God and God alone is the active agent in the salvation of humanity, for the human will has been universally, wholly, and surely corrupted by the effects of the fall. For the revivalists of the late nineteenth century, the will has been affected by the fall, but not to the point of total inability. Though misshapen and bent, the will remains both relatively able and free to respond to the offer of salvation.

As noted earlier, an essential soteriological shift took place between the First Great Awakening (personified in New England theologian and revivalist Jonathan Edwards) and the Second Great Awakening (represented by theologian and preacher Charles G. Finney). Both Edwards and Finney were of Calvinist stock, but as has been demonstrated, their Calvinisms were not identical. Finney exerted significant effort in directly rebutting Edwards's view of the inability and bondage of the will.[67] He took an apologetic and polemical posture because he was opposing the reigning orthodoxy and thus needed to demonstrate that his

66. "Revivalists varied in their orthodoxy, but the common thread was that they defined the individual as the unity that approaches God and chooses to be saved or not. A central belief was that an emotional, life-changing experience marked salvation." "Freedom of choice was basic to nineteenth-century revivalism. God was viewed as a somewhat passive actor whose will was accomplished through the free activity of individuals" (Thomas, *Revivalism and Cultural Change*, 67–68).

67. Finney dedicates an entire lecture in his *Systematic Theology* to his disagreement with Edwards on this very issue and goes on in subsequent lectures to clarify his own position (Finney, *Finney's Systematic Theology*, 303–42).

view was the most biblical, reasonable, and true to common experience. Though he still identified himself with Presbyterian Calvinism, Finney placed the responsibility for the salvation of humanity squarely upon the shoulders of both God and humanity. For Edwards, not only is humanity wholly dependent upon God for something as large as revival, but it is also wholly dependent upon God for personal salvation. Finney took exception to the doctrine of human inability and consequently opposed the notion of human irresponsibility in the area of salvation. Human beings, he asserted, by an act of their will are able and responsible to choose salvation.

The Synergistic Exercise of the Will

By the last quarter of the nineteenth century, much of the contention over the human will had evaporated. In the writings of A. T. Pierson, for example, the "very threatening Arminianism" of which Edwards was so fearful, and against which he had battled so strongly, shows its influence.[68] The moderate Calvinism that the Presbyterian Pierson represented was a full step away from what Edwards and others had been promoting only a century prior. Though the Princeton theologians were at their apex of activity and influence during his time, the preaching and teaching of Pierson is not apologetic. The battle that Finney had fought was finished by the latter part of the century. Pierson felt no need to defend his theological position,[69] because for him and his revivalist contem-

---

68. "But man was made in the image of God, and that image partly remains to man, even after the fall, in the independent power of thought and choice. I say with great reverence, that God respects the creature that he has made, and the consequence is that he does not, and will not, deal with a human being as you would with a machine, which, if it needs repair, you remodel, after which, if you cannot make anything out of, you do not hesitate to smash into pieces" (Pierson, *Heart of the Gospel*, 203–4). "The Creator respects the mind, capable of thought; and the heart, capable of love; and the conscience, capable of judging; and the will, capable of choosing; and therefore he puts salvation before us as a something to be chosen, accepted and appropriated. You could not earn it, obtain it, work it out; but you can take it, and it never will be yours if you do not" (Pierson, *Heart of the Gospel*, 204).

69. "Whether the human act or the divine act has the precedence, we are neither concerned to inquire, nor are we capable to determine. There is a profound mystery about the whole subject upon which the Word of God sheds no decisive light; but the paradox is not a contradiction, nor does the mystery involve an absurdity. It is sufficient for us to know that we shall never enter in Christ save by our own consent, and to know with equal certainty that we shall never enter into Christ without God's new creative act" (Pierson, *In Christ Jesus*, 54–55).

poraries, belief in human ability to choose for or against the offer of
salvation had already attained the status of a theological assumption.[70]
For Moody, salvation was essentially something accomplished through
an act of the will. In reply to a charge that sin is what stands between
man and Christ, Moody replied, "It isn't, it's your own will! That is what
stands between the sinner and forgiveness."[71] In regard to salvation, all
is in place except for the decision of the will.[72] A. J. Gordon, too, boldly
asserted that

> the relation of the human to the Divine is mutual. God's willing-
> ness to give is exercised through our willingness to receive; and
> in the order of divine providence, the Lord needs the action of
> our will as much as we need the action of His will. . . . God's will
> is dependent on the submission and choice of our will in order
> that he may bless us and give us the things that we need.[73]

The assumed ability of the human will to choose or reject salvation
colored all facets of late nineteenth-century revivalistic soteriology, if
not all late nineteenth-century theology. Certainly belief in the capacity of the will affected anthropology, but it also influenced and shaped
theology proper. Though they agreed with Edwards that God remains
sovereign, the revivalists came to a different understanding of how he
exercises that sovereignty, namely, that he has chosen to work in cooperation with and even to be limited by the exercise of the human will.

Though raised and trained in a staunch Old Presbyterian environment, Simpson did not continue to hold to the doctrine of "total
depravity," or to regard humanity as an essentially passive character in
the drama of its own salvation.[74] Like his contemporaries, he saw the

70. Pierson reveals his volitional soteriology when he says that to come to Christ
"you take a step in the direction of Christ. Every step is the effect of a will. You may not
be conscious at the time that you are making a will, or a choice, or a decision, but you
cannot take a step without an act of the will" (MacLean, *Dr. Pierson*, 76).

"By 'evangelization,' A. T. Pierson meant the preaching of the word to all persons so
that they could choose whether or not to become Christians" (Robert, "Origin of the
Student Volunteer Watchword" 147).

71. Robertson, *Chicago Revival, 1876*, 113.

72. D. L. Moody said, "[Christ] comes and offers salvation. You can be saved now if
you will" (Moody, *Best of D. L. Moody*, 174).

73. Gordon, *A. J. Gordon*, 195–96 (emphasis added).

74. In his Knox College days, Simpson won an award for a paper titled "Infant
Baptism," which defended the historic Presbyterian practice of baptizing children and

positive action of the human will as a necessary component of salvation. It was not merely something consequent or responsive to a salvation already received. This is not to say that he denied that the first move in the overall work of salvation was God's, or that human ability was unaided by divine grace. In fact, he asserted that even those apparently subjective aspects of salvation are not completely humanity's own doing.[75] Still, in contrast to his classically Reformed upbringing, Simpson was a strong proponent of the responsibility of the human will to actively and necessarily appropriate the grace of God. Though God in Christ has furnished all that is necessary for salvation, and while God alone is able to save,[76] the individual must personally appropriate that grace to make it effective.[77] On this he is clear:

> Every man's salvation hinges upon his own choice and free will. It is an awful thing *to have the power of salvation* and to throw that opportunity away. And yet it is left to our choice. We are not forced to take it. We must *voluntarily* choose it or reject it.[78]

> God calls each of us through the Gospel to accept His free offer of salvation. But the Holy Spirit also comes with a personal pressure, and then it becomes with each of us *a matter of individual choice*. We may refuse and lose our heavenly calling, or we may "lay hold upon eternal life."[79]

> Salvation is not a mechanical process, but a *voluntary* one in which every human effort must *cooperate with God*.[80]

---

of doing so by sprinkling rather than by immersion. Years later, he would find himself retracting these well-thought-out "arguments and doctrinal opinions, which [he had] so stoutly maintained in [his] youthful wisdom." Simpson's soteriology no longer allowed him to be so convinced of a salvation apart from an independent and personal exercise of the human will (Simpson, "Simpson Scrapbook," 13–14).

75. "God has provided all the resources, even the grace, repentance, and faith, if we will take them" (Simpson, *Fourfold Gospel*, 22).

76. "Jesus Christ is the only remedy for man's lost condition" (Simpson, *Kings and Prophets*, 9; Simpson, *Missionary Messages*, 54).

77. "God does not love us or save us in groups but one by one. Each of us has an individual value and personal relation to Him shared by no other" (Simpson, *Earnests of the Coming Age*, 72).

78. Simpson, *Fourfold Gospel*, 21 (emphasis added).

79. Simpson, *Earnests of the Coming Age*, 72 (emphasis added).

80. Simpson, *Missionary Messages*, 62 (emphasis added).

One remains unsaved, too, because of an action of this will. In this case, however, it is because of a rejection of the love of God in Christ.[81]

Yet even the action of reception remains in a sense passive. It is not a work worthy of commendation but merely a trusting and reliance on Christ to make good on the salvation he has provided and offered and, at the same time, a rejection of one's own strivings to save oneself. "The only way to get saved," for Simpson, "is to stop everything and let Him save you."[82]

Simpson, Presbyterianism, and Knox College

While the questions of how, why, and when Simpson changed his mind may be next to impossible to answer, the fact that his soteriology underwent a distinct change is indisputable. The Covenant Presbyterians, whose doctrines and devotion shaped Simpson's rigorous religious upbringing, were both deeply pious and strongly and traditionally Calvinistic in their soteriology, especially where human participation in salvation is concerned. Their standard of doctrine was the Westminster Confession of Faith, which teaches (in chapter 10, "Of Effectual Calling") that

> this effectual call is of God's free and special grace alone, not from any thing at all foreseen in man, who is altogether passive therein, until, being quickened and renewed by the Holy Spirit, he is thereby enabled to answer this call, and to embrace the grace offered and conveyed in it.[83]

In the chapter "Of Free-Will," the Confession clarifies this idea of human inability in regard to salvation:

> Man, by his fall into a state of sin, *hath wholly lost all ability of will to any spiritual good accompanying salvation;* so as, a natural man, being altogether averse from that good, and dead in sin, is not able, by his own strength, to convert himself, or to prepare himself thereunto.[84]

---

81. "If we are lost it is because we have neglected and defied God's love" (Simpson, *Fourfold Gospel*, 23).

82. Simpson, *Kings and Prophets*, 18.

83. Committee for Christian Education & Publications, *Confession of Faith*, 37.

84. Ibid., 34–35.

Accordingly, regeneration is divine work alone; the role of humanity is merely to live in a manner worthy of that previous gift of regeneration. This point dissolves any possibility of a synergistic understanding of regeneration, for not only does the will not cooperate in salvation, it is unable to do so.

Knox College, Simpson's alma mater, was also strongly Calvinistic, and during his time there also held closely to the Westminster Confession of Faith, including to the sections "Effective Calling" and "Of Free-Will." The task of a professor was to "[pass] on . . . the denomination's identity and especially its belief system."[85] The goal of the Knox faculty, therefore, was not a "liberal" education. That is, the faculty did not consider it their duty merely to present their students with a smorgasbord of theological options and allow them to choose for themselves. Rather, "[from] the beginning, [Knox's] intent was to educate students to be persuasive promoters of a particular interpretation of Christianity."[86] Its goal was to indoctrinate those who would in turn indoctrinate others with their particular species of Protestant Christianity. In this sense, they were quite unecumenical, even within Protestant circles. They sought not merely to defend Christianity but to "defend the intellectual integrity of the Presbyterian system of doctrine as revealed by God in the Scriptures and systematized most fully in the Westminster Standards."[87]

What was the content of this particular interpretation of Christianity? "[The] five points of Calvinism defined at the Synod of Dort (1618–1619) formed the core doctrine around which the faculty designed the curriculum. The five propositions said that human beings, by nature, were totally depraved and could not contribute to their salvation in any way."[88] While one may want to describe the Knox faculty during Simpson's time as "evangelical," they were certainly not evangelical if by that one means revivalistic and having a positive, "Arminianized" view of human ability in relation to salvation. Indeed, one of the reasons for Knox College's suspicion of American Christianity, including American Reformed thought and even American Presbyterianism, stemmed from the New England or "New Light" fascination with the

85. Fraser, *Church, College, and Clergy*, 9.
86. Ibid.
87. Ibid., 14.
88. Ibid., 28–29.

role of human agency in the work of salvation. Michael Willis, principal of Knox's Theological Department during Simpson's student days, identified American theology of this stripe as smacking of the "Arminian heresy."[89]

American Presbyterianism, given the almost universal popularity of revivalistic theology, remained suspect at Knox but was not wholly ignored. The early Princeton divines were a notable exception to this rule; the works of Archibald Alexander and Charles Hodge were both used in the Knox classrooms in the mid-nineteenth century.[90] Following the Civil War, the Emancipation Proclamation, and the arrival of William Caven to Knox, the American Presbyterian theologians, especially those who taught at Princeton, made a major impact on Knox College.[91] Princeton theology popularized "Old School Presbyterianism" and restored its respectability on the American scene. At its core, Old School Presbyterianism, too, held closely to the definition of the faith as articulated in the Westminster Confession. American Presbyterian thought was accepted at Knox as long as it was Princetonian, and only as long as it adhered to traditional Calvinistic categories, including total depravity and human inability.

Despite the growing influence of Princeton theology in his own day, and in the face of his own theological heritage, Simpson, like so many of his contemporaries, did not engage in an extended theological defense of his view of human responsibility and ability. However,

89. Ibid., 58. It is interesting to note, however, that Willis's characteristically Calvinistic rejection of Arminianism did not diminish his zeal or totally overshadow his concern for evangelism and the human "duty" to accept "the common salvation which is proffered to us in the most unrestricted terms." This should not be understood, however, as evidence that he believed in the ability of humanity to achieve salvation apart the antecedent work of God in regeneration (Vaudry, *Free Church in Victorian Canada*, 49).

90. Fraser, *Church, College, and Clergy*, 15, 54.

91. To overstate the Princeton-Knox connection would be to do an injustice to the independence and individuality of the Knox faculty. Though Knox and Princeton shared more than just common doctrinal positions (e.g., an aversion to an oversimplified Presbyterian reunification and a respect for Presbyterian polity), it is interesting to note that many of the popular practices of the nineteenth century to which Princeton and Old School Presbyterianism felt an aversion (e.g., voluntary societies, foreign missions) were alive and well among Knox's faculty and students. "From the Old School perspective, such efforts threatened the purity of the church, and hence were suspect" (*Dictionary of Christianity in America*, s.v. "Old Presbyterians").

his convictions show themselves in his unheeding and universal call to those who wished to be saved to make a conscious decision of their will to receive Jesus. Repeatedly, and throughout his career (especially the post-Presbyterian portion), Simpson did not encourage people to rest in the assurance of their salvation, unless that resting had been preceded by an act of the will to appropriate the salvation made possible for them. He believed that the security of one's salvation is based on the character of an unfailing God but also on the historic reality of an exercise of the will in favor of this unfailing God: both elements are necessary for salvation.

The Critical Nature of Salvation

The revivalists considered salvation to be a punctiliar or sudden event, though it looked toward growth and development. Related as it is to a decision of the will, "saved" is something one either is or is not. The moment of decision, should it be in the affirmative, is the point at which one becomes saved, justified, and regenerate. Salvation undoubtedly presupposes growth and maturity, but the salvation event, in and of itself, is not this process.[92]

This view of salvation was not, of course, without its contemporary critics.[93] John Kennedy, a leading Scottish Free Church minister, for example, responded to Moody's successful campaign in Great Britain by attacking Moody on this very issue. In his opinion, "Real repentance . . . was a process which required some considerable time to be accomplished. The work of conversion includes what we might expect to find

92. D. L. Moody used the biblical examples of the thief on the cross and Zacchaeus to support his belief in conversion as a punctiliar phenomenon: "Any man who objects to sudden conversions should give attention to how this man was converted. If conversions are gradual, this poor thief could not have been converted." The example of Zacchaeus illustrates both the distinctness of the event and the changed life that normally ought to follow from it: "Some people do not believe in SUDDEN CONVERSION. I should like them to answer me—when was Zacchaeus converted? He was certainly in his sins when he went up into the tree; he certainly was converted when he came down. He must have been converted somewhere between the branch and the ground" The proof of this critical change, said Moody, was seen in his consequent change in attitude and action (Moody, *Best of D. L. Moody*, 167, 131).

93. James Findlay notes that this aversion to preaching on hell differentiated Moody from the camp-meeting preachers of the earlier part of the century and opened him to much criticism from many of his contemporaries (Findlay, *Dwight L. Moody*, 228).

detailed in a process."[94] He would go on to argue that the instantaneous nature of the Moody-related conversions proved that they were merely human acts and not the gracious work of God. These competing notions may have led the revivalists to emphasize the critical nature of salvation. The revivalistic doctrine of salvation came into prominence at the same time that Horace Bushnell's theology of nurture was gaining popularity. Bushnell believed salvation to be the result of a process of nurture and instruction, if not the process itself. For the revivalists, the operative question was, are you saved or not? whereas for Bushnell it was, at what point are you on the road of salvation? The revivalists considered salvation to be necessarily dependent upon a conscious decision of the will at a moment in time. Bushnell, by contrast, believed that salvation is a road that many, if not all, are already treading. The question for Bushnell, then, is not an exclusive, are you in, or are you out? Rather, the question, if there is a question at all, is one of degree or maturity.

Given his understanding of the role of decision in the attainment of salvation, Simpson, too, saw salvation as a punctiliar event. The momentous arrival of Christ brings life, and from this new vitality, one subsequently grows and matures. Growth and maturity do not lead to salvation, they flow from it. As Christ arrives in an instant, so too, life arrives in an instant.

> Now all this comes through Christ. It is not a character slowly built up. It is not mere merit painfully attained . . . but it is a Person—a living, loving, real Man, Christ, our Brother, our Saviour, our living Head, who has wrought it all out for us and who waits to give it to us *the moment we accept Him.*[95]

The Disadvantaged—The Special Objects of Salvation

As the revivalists of the late nineteenth century adhered to a particular soteriology, so too, they brought their message of salvation to a

94. Ross, "Calvinists in Controversy," 54.

95. Simpson, *Missionary Messages*, 55–56 (emphasis added). Again, Simpson also believed in a "Full Salvation" that moves beyond the attainment of life, a salvation that is the greater will of God for humanity. However, this does not diminish the reality and completeness of the real salvation acquired in the momentous event of receiving Jesus Christ. One is truly saved even before growth and maturity occur, not because of them. Maturity is a consequence of salvation, not its effect.

particular audience. That is, they evidenced what modern observers might call a "preferential option for the poor,"[96] and focused their evangelistic efforts especially on the disenfranchised. This focus was by no means wholly innovative. It had characterized the lives and ministries of their predecessors, including John Wesley and George Müller.[97] This is not to say, however, that they neglected other groups. They preached to all classes, ethnicities, and ages. Indeed, they went out of their way to enlist the support of the rich and privileged, and though many of the well-to-do were moved and changed in the meetings, they focused their efforts on the poor.

The revivalists did not believe that the lower classes necessarily had any spiritual advantage.[98] Their preference for the poor stemmed rather from their perception that the contemporary church had neglected the poor, if not treated them with disdain. They sought them out in spite of the hardships associated with such a ministry.[99] Moody started his ministry with the poorest of the poor, the children of the slums of Chicago. Pierson, whose biography bears many striking resemblances to that of Simpson, left his parish ministry in an effort to reach out to the underprivileged classes of Detroit. Gordon, like Simpson, struggled with his fashionable congregation over his personal commitment to overcome any ostentation that might stand between the Clarendon Street Church

---

96. Though this term is commonly used by modern-day liberation theologians to refer to God's attitude toward the poor, it is also a fitting description of the related view of the late nineteenth-century revivalists. Related liberative issues of the second half of the twentieth century may, but need not necessarily, be read into this choice of phrase.

97. Dayton, "Presidential Address," 10–12. For Pierson's account of Müller's life, see Pierson, *George Müller of Bristol.*

98. Some revivalists, however, believed that the poor were more receptive to the gospel because of their greater experiential realization of need. Unlike those of the middle- and upper class, they had not been lulled to sleep by the ease and comfort of American life. They were more than willing to throw aside what they had in order to gain what the gospel offers to them. A. J. Gordon believed that throughout history the gospel has always first taken root among the poor, and once established there, moves its way through the ranks to the upper classes (Gordon, *Yet Speaking,* 87; Gordon, *Holy Spirit in Missions,* 135).

99. "No matter how troublesome the persons they helped—former prisoners, prostitutes, unwed mothers, vagrants, or the unemployed—revivalists accepted them with openness and warmth. Placing the blame largely on environmental pressures, rescue workers argued that given a proper chance even the most difficult persons would perform creditably" (Magnuson, *Salvation in the Slums,* xvii–xviii).

and the poor, including the practice of pew rental.[100] The revivalists did not completely disparage the ministries that the more conventional churches of their day were undertaking. Yet they believed that these ministries were, partly by design though perhaps not completely by intent, ignoring the real need of those beyond the church doors. Hence by focusing on the poor, the revivalists were simply attempting to reach an identifiable socioeconomic group that had not yet been touched by their gospel.

Another reason that the revivalists focused their message on the poor was simply a concern for the welfare of their fellow human beings. The burgeoning growth of the late nineteenth century, otherwise known as the "Gilded Age," had led to tremendous industrial growth and the accompanying phenomenon of the self-made multimillionaires, exemplified in the likes of Andrew Carnegie, John D. Rockefeller, and Cornelius Vanderbilt. However, on the dark side of this age of affluence lay an equally great squalor. Following reasoning that would later be refined by Abraham Maslow, the revivalists realized that should they wish to reach the poor with their gospel, it would be wise to first address the pressing physical needs that daily consumed them. Donald Dayton, Norris Magnuson, and others have shown that a passion for evangelism fueled many of the social relief agencies at the end of the nineteenth century.[101] Despite their premillennial eschatology, which carried with it the possibility of a world-abandoning despair,[102] the revivalists persisted in their social relief work, so as to prepare their designated audience as a fertile soil in which the gospel could germinate, grow, and yield its fruit. Even Moody, whose famous quotation, "God has given me a lifeboat and said, 'Moody, save all you can!'"[103] revealed his own

---

100. It is noteworthy that the issue of pew rentals and the poor became important in one way or another for all the subjects of this study. The pastors (Simpson, Pierson, and Gordon) had to deal with it within their own churches, while Moody had to deal with it as one who sponsored a pew that he filled with "people [that he] brought in from street corners and boarding houses" (Gundry, *Love Them In*, 33; Robert, "Legacy of Arthur Tappan Pierson," 121; Robert, "Legacy of Adoniram Judson Gordon," 176; Russell, "Adoniram Judson Gordon," 66).

101. Dayton, *Discovering an Evangelical Heritage*, 4–5; Magnuson, *Salvation in the Slums*, xvi.

102. This particular view of eschatology will be more thoroughly discussed in chapter 5.

103. Moody, "Second Coming of Christ," 28.

pessimistic view, did not wholly disparage the use of social ministries in his gospel work.[104] He and his fellow revivalists realized that once their audiences' physical needs were met, they could more easily and more intently turn their minds to issues of a spiritual, eternal, and less immediate nature. The revivalists regarded social relief as a form of pre-evangelism.[105] By providing for the physical and social needs of their audience, the revivalists were attempting to remove any unnecessary and even diabolical encumbrances from their path and thereby were freeing up their ability to choose.

One would be amiss, however, to assume that the notions of simple human compassion and mercy did not play a role in the revivalists' relief work. They did not regard such effort as merely a means to serve the end of evangelism. As they drew nearer to the poor and underprivileged, many revivalists became more aware of and more concerned about their physical and social plight. Though they had many rich and privileged supporters, the revivalists did not simply champion the status quo, for more often than not it simply increased the poverty and oppression of the poor. According to Norris Magnuson,

> the openness of the revivalists toward the underprivileged, their criticism of the social order, and their support for labor and for various progressive reforms, ought to weigh heavily against their being identified with an irrelevant or reactionary position. Indeed, ... in a number of statements and interests the revivalists moved close to the radical critics of the established order.[106]

Though the revivalists were involved in social action, it would be incorrect to fully equate their ministry with that of their contemporaries in the Social Gospel movement. Both groups were involved in social

104. George Marsden, while acknowledging the social impact of Moody's early work, believes that Moody later "dropped direct social involvement for the same reason that he avoided controversial theology—both threatened to distract from his primary concern for evangelism." Which is to say that Moody abandoned social relief work for reasons of political expediency and not because he objected to it on theological grounds (Marsden, *Fundamentalism and American Culture*, 37).

105. A. T. Pierson, while not completely denigrating the role of social work, certainly attempts to keep it in perspective with regard to what he considers the highest work: "Even if you try to feed the hungry and clothe the naked, do it as Christ did, that your ministry to the body may be the preparation of your ministry to the soul" (MacLean, *Dr. Pierson*, 120–21).

106. Magnuson, *Salvation in the Slums*, xviii.

relief and both spoke of "salvation," but each defined the term differently, and each attempted to bring it about in different ways. How it looked and how it was achieved was radically different. Those involved in the classic Social Gospel movement sought to create better individuals by creating a better society with just social structures that would foster people of justice. Hence they concentrated their efforts on changing the corporate realm and sought to convert social structures, not individuals per se. Individual conversion would result from the process of renewing the social structures to which individuals belong.[107] Such a soteriology may be labeled "cosmological," in that focus is on the larger structures, and only consequentially does it affect the smaller, constituent members of that society. The move for those who practiced such a method of salvation is from the larger to the smaller—a just, righteous social superstructure creating the proper environment in which to nurture and produce just, righteous individuals.[108]

The inverse is true of the late nineteenth-century revivalists. Within late nineteenth-century evangelicalism, there was a hierarchy of individual conversion over social reform in both theory and practice. Though such societal reforms were not viewed as inherently bad, no hope was held out for the ultimate transformation of society. Not only was society too large, complex, and intangible a hydra to tackle, but the revivalists' eschatology dismissed out of hand any hope of lasting societal change. The revivalists understood that the ultimate fate of society was sealed. To work at improving it and achieving some type of heaven on earth was futile. Their premillennialism was ultimately pessimistic regarding the possibility of human effort improving the world. Rather, the best they could hope to do was to relieve the suffering of those caught up in the downward spiral of world history.[109]

107. Daniel Evearitt has pointed out, with multiple examples, the growing tendency of American Christianity, as exemplified in Walter Rauschenbusch, to equate salvation with the improvement of social relationships in the here and now and to eschew the church's traditional perception of salvation as an essentially individual category that finds its fulfillment in some otherworldly eschatological event. "So, the older theology of personal salvation, with the kingdom of God off in the future, was to be left behind by the new social theology of the late 19th century" (Evearitt, *Body and Soul*, 34).

108. "[In] Moody's judgment the basic ill of society was the need of individual regeneration which would produce moral integrity" (Gundry, *Love Them In*, 151).

109. Douglas K. Matthews describes the ways in which the exponents of the forms of premillennial eschatology view the role of social involvement and relief work.

The revivalists knew that the individual was more easily definable, easier to work with, and the proper object of the gospel. Theirs was an "atomic" soteriology.[110] They believed that to try to affect society without changing the hearts of individuals was a waste of both time and resources, for it is sin-infested and tainted individuals who determine the character of a given society, and not the other way around. Therefore, as long as individuals were not transformed, any change in society would be temporary at best. Only redeemed individuals would have a prolonged transformative effect on unrighteous social structures.[111] Conversion ought not simply to lead to some type of personal spiritual gain but should also manifest itself in the social life and concern of the believer, even if the results of such engagement were minimal and fleeting.

Despite his conviction of the universal need for the gospel,[112] Simpson did not direct his ministry, either at Thirteenth Street Presbyterian Church in New York City or at the Gospel Tabernacle, to *just* anybody. In fact, his very focus on the economically underprivileged and the culturally marginalized contributed to his resigning his Presbyterian pastorate and striking out on his own. The pew-rental system in place at the church de facto kept unsophisticated people at

---

Matthews explicitly links Simpson with "symptomatic or relief-oriented premillennialism," which excels at relief work but believes that society will ultimately degenerate to the point of an "inevitable slide to Armageddon" (Matthews, "Approximating the Millennium," 63–64).

110. David Moberg has labeled these two categories "social salvation" and "religious individualism." The classifications "cosmological" and "atomic," however, speak more directly to the flow of the methodology that underlies each category (Moberg, *Inasmuch*, 18).

111. A. J. Gordon believed that this was indeed the divine prescription for change: "The seed of the Word germinating in single hearts, and these renewed hearts in turn becoming the germ principle of a new society—this is the divine order" (Gordon, *Holy Spirit in Missions*, 136).

112. The work of Christ is categorically the only foundation for salvation for Simpson, but this foundation is available to all: "Christ's blood is the only passport . . . to the presence of God, either in earth or in heaven. With it, we are accepted either on earth or in heaven to the very presence of God.

"Further, [the blood of Christ] was accessible to the highest and the lowest, to every class of people. This indicates the fullness and graciousness of the great atonement that Christ has made for the sins of the whole world, sufficient for all, though effectual only for those who believe" (Simpson, *Christ in the Tabernacle*, 28).

"[The gospel of Jesus Christ] is the only remedy for a guilty conscience and a sinful heart" (Simpson, *Missionary Messages*, 54).

the margins at best. Simpson called the practice "wrong and we believe most unscriptural."[113] It offended his evangelistic sensitivities. Though he did not despise the rich and affluent, Simpson encouraged a special "loving consideration, a spirit of considerateness for those in humbler places, the graciousness that in every way covers our social differences by Christ's own law of love."[114] Simpson, to at least a practical degree, had a "preferential option for the poor."

This preference was based on their status as those beyond the current scope of the gospel. Their attractiveness for Simpson was one of pathos. He sought them out for the precise reason that others in the church were not doing so. After all, the kingdom of God was not to be declared to an exclusive few, but universally. While the church of Simpson's day had a strong and long relationship with the affluent majority, it had neglected the poor, the socially marginal, and the newly immigrated. The church must declare the gospel to those within its own sphere of influence, but it also had an obligation—perhaps a greater one—to declare it to all who might benefit from it.[115] Here, then, in these "region[s] beyond even in the Christian work at home"[116] is where Simpson would minister. He would reach the unreached. The gospel was for all, and Simpson wanted to make sure that all would hear it.

Simpson's understanding of the mission of the church in the world also contributed to his concern for the poor and to his desire for social reform. He understood that part of the ministry of the church was to "mother" not only those within its immediate sphere but those within its wider scope of influence and contact. The church has a responsibility to care not only for those within its fellowship but for the wider society as well. Though a revivalist, Simpson believed in the responsibility of the church to care for more than just the souls of people. The church was to be

> complete in every department of work; He [God] wants us to
> have not only the mere preaching of the Gospel, but work for

113. Simpson, *Practical Christianity*, 75.

114. Ibid., 76.

115. "It is not a matter of beneficence to give the gospel to the nations, it is simply a matter of obligation." "We are simply guilty of breach of trust and spiritual dishonesty and crime, if we withhold the gospel from any of our fellow beings whom it is within our power to reach" (Simpson, *Epistle to the Romans*, 272).

116. Simpson, *Epistle to the Romans*, 282.

the poor and lowly; work for the destitute and the sick; work for the rich and worldly. He wants us to be a people who will combine under Christ's name every department of Christian beneficence which it is right for the church of God to sustain.[117]

Those most in need of this extended care were the poor and the socially and economically disenfranchised. Late nineteenth-century New York City was teeming with such people. Although Simpson believed that social relief could be an instrument by which to evangelize these people,[118] he was convinced that the meeting of these needs, in and of itself, was a church responsibility, regardless of its outcome. The ministry of the church was to be as full and wide ranging as were the legitimate needs of humanity. Even though the "last great mission"[119] of the church is to evangelize the world and win souls, Simpson was convinced that

> we should aim to bring all the work of God within the sphere of the church of Christ. God, it is true, is doing His work in every way and we cannot limit His mighty providence even by the church; but we should work within His prescribed moulds as far as practicable. There is no form of Christian effort but may be embraced under a fully developed plan of church organization. This is room not only for the worship of God, the teaching of sacred truth and the evangelization of the lost, but also for every phase of practical philanthropy and usefulness. There may be, in perfect keeping with the simple order and dignity of the church of God, the most aggressive work for the masses and the widest welcome for every class of sinful men; the ministry of healing for the sick and suffering administered in the name of Jesus; the most complete provision for charitable relief; industrial training and social elevation for the degraded classes, workshops for the unemployed, homes for the orphaned, shelter for the homeless, refuge for the inebriate, the fallen and the helpless; missions for the heathen; Christian literature for the instruction of the people; and every agency needed to make the church of God the light of the world and the mother of the suffering and the lost.

117. Simpson, *Fullness of Christ*, 25.

118. "The world needs to see our love and then it will understand the love of our God. So He wants to put His own love in us and make it a passion and a delight and a necessity of our nature to bless others. When Christ comes into our heart this always comes to pass. It should become the first business of our life" (Simpson, *Missionary Messages*, 110).

119. Simpson, *King's Business*, 147.

And there is no work that will be more glorifying to God than
a church that will embrace just such features and completeness.
May the Lord help us yet to realize the vision and present at His
own blessed coming His own fair bride and her multitudes of
children.[120]

Like the other revivalists, Simpson both believed in the intrinsic
worth of relief work and knew that such philanthropy would open
doors for the gospel. Not only could such works remove the barriers of
constantly pressing physical needs, but they would also arouse the curi-
osity of those ministered to in regard to the message that the benefactor
was proclaiming. Citing the example of Jesus, Simpson said, "He came
to heal as well as to save. To help the multitudes and practice His own
precepts as well as point the way to heaven. Our acts of love and help
may be His links in bringing them to see the attraction of His love and
listen to the Gospel of grace."[121] Not only was this Jesus's example for
us, but this was also part of the divine plan: "It is probable that God lets
every human being that crosses our path, meet us, in order that we may
have the opportunity of leaving some blessing in his path, and drop into
his heart and life some influence that will draw him nearer to God."[122]

Though genuinely interested in the social welfare of the poor,
Simpson still warned against emphasizing social ministry at the expense of soul care and evangelism. At points, Simpson appears to give
conflicting messages regarding the value of social ministry. Sometimes
he seemed to disparage of the whole social enterprise. In such cases
Simpson was responding to what he perceived to be a drastic imbalance
in the fledgling Social Gospel movement. Social involvement, though
an important and necessary task of the church, should never be allowed
to become the primary task of the church. Ultimately the church's task
was to evangelize in such a way as to bring about regeneration. Progress
on the physical and social levels, however great, would all be for naught
if it did not lead to regeneration of the soul. John Dahms rightly
identifies this move later in Simpson's career as a corrective to what
Simpson perceived to be an overemphasis of a good yet secondary task
of the church. Simpson believed that social action has a legitimate and

120. Simpson, *King's Business*, 149–50.
121. Simpson, *Practical Christianity*, 80.
122. Simpson, "Mutual Responsibility," 149.

important place in the overall ministry of the church, but it must be kept in its place.[123]

Simpson also believed that spiritual conversion ought always to take precedence over, though not obliterate, social action; that lasting change could only occur from individuals to society, not the other way around. The Social Gospel movement held the opposite opinion. Walter Rauschenbusch, the father of the Social Gospel movement, was serving at Second German Baptist Church, "in a particularly depressing section of West 45th Street, near Tenth Avenue,"[124] a mere three blocks away from Simpson's Gospel Tabernacle.[125] As was noted above, the Social Gospel movement held that the relative health of the societal structures of a given culture determines to a great degree the relative health of the individuals that are produced by and inhabit those social structures. The greater affects the lesser. If, then, one wants to have a society of good people, one must work at effecting change at the structural level and not at the level of the individual.

Though Simpson did not wholly deny either the impact that an immoral society could make on the individual or the positive impact that the right environment could make on the individual,[126] the aim of his relief work was individual and not corporate. The ultimate destiny of human society was sure—it would not survive intact. It was not just that it was corrupt beyond hope, but that Scripture had forecast its downturn and ultimate destruction. The same was not true of individuals. Though Simpson was somewhat fatalistic regarding the possibilities for human society, he was an optimist regarding individuals. Indeed, God did not intend the gospel for societies per se, but for individuals.[127] Though the

123. Dahms, however, also considers the possibility that such a move was not simply a corrective but a "retrograde step" (Dahms, "Social Interest," 66).

124. Minus, *Walter Rauschenbusch*, 50.

125. For a comparison of the ministries and methods of Rauschenbusch and Simpson, see Evearitt, "Social Gospel vs. Personal Salvation," 1–18.

126. On of the main reasons that Simpson is said to have moved the Missionary Training Institute from New York City to Nyack was to provide better surroundings for the cultivation of Christian workers (Pardington, *Twenty-five Wonderful Years*, 42; see also Turnbull, "Christian Educator," 218).

127. Simpson, *Missionary Messages*, 24. Simpson states that the "mistake" of the church lay in its extended efforts "to convert the whole of one country[,] i.e. social renewal at the expense of relaying the gospel message to all lands" (Simpson, *Missionary Messages*, 26).

ministry of the Gospel Tabernacle included social relief, it was done to minister to and in some measure to rehabilitate individuals. It sought neither to reverse the downward momentum of society nor to divert attention from its primary task: the evangelization of individuals. If social change were to occur through the ministry of the Gospel Tabernacle, it would come as a consequence of the redemption and salvation of individuals and would be minimal and temporary.

Conclusion

That which sets Simpson apart from his contemporaries in regard to soteriology has nothing to do with major points of doctrine. Like his fellow revivalists, Simpson held to a penal-substitution theory of the atonement that included a belief in the reciprocity of exchange between Christ and the Christian; he also staunchly advocated the exercise of the will as a prerequisite to the actualization of salvation through the indwelling of Christ, and he concentrated his evangelistic efforts on the poor and marginalized. Any differences there may have been had to do merely with nuance of expression or difference in emphasis.[128]

128. According to David J. Smith, "While Simpson echoed mainstream, evangelical, nineteenth century Protestantism, the unique contribution of Simpson was to view salvation as a spiritual union of the believer with Christ. The initial encounter with the Risen and Living Lord Jesus Christ was considered a salvation experience of conversion" (Smith, "Albert Benjamin Simpson"). However, Simpson does not make a unique contribution even here, for this same emphasis on spiritual union can be found in A. J. Gordon's *In Christ* and A. T. Pierson's *Vital Union with Christ*, to name but two such works by Simpson's revivalist contemporaries.

The one area where Simpson is clearly distinct from his contemporaries is in his clear endorsement of divinization. Neither Moody nor Gordon nor Pierson takes the same stand as Simpson on this issue (Van De Walle, "How High of a Christian Life?").

"I Will Say 'Yes' to Jesus"

I will say "Yes" to Jesus;
Oft it was "No" before,
As He knocked at my heart's proud entrance,
And I firmly barred the door;
But I've made a complete surrender,
And given Him right of way;
And henceforth it is always "Yes,"
Whatever He may say.

I will say "Yes" to Jesus,
"Yes, Lord, forever yes.
I'll welcome all Thy blessed will
And sweetly answer Yes."

I will say "Yes" to Jesus.
His promises I'll claim,
And on every check He endorses
I'll dare to write my name;
I will put my "Amen" wherever
My God has put his "Yea,"
And ever boldly answer "Yes,"
Whatever He may say.

I will say "Yes" to Jesus,
To all that He commands,
I will hasten to do His bidding
With willing heart and hands;
I will listen to hear His whispers,
And learn His will each day.
And always gladly answer "Yes,"
Whatever He may say.

I will say "Yes" to Jesus,
Whate'er His hands may bring;
And, though clouds hang over my pathway,
My trusting heart will sing.
I will follow where'er He leadeth;
My Shepherd knows the way,
And while I live I'll answer "Yes,"
Whatever He may say.[129]

129. Simpson, "I Will Say 'Yes' to Jesus," in *Hymns of the Christian Life*, 217.

3

Christ, Our Sanctifier

As was noted in the preceding chapter, the history of the American religious scene is the history of the rising and fading of movements known as "revivals." Though they are called by the same name, these phenomena were not homogeneous. They differed not only in duration, in the primary geographical area they affected, and in the identities of their leading figures, but also in their central emphases. Nevertheless, all nineteenth-century revivals centered on the revivification of a life of "practical holiness" or "sanctification." Most people today would associate "revival" with mass evangelism, and initial Christian conversion was indeed a component of all nineteenth-century revival movements, but nineteenth-century popular religion and revivalism were not primarily interested in initial conversion but in the holiness of life that ought to flow from it.

Those who led the revivals of the nineteenth-century had as their goal the resuscitation of what they believed to be a dead or anemic church. The church, and not society in general, was their primary target. They wanted those who had already experienced conversion to move on to experience the "full gospel," "full salvation," or their "full inheritance."[1] This fuller experience, the revivalists believed, was not just for a special pious few: It was the will of God for all, even though it was not a common experience. They did not understand spiritual poverty as preferential, inevitable, or necessary, but rather as a deficiency that could and must be overcome. The common attainment of the "victorious Christian life" was the goal of the nineteenth-century holiness revival.

1. According to Melvin Dieter, the "main thrust" of the Holiness movement, though it "eventually resulted in bringing thousands of new converts into the Christian faith and churches," was "to reform the church itself" or to "*Christianize* Christianity" (Dieter, *Holiness Revival*, 6).

A. B. Simpson was not unaffected by this emphasis on holiness. Indeed, the doctrine of sanctification may be said to lie at the heart of Simpson's "Fourfold Gospel."[2] Some might think that his teaching on sanctification, though not entirely original, was a distinct and special gift to evangelicalism. However, a close comparison of the writings on sanctification of Moody, Pierson, and Gordon with those of Simpson reveals that, although Simpson contributed to the shape of the late nineteenth-century doctrine of sanctification, he was in almost no way unique, in either terminology or emphases. Rather, even against his own protestations, his doctrine of sanctification clearly falls under the larger umbrella known as Keswick theology, which was a very popular option of the period.

Shapers of the Nineteenth-Century Doctrine of Sanctification

John Wesley

Following his own conversion, which was the result of a chance meeting with Moravians, John Wesley (1703–1791) visited their settlement at Herrnhut, and spent time with their leader, Count Nikolaus von Zinzendorf (1700–1760). From this point on, Wesley made it his life goal to revive the Church of England and, in his own words, "to spread Scriptural holiness throughout the land."[3] This emphasis on holiness, though it had not been entirely absent before the eighteenth century, returned to the fore of both church life and theological discussion with Wesley. Following his alienation from the Anglican Church over his particular methods and his focus on holiness, Wesley pursued his goal through itinerant, open-air preaching and the Methodist movement was born. Within one hundred years of his death, the various denominations and organizations that traced their lineage back to Wesley easily comprised one of the largest groups in American Christianity.

In addition to reviving the doctrine of sanctification within the church, Wesley impressed it with his own particular theological stamp. Central to this theological innovation was his own doctrine of sin.

2. "Quite central in A. B. Simpson's writings stands the doctrine of sanctification" (McGraw, "Doctrine of Sanctification," 124).

3. Wesley, "Minutes of Several Conversations," 299.

Furthermore, though he linked sanctification closely to the work of justification/conversion, Wesley understood the former to be a distinct work of its own and one that the church of his day needed to understand and reclaim.

For the most part, the ruling doctrine of sin prior to Wesley focused on sin in an absolute sense. Following Augustine, it unequivocally identified sin as any human transgression or deficiency relative to the will and character of God. Sin continued in the lives of believers because even after justification/conversion, according to the Westminster Confession, "there [abides] still some remnants of corruption in every part, whence ariseth a continual and irreconcilable war, the flesh lusting after the Spirit, and the Spirit against the flesh."[4] Indeed, according to the anthropology of the Westminster divines, and that of much of the Christian world, Christians must contend with two opposing natures, the bad and the good; and they would not be free of the former until death.

For Wesley, however, sin was neither so exhaustive nor so necessary. He denied that "mistakes," "ignorance," or "infirmities" due to primeval finite human nature were sin.[5] Those misdeeds that occurred due to human frailties were simply that—frailties—not sin. The nature of sin, rather, is closely tied to intent. It does not consist simply in falling short of or transgressing the law of God. Rather, it involves anything that comes from a heart less than full of love for God or one's neighbor. Wesley based this belief on his understanding of Jesus' distillation of the Law and the Prophets to the single concept of love for God and humanity. If the Law and the Prophets could be summed up in the love commandments of Matthew 22:37–40, then surely love, or more precisely a lack of love, must lie at the heart of what constitutes the nature of sin. It does not consist of a set of specific actions or omissions but of an attitude or inner disposition. Indeed, sin has to do with the motives and attitudes that lie behind any act. Consequently, knowledge of the offence is key. If one trespasses in actuality, but does not do so intentionally but mistakenly or out of ignorance then, to Wesley, the act of trespass, while regrettable and unfortunate, is not sin.

4. Committee for Christian Education & Publications. *Confession of Faith*, 44.

5. Wesley, "Plain Account of Christian Perfection," 374.

Sin, argued Wesley, may be common but it is not necessary. Though sin may be pervasive and even universal, it is not inevitable, and it remains unwarranted—even after the fall. It remains in the life of the believer only as long as it is given ground. The continuing sin of the biblical "saints" may prove the deep-rootedness of the problem, but Wesley would not allow that such evidence constituted its necessity. While granting the commendable behavior of biblical heroes, he would not concede that their own stumblings were the apex of Christian behavior beyond which one could not hope to go.

Challenging the majority opinion of his day, Wesley did not believe that two natures, one fallen and one regenerate, will continue to wage war with one another throughout the life of the believer. The old nature is not merely suppressed or kept in check by an equally strong regenerate nature or alien force. It has rather been removed altogether. Given the possibility of the removal of the fallen nature, he rejected the prevailing conviction, that the ultimate goal of sanctification is achievable only at death, when the old nature will be forever obliterated. Instead, he believed that sanctification is achievable in this life, not only in part, but to the fullest extent that humanity, by nature, can attain. To act in "perfect love" is a real possibility, but it requires deliverence from an evil heart.

In keeping with his definition of sin and of human nature, Wesley believed that Scripture teaches that believers can experience "entire sanctification" or, as Wesley preferred to call it, "perfect love." By this he did not mean that human beings can attain to the same "perfections" that inhere in God by nature, that they can somehow independently overcome their human frailties, or that they will arrive at a place where they were unable to sin. Rather, human beings, relying constantly on the power of the Holy Spirit, can attain a state where they do not knowingly sin. Yet "entire sanctification" comes, not by human nature, effort, or striving alone, but by a gracious act of God subsequent to the grace of justification/conversion.

For Wesley, sanctification is related to the works of justification and regeneration but is distinct from these more basic principles. The Reformed theology that ruled American religious life before the nineteenth century, however, held that sanctification, though distinct in nature from these other works, was not distinct in time and flowed from the one crisis of salvation. Hence sanctification, in the sense of personal holiness, is not experienced by all Christians. Rather, it is the "more excellent way" experienced only by some.

Phoebe Palmer

No other person had a greater impact on the doctrine of sanctification in the nineteenth century than Phoebe Palmer (1807–1874).[6] Though she occupied neither pulpit nor academic chair, Palmer was still able to influence both the social elites and those of more humble station.[7] Her avenues of propagation were primarily two: her Tuesday Meetings and her various publications. She and her sister, Sarah Lankford, ran a series of meetings out of their Manhattan homes that became known as the "Tuesday Meetings for the Promotion of Holiness." Palmer eventually took sole leadership of these meetings. In time, many of the greatest names of nineteenth-century revivalism attended and identified themselves with this simple parlor meeting, which gave rise to a large number of satellite meetings throughout the nation, all of which retained the emphases of the New York meetings. Palmer's writings had an even broader influence than her Tuesday Meetings. Most important to the dissemination of her views was *The Guide to Holiness*, a popular magazine that her husband, physician Walter Palmer, had purchased from Methodist churchman Timothy Merritt in 1864.[8] Her books also had a wide audience. Though she was influenced by Wesleyan soteriology and though, she, like Wesley, defined sanctification as an attitude of the will,[9] Palmer's own ideas in regard to sanctification, which she called the

6. Donald Dayton has identified Palmer's Tuesday Meetings with the start of the Holiness movement, which was arguably the most influential American religious movement of the nineteenth century (Dayton, "Preface," 9). Charles Jones also notes the seminal role that Palmer played in the development of the American Holiness movement (Jones, *Perfectionist Persuasion*, 2–6).

7. Thomas Oden goes into a long defense of the great yet often unheralded role that Palmer played in the formation not only of the modern American religious landscape but, to a degree, of America itself (Oden, "Introduction," 1). In the same vein, Albert Truesdale contends that "Without Phoebe Palmer's influence, the American holiness movement would not have achieved the significance it did as an American religious movement. As a theological formulator, and directly through her teaching, she was indeed one of the more important—perhaps the most important—figure" (Truesdale, "Reification," 113).

8. Jones, *Perfectionist Persuasion*, 3.

9. Palmer identifies her search for sanctification as "*Conformity to the will of God in all things.*" (Palmer, *Devotional Writings*, 32, emphasis original).

"crowning doctrine of the crowning dispensation,"[10] were distinct from those of Wesley.[11]

Charles White contends that Wesley continued to hold in tension the elements of crisis and process, despite the latter's championing of the possibility of "entire sanctification."[12] That is, although he affirmed the possibility of attaining "perfect love," he also believed that journey in sanctification involves a journey to this higher plane. This journey consists in growth and progression toward the zenith, with each period of growth characterized by its own achievements and characteristics. Palmer, by contrast, purposely eliminated the idea of process in relation to sanctification.[13] For her, sanctification involves a "state of grace" that believers enter instantly and fully, and in which they should presently live.[14] It was not something that one strived for, hoped to attain, or worked out. "Phoebe Palmer's insistence on present availability directly contradicted the theory of gradual attainment of perfect love."[15] Donald Dayton has described Palmer's doctrine of sanctification as a hybrid of the Wesleyan doctrine of entire sanctification and "Finneyite new measures revivalism." The synthesis that results is the doctrine of immediate and entire sanctification.[16] Sanctification, like justification/conversion, is the free offer of God's grace to humanity and it is to be seized, received, and experienced in all its fullness in a moment in time. Consequently, "[You] may have this full salvation now—just now."[17]

This crisis event of sanctification is a radical disjuncture from the previous state of the believer. Sanctification is not a process that one enters gradually and only anticipates completing fully in the distant future. Instead, sanctification is a state of grace. The state of "entire sanctification" is not simply the distant terminus and aspiration of some process, it is all that there is of sanctification. It is a gift that God bestows upon

---

10. Palmer, *Pioneer Experiences*, vi.

11. Howard, "Wesley versus Phoebe Palmer," 36.

12. White, *Beauty of Holiness*, 129–30.

13. Jones, *Perfectionist Persuasion*, 4–6.

14. Palmer, writing about herself in the third person, says, "She now saw that holiness, instead of being an attainment beyond her reach, was a state of grace in which every one of the Lord's redeemed should live " (Palmer, *Devotional Writings*, 33).

15. Jones, *Perfectionist Persuasion*, 5.

16. Dayton, "Whither Evangelicalism?" 150.

17. Palmer, *Devotional Writings*, 58.

people, in all of its fullness, all at once. There are no progressions or stations along the road to sanctification apart from the terminus itself. One is either entirely sanctified or one is not sanctified at all.

Sanctification is not attained on the basis of human merit, but like all aspects of salvation, is fully an act of God's sovereign grace based on the merits of Christ alone. This assertion has been labeled Palmer's "altar theology." By consecrating one's entire being to God in a decisive act of laying oneself upon the "altar" before God, one is sanctified. Yet it is not the life offered in consecration on the altar that results in entire sanctification. Rather it is the altar itself upon which the gift is offered that is key. For Palmer, "The ALTAR *sanctifieth the gift.*"[18] The effectiveness of this particular altar is based on its identity, for it is none other than Christ himself.

> You come to the Christian's altar. "We have an altar." Your final conclusion is that you have consecrated all upon this altar, which is Christ. In view of his sacrificial sufferings and death, should I ask whether there is virtue sufficient here to cleanse from all unrighteousness; to sanctify wholly; what would you say? I know you would tell me that the virtues of this most holy altar are amply sufficient for the cleansing of a world of polluted mortals.[19]

In another move that set her apart from Wesley, Palmer denied the value or need for the emotions to testify to or guarantee the sanctifying work of God in the believer's life. Wesley, believed that the promise of God must always be coupled with experience.[20] Palmer, however, held that surety comes from the constant and trustworthy character of God alone and not from the possible vacillations or vagaries of the human condition.[21] One can be sure that one is sanctified not only because of the sufficient power of the altar, but also because God is always true to his word, even apart from the apparent evidence itself.[22] Palmer

---

18. Ibid., 101 (emphasis original).

19. Ibid., 111–12.

20. Howard, "Wesley versus Phoebe Palmer," 32.

21. Palmer, *Devotional Writings*, 38.

22. "Do you believe God's promise constitutes reliable ground for your faith? *Is his word evidence* sufficient to rest your faith upon? If you have come to the point to rely upon it fully as the foundation of your hope, you will not hesitate in making confession with your mouth. If you are not willing to do this, it proves that your faith is defective;

described her own taking of this promise as nothing more than "[taking] *God at his word*."[23] She believed that God had said that if the requirements were met, then the results would follow. Even if personal experience and emotions did not seem to attest to sanctification, believers can rest in the fact, should they have fully observed the requirements, that God will be true to his own word.[24] One may ask, however, what these requirements are.

To begin with, although she affirmed sanctification as the work of God alone, Palmer did not consider its human subjects to be merely passive participants. On the contrary, she constantly affirmed that work of sanctification requires a fundamental attitude and three distinct steps. Sanctification will only come to the humble, for, only the humble realize their own spiritual poverty and their need for outside help if they are ever to attain sanctification. Those who lack the fundamental attitude of humility will neither search for God nor realize their need for his gift of sanctification. The three distinctive steps that the faithful must take in their appropriation of this state of sanctification are entire consecration, faith, and confession. By "entire consecration," Palmer meant a full and final[25] abandonment of trust or hope in any avenue of sanctification other than Christ himself. This meant abandoning even the slightest hope in human capability.[26] One must be convinced that

---

for you will speak with a confidence precisely proportionate with what you deem to be the authority and faithfulness of Him upon whose word you rely" (Palmer, *Devotional Writings*, 113, emphasis original).

23. Ibid., 38.

24. "If God hath said, 'The *altar* sanctifieth the gift,' it sure is not left optional with yourself whether you will believe or not; it is presumptuous to doubt. You cannot dishonor God more than by doubting his word" (Palmer, *Devotional Writings*, 160, emphasis original). See also Jones, *Perfectionist Persuasion*, 5–6; Dieter, *Holiness Revival*, 26.

25. In a passage that is undoubtedly at least somewhat autobiographical, Palmer states that the decisive step on the road to present holiness is the determination of an ongoing consecration or offering of oneself before God (Palmer, *Devotional Writings*, 21).

26. Palmer did not understand consecration as a meritorious act. It was not an act of humanity delivering to God either something it already owned or something God did not already own. By way of illustration she writes, again in the third person, of her own experience: "Instead of perceiving anything meritorious in what she had been enabled, through grace, to do, that is, in laying all upon the altar, she saw that she had but rendered back to God that which was already his own" (Palmer, *Devotional Writings*, 34).

only God in Christ can sanctify. Faith is that sure confidence that the consecrated one trusts God, without a shade of doubt, to sanctify as he has promised. One must not doubt one's acceptance by God but trust wholeheartedly in his promise to accept all those who so offer themselves. Palmer also held unswervingly to the need to confess the obtainment of sanctification, regardless of the presence or absence of emotion or any other evidence. By this act of confession, not only do the newly sanctified secure this fact in their own hearts, but glorify God by the communication of it to others. Though she would continue to promote this tripartite formula throughout her ministry, Palmer encapsulated this understanding in her "Altar Covenant" of July 27, 1837.

> There are distinctive steps in the attainment of the great salvation! In that of ENTIRE CONSECRATION, I had so carefully pondered the path of my feet, that the way back again to self, or the world in any degree, was returnless. The next step, FAITH, in regard to Divine acceptance of all, had also been distinctly taken. And now, as I plainly saw the third step clearly defined in the Word, I took the advance ground—CONFESSION.[27]

Palmer believed that all Christians are commanded by God to enter into this state of grace and that it is their duty to do so immediately.[28] Though not denying the inaugural value of justification/conversion, she stressed that it was an insufficient basis on which to meet God. Holiness is not an option for the Christian. Rather, "it is absolutely necessary that [one] should be *holy*, if [one] would see God."[29] Palmer stressed this to the point of saying, "If you are not a *holy* Christian, you are not a *Bible* Christian."[30]

Since she believed that the state of entire sanctification is the gracious gift of God to humanity, that it is available in a moment by the sufficiency of the work of Jesus Christ as the altar,[31] and that sanctification

---

27. Palmer wrote this Covenant the day after her "Day of Days," on which she had experienced her crisis of "entire sanctification" (Oden, *Phoebe Palmer: Selected Writings*, 121).

28. "Hath he given the command 'Be ye holy,' and not given the ability, with the command for the performance of it" (Palmer, *Devotional Writings*, 34–35; Oden, *Phoebe Palmer: Selected Writings*, 121)?

29. Oden, *Phoebe Palmer: Selected Writings*, 187 (emphasis original).

30. Ibid., 186.

31. "The sacrifice is presented; and the very moment it touch that '*altar* most holy' it is sanctified. The sanctification of the gift did not depend on any inherent good in the

is not optional for those who desired to encounter God, the appropriation of sanctification was for her an urgent matter; and she regarded it with a gravity that the revivalistic tradition normally reserved for justification/conversion. One does not only have the option of acquiring sanctification now, one must do so now, given the frailty of human life.[32] One need not expect a long interval between the time of justification/conversion and the time of sanctification,[33] nor would one want to arrive on the other side of death apart from having secured sanctification. Such would result in doom, not in deliverance.

In addition to bearing eternal consequences, sanctification also has present implications. One requires it not only if one desires to abide with God on the other side of death, but also if one expects to have an effective ministry in this life. Holiness is not only a prerequisite for seeing God, it is also prerequisite for being used by God.[34] In fact, sanctification and its accompanying holiness "is the 'Gift of Power' that brings the world to Christ. Purity and power are identical."[35]

Palmer understood sanctification not only as an attainable goal in this life, as had Wesley, but like justification, as the gift of God received in all of its fullness in a moment through the exercise of faith. Though it still involved a synergism—humanity had to consecrate itself in an act of faith—the idea of progress was gone. Sanctification, according to Palmer was a complete work of God, fully present and effective at its implementation.

William E. Boardman

William E. Boardman (1810–1886) was raised in, trained in, and continued to identify throughout his life with the Reformed tradition. Despite the fact that he was at one time a Presbyterian minister, it would

---

offerer, but upon the sanctity of the altar upon which it was laid. The ALTAR *sanctifieth* the gift" (Palmer, *Devotional Writings*, 101, emphasis original).

32. "Let me assure you, dear friend, that as surely as you need holiness *now*, so surely it is for you *now*. The provisions of the Gospel are all suited to the exigencies of the present time. Are you commanded to be ready for the coming of the Lord *now*? Then holiness is a blessing which it is now your privilege and also your duty to enjoy" (Oden, *Phoebe Palmer: Selected Writings*, 187).

33. Palmer, *Devotional Writings*, 54.

34. White, *Beauty of Holiness*, 133.

35. Palmer, *Pioneer Experiences*, vi.

be a great mistake to say that he, like so much of the rest of America, was untouched by Wesleyanism, especially its distinctive doctrine of sanctification. Boardman, like so many notable figures of the day, attended Phoebe Palmer's "Tuesday Meetings" and was undoubtedly influenced by them. One biographer has credited him with making the "despised doctrine of the early Methodists the glorious heritage of all denominations."[36] That is, his connections with the larger popular religious movements of the time enabled Boardman to inject into popular revivalistic piety a new form of this once exclusively Wesleyan doctrine of entire sanctification.[37]

Boardman's widespread influence came first through *The Higher Christian Life*, which he wrote in 1858 after his wife's failed attempt to write a book about the couple's experience and understanding of the doctrine of sanctification. He declared that he had been given the "plan of a book"[38] by divine inspiration, a claim that seemed to be borne out by the book's phenomenal sales, which were, according to Mrs. Boardman,

> rapid beyond all precedent in the class of solid Christian literature. It was impossible for many weeks to supply the demand. People thronged, and even waited outside the store in order to obtain the book, and while it was thus called for in America, it found its way across the great Atlantic, and was taken up in London by several publishers, who gave it wings in England and other countries.[39]

In the end, *The Higher Christian Life* sold thousands upon thousands of copies, in a multitude of printings, on both sides of the Atlantic. Its impact on the wider revivalistic culture would be dramatic; Holiness historian, Melvin Dieter, claims that it "opened the doors of non-Methodist churches to the revival's teaching more widely than any volume

36. Pearse, "Preface," v–vi.

37. Given his acceptance of this Wesleyan doctrine, despite any alterations he may have made, Boardman has been variously categorized as Wesleyan, Reformed, and neither. For example, despite Boardman's own background, David Bundy identifies him as Wesleyan. Myung Soo Park, on the other hand, categorizes Boardman and the Higher Life Movement that would lie in his wake as Reformed. The truth is that what we have in Boardman is a *tertium quid* or a synthesis of the prior two (Bundy, "Keswick," 167; Park, "Concepts of Holiness," 144).

38. Boardman, *Life and Labours*, 104.

39. Ibid.

which had preceded it."[40] Its success made Boardman a popular speaker at conferences, and it was to this enterprise, rather than to writing, that he would dedicate the remainder of his life.

Boardman's doctrine of sanctification was not wholly innovative: like both Wesley and Palmer, and contrary to his own Reformed heritage and training, he believed sanctification to be distinct from justification/conversion in both its nature and its timing. Sanctification, though part and parcel of the overall work of salvation, is neither identical to nor simply a subset of conversion, but rather "a second experience, distinct from the first—and as distinctly marked, both as to time and circumstances and character as the first—a *second conversion,* as it is often called."[41] The first "conversion" is the act through which God frees believers from the consequences of sin; sanctification brings the believer freedom, not simply from the eternal and future consequences of sin, but from the "dominion of sin" presently.[42] Borrowing a phrase from Wesley, sanctification is the work of God that enables one to be "holy in heart and life."[43] It has not only eschatological implications, but immediate consequences as well.

Boardman affirmed that sanctification may begin at a point subsequent to conversion. However, he did not believe that this possible hiatus was necessary. Nor did he believe that it needed to be a protracted struggle leading to failure and the eventual abandonment of self.

> Let it not be supposed, however, that in every instance there must be two distinct experiences, separated by a gulf of vain strugglings. It is not necessary that there should be one even. Let Jesus be received as the all in all, and that is enough! Whoever can say, "Jesus is mine and I am his, that he is complete and I am complete in him," and say the truth, has the experience whether he has an experience to relate, or not.[44]

---

40. Dieter, *Holiness Revival*, 49.
41. Boardman, *Higher Christian Life*, 47.
42. Boardman, Mary, *Life and Labours*, 48, 53.
43. Boardman, *Higher Christian Life*, 52.
44. Ibid., 53.

Here we find Boardman asserting, much like Palmer, the dispensability of experience. Sanctification may involve a distinct experience, but such an experience does not constitute the evidence of actual reception.[45]

Sanctification is not a state that only a spiritual elite can attain, for God intends it to be "an experience for common people and for common circumstances."[46] A full salvation, a "Higher Life," that includes both conversion and sanctification, is not only "the provision and the demand of the gospel, [it is] of course the privilege and duty of all."[47] By a full salvation, Boardman meant the meeting of the twofold need of humanity: justification, "to be *just* in the eye of the law;" and sanctification, to be "holy in heart and life."[48] Justification/conversion takes care of the first matter; sanctification takes care of the second. Since the need for both is vital, the provisions for both are necessary.

In *The Higher Christian Life* Boardman offers his own analysis of the prevailing views on sanctification. He observes that the Oberlinians and Wesleyans generally agree on the subject of sanctification but that they tend to disagree on "whether this experience is that of *entire instantaneous sanctification* or not."[49] The Oberlinians (his term for the followers of Asa Mahan and Charles Finney) unequivocally affirmed that sanctification always comes in its entirety, hence their use of the term *entire sanctification* to describe their position.[50] That is, their "view of the claims of the law as graduated to the sinner's ability, enables them to hold and profess perfect sanctification when they come to yield wholly to the known will of God, and take Christ wholly as their righteousness and true holiness."[51] The Wesleyans, on the other hand, do not make such bold claims about the possibility of achieving entire or "absolute [perfection], like the spotless purity of Jesus, and the holy angels" but instead prefer to assert only "*Christian* perfection, making a broad distinction between Christian and angelic perfection."[52]

---

45. Ibid., 47.

46. Pearse, "Preface," v–vi.

47. Boardman, *Higher Christian Life*, 45.

48. Ibid., 52.

49. Ibid., 56.

50. Ibid.

51. Ibid., 41.

52. Ibid., 42.

Boardman, in propounding his own views, chose not to criticize the assertions of these parties. Instead, he switched the focus from the extent of sanctification to the content or means of sanctification. Laying aside the debates over "entire" versus "Christian" perfection, Boardman contended that one does not receive some abstract ability or energy at this second crisis but rather *someone*—Jesus Christ, and him in all of his fullness. For Boardman, the crisis of sanctification does not consist in an arrival at some self-constituted state of final purity. Rather, it constitutes the point at which the believer has coupled himself or herself to Jesus Christ, not only for justification/conversion, but for sanctification as well.

This more intimate union with Christ, however, is "the beginning and not the end."[53] Like conversion, it is another inaugural point in the life of the believer, an entrance "fully and consciously, by the right principle, [into] the process of sanctification—not sanctification completed."[54] For Boardman sanctification, though it has a punctiliar beginning, is not achieved or even received in all its potential fullness at that point, for it necessarily involves a progression of indeterminate length.[55] Justification/conversion occurs instantaneously; the second work, though it begins at a point in time, "unfolds."[56]

Sanctification, then, comes about as a result of a deepening or enhancing of one's relationship to Christ, and it leads to a qualitative difference of life. It "is a higher height, and a deeper depth, in the comprehension of both of the love of Christ which passeth knowledge, and of the way of salvation by faith;"[57] and "a *deeper work of grace*, a fuller apprehension of Christ, a more complete and abiding union with him than the first."[58] As one trusts in Christ for one's conversion, so too, should one, by a distinct act of faith, trust Christ for one's sanctification.[59] "Jesus is *the Way* not only for . . . justification but also for . . .

53. Ibid., 69.

54. Ibid., 60.

55. "There is a radical difference between the pardon of sins and the purging of sins. Pardon is instantaneously entire, but cleansing from sin is a process of indefinite length" (Boardman, *Higher Christian Life*, 116).

56. Ibid., 117.

57. Ibid., 50.

58. Ibid., 48 (emphasis original).

59. Cf. David Bundy's observation that "William Edwin Boardman . . . [in] his very influential book, *The Higher Christian Life*, . . . argued that every Christian must achieve

sanctification."[60] He satisfies not only the need of the past—to be justified and converted—but the need of the present and future need—to live a life—as well. He not only saves humanity from the penalty of sin in the future, but he is also able and willing to deliver it from the reign of sin in its life now. Many Christians "see and believe in Jesus as our atonement on earth, and our Advocate and Mediator in heaven, but . . . [fail] to see and receive him as [an] ever-present *Saviour from sin* now here with us in the hourly scenes of the daily journey heavenward."[61] So then, believers who seek sanctification ought to be "taking Christ for [their] sanctification, just as [they have] already taken him for [their] justification."[62] Jesus' sufficiency does not change with the challenges, for the Scriptures

> everywhere teach us the same thing. They always answer the question, "What must we do?" by the assurance, "Believe in the Lord Jesus Christ and thou shalt be saved." Whether the question relates to justification or sanctification the answer is the same. The way of freedom from sin is the very same, as the way of freedom from condemnation. Faith in the purifying presence of Jesus brings the witness of the Spirit with our spirits that Jesus is our sanctification.[63]

Boardman's doctrine of sanctification is thus radically Christocentric. Jesus is the answer, regardless of the question. In the search for sanctification, one must seek Jesus Christ and him alone. The mistake that many make in the search for sanctification is that they seek for deliverance from a "something" apart from the aid of a "someone."[64] Sanctification is indissolubly related to the person of Christ. Christ is the Sanctifier. "Christ. Christ in all his fullness. Christ is all in all. Christ is objectively and subjectively received and trusted in. That is all. And that is enough."[65]

---

a higher plane of Christian life, enter by an act of faith as at justification" (Bundy, "Keswick," 127, fn. 12).

60. Boardman, *Higher Christian Life*, 53 (emphasis original).

61. Ibid., 52–53 (emphasis original).

62. Ibid., 52.

63. Ibid., 94.

64. Ibid., 119.

65. Ibid., 58.

The Keswick Movement and the Revivalists

William Boardman's doctrines exerted a formative influence on the Keswick movement, which had its origins in British camp meetings. These gatherings had been spawned by a movement of renewal within the Anglican church and by the lingering impact of such revivalists as Moody, Mahan, and Finney who had toured Great Britain during the early and mid-nineteenth century. Following on the success of meetings in Brighton and Oxford, a conference was organized at Keswick in 1875 at the invitation of Canon T. D. Harford-Battersby, an Anglican cleric who had attended the Oxford meetings. These meetings, originally called the "Union Meetings for the Promotion of Practical Holiness," continue to be held annually. However, the Keswick movement itself and the theology of sanctification associated with it owe their distinctive characteristics more directly to the impact of William Boardman and the husband and wife team of Robert Pearsall and Hannah Whittall Smith.[66] The Smiths' and, more particularly, Boardman's Reformed reinterpretation of the Methodist doctrine of sanctification came to shape the message of Keswick.[67] Keswick, in turn, steered many Reformed people and organizations in a Wesleyan direction, especially in regard to the doctrine of sanctification.[68]

Though the influences of Keswick are fairly easy to trace, and though there is near unanimity on who and what these influences were, to determine the exact content of its teaching is not nearly so simple. This lack of clarity stems from the fact that the convention was never organized in any formal way. It was, simply, a fraternal gathering of likeminded people that revolved around a common interest in and an

---

66. Barabas, *So Great Salvation*, 15–16; Bundy, "Keswick," 123–24. C. F. Harford, the nearest thing to an official spokesperson for Keswick, expanded the umbrella of identified influences when he wrote, "the roots of the distinctive [Keswick] teaching can easily be traced in the writings of Walter Marshall, William Law, John Wesley, Fletcher of Madeley, Thomas à Kempis, Brother Lawrence, [and] Madame Guyon" (Harford, *Keswick Convention*, 223). David Bundy traces other influences to Keswick (Bundy, "Keswick and the Experience of Evangelical Piety," 119).

67. Bebbington, *Holiness in Nineteenth-Century England*, 73.

68. "The most significant Wesleyan penetration into the Reformed evangelical traditions was the spread of holiness/higher-life teaching prompted by the English Keswick Convention. It became the most popular and pervasive of the non-Wesleyan expressions of the holiness revival" (Dieter, *Holiness Revival*, 249).

emphasis on practical holiness.[69] The movement did not possess official or prescriptive statement of faith, and its "organ", *The Keswick Week*, contained mostly descriptive reports. It should not be surprising, then, that it is not only difficult but, indeed, impossible to define Keswick teaching precisely.[70] Since it was not restricted by a creedal statement, the teaching at Keswick varied from participant to participant, sermon to sermon, speaker to speaker.[71] This cacophony of opinion charaterized Keswick even in its earliest days.[72] As such, "The Keswick Movement presents special problems [of categorization] due to its lack of institutional structure and its fluid character which make precise identification difficult."[73] However, despite differences in nonessentials,[74] most, if not all of those who attended the meetings had a similar understanding of both hamartology and the "Higher Christian Life";[75] and their views on the former shaped their views on the latter.

At the heart of Keswick teaching, and at the heart of the human predicament, lies a search for a solution to the problem of sin. Justification addresses the penalty of sin; sanctification deals with the ongoing dominion of sin. Those who spoke at Keswick did not preach that sin is part of God's primordial design for humanity, but rather that it has become part of universal human experience through the Fall. Humanity, however, is not necessarily bound to follow the lead of sin. Sinfulness is rather a tendency, but a tendency that has become a part of the human condition. By the term "tendency," Keswickians did not mean merely that human beings are liable to sin, but rather that sin

69. "The Keswick Convention is . . . an amorphous conglomerate of individuals and groups who are in sympathy with the teachings and lifestyle as taught at the annual meeting and proclaimed in the official record of the Keswick Convention, *The Keswick Week*, an annual report of the meeting at Keswick" (Bundy, "Keswick," 119).

70. "[Since] Keswick is a broad fellowship encompassing those of varying theological convictions, it should not be surprising that differences would arise among the leaders, even on doctrines relating to the Christian life" (McQuilkin, "Keswick Perspective," 156).

71. "Speakers from the Keswick platform were not clamped to a party line. They signed no statement of doctrine" (Pollock, *Keswick Story*, 73).

72. Pollock, *Keswick Story*, 65.

73. Kostlevy, *Holiness Manuscripts*, ix.

74. "In these areas of ambiguity one should not seek to establish an official Keswick position, for there is none" (McQuilkin, "Keswick Perspective," 156).

75. Bundy, "Keswick," 153.

exerts a constant downward draw. Sin is a resident, though still alien, disposition.

In the Keswick tradition, sanctification does not consist in a final state of separation—as either a present experience or a future aspiration—from this tendency to sin. The proclivity would always remain. Here, Keswick teaching challenges traditional Wesleyan hamartology. Whereas traditional Wesleyanism finds the solution for the problem of sin in what may be called the replacement, removal, or eradication of the sinful nature, Keswick denies that sin may be completely removed in this life. [76] Instead of counting on the elimination of the tendency, Keswick declares that the solution to the problem of sin lies in its being overcome or, to use a phrase customary to Keswick, "victory over sin."[77] Melvin Dieter describes the difference:

---

76. "The predominantly Anglican Keswick Movement questioned the possibility of amoral purity and suggested that suppression of evil tendencies might, after all, be all that was possible to mortal men. Emphasizing spiritual growth, Keswick spokesmen have preferred to talk of the Deeper Life instead of Holiness" (Jones, *Guide to the Study of the Holiness Movement*, xviii). "The view of sin held unofficially by Keswick is Reformed and Anglican, rather than the Wesleyan understanding of Mahan, Boardman, and Arthur" (Bundy, "Keswick," 167). Ian M. Randall has written that it was the explicit intention of Evan Hopkins to "provide a Keswick theology of sanctification and power which would be acceptable to British evangelicals and in particular to the Anglican constituency. Any notions of Wesleyan perfectionism were repudiated" (Randall, "Spiritual Renewal and Social Reform," 68–69). Despite the differences, Ralph W. Thompson has identified six areas of agreement between the Keswick and Wesleyan doctrine of sanctification. These are

1. that humanity is "a sinner by nature" and "unable to cease from sinning or save [itself] from the wrath of God,"

2. that "justification is by faith in Christ,"

3. that "although transgressions are forgiven in justification, at which time sanctification is begun, yet the principle of sin with which man is born remains in the justified believer";

4. that Wesleyans and Keswickians "agree that a life of complete victory in Christ comes usually through a definite crisis experience, or second work of grace";

5. "that the sanctified believer continues to grow in grace so long as he lives"; and

6. that this sanctification can be lost.

(Thompson, "Appraisal of the Keswick and Wesleyan Contemporary Positions," 13–14).

77. Dieter, *Holiness Revival*, 249.

The experience of daily victory [over] sin was the promise of both theologies. The Calvinistic Keswickians, however, would claim only that, in the fully consecrated believer's life, the power of the old nature of sin was countered by the presence of the indwelling Spirit, not cleansed away as commonly maintained by their Wesleyan compatriots.[78]

Ralph W. Thompson describes the difference in this way:

Wesleyanism teaches that the soul itself is delivered from all sin. Keswick, on the other hand, teaches that the sanctified themselves are not made holy, but only that they are made completely victorious over the sin nature, which still remains in their hearts. They distinguish between a state of holiness and a condition of holiness. They say that if the sanctified were in a state of holiness he would have no need for God to keep him thus, therefore they reject it as untenable.[79]

Continual and progressive victory over this tendency to sin, rather than its eviction, is the role of sanctification according to Keswick. While this tendency remains, it is countered by a stronger and contrary impulse that leads not to the elimination, but rather to the "suppression"[80] or "repression"[81] of sin. Evan Hopkins, a noted proponent of Keswick, calls sanctification that "*counter-action* in which the soul is delivered, and kept, and led from strength to strength only through the grace and mightiness of One who dwells within it, a sin-restraining and sin-conquering Saviour."[82] Other supporters of the Keswick alternative have likened it to a lighter-than-air balloon. Though gravity maintains its constant earthward pull upon the balloon, the power resident within the balloon does not eradicate the gravitational tendency of the balloon, but it does overcome it so that the grip or "dominion" of gravity is lost.[83]

78. Ibid.

79. Thompson, "Appraisal of the Keswick and Wesleyan Contemporary Positions," 14.

80. Bundy, "Keswick," 119, 122, 153; Jones, *Guide to the Study of the Holiness Movement*, xviii; Kostlevy, *Holiness Manuscripts*, ix–x.

81. Bebbington, *Holiness in Nineteenth-Century England*, 83.

82. Pollock, *Keswick Story*, 76 (emphasis original).

83. Barabas, *So Great Salvation*, 49.

One of the issues that the Keswick Conventions seek to address is not only holiness, but more particularly, the lack of holiness and, consequently, the impotence of the church. Keswick believes that the church lacks the holiness that it could and should have because it has sought it in all the wrong places. Keswick does not seek to evangelize the world with its message but, instead, to evangelize the church. It delivers a message of freedom from the power of sin through the "Higher Christian Life." Though Keswick does not doubt the justification/conversion of those within the church, it does not hold such an optimistic view of their sanctification. According to Keswick, the problem with so many in the church is that though they have been justified, they have not yet been sanctified. For Keswick, though justification/conversion and sanctification are related, they are neither identical nor coincidental. The cause of the church's lack of sanctification is the conflation and confusion of these two distinct works. Though some slight measure of sanctification may begin at the point of justification/conversion, sanctification as a work does not begin in earnest apart from the conscious decision of the believers to receive Jesus as their holiness, just as they had accepted him as their righteousness.[84] Just as justification, the deliverance from the penalty of sin, is received through a conscious decision on the part of the believer, so too, sanctification is available to those who claim it through an act of conscious decision and consecration.[85] As such, though sanctification remains a lifelong process, it begins in a moment in time, subsequent to and different in nature from justification/conversion.[86] Little time need elapse between the crisis of sanctification and the crisis of justification/conversion. They may (and should) fall one immediately after the other, but a separation, even if imperceptible, exists.

84. Ibid., 115.

85. David Bundy identifies Boardman as a key influence in Keswick's adoption of this concept of subsequence. See Bundy, "Keswick," 127, 164.

86. This process, generally understood, does not attain its goal in this lifetime. Yet it is still a goal to be thoroughly pursued. The Keswick view has been summarized in the following way: "Sanctification is not complete in an instant but should progress, cultivated by prayer, study of the Scriptures, worship and the Breaking of Bread. Discipline and effort are not redundant but of different quality and for a different purpose: not self-centred climbing toward blessedness but vital accessories of the service which is perfect freedom" (Pollock, *Keswick Story*, 76–77).

Keswick understands sin, in all of its varied manifestations, to be a desire on the part of humanity to live and to act independently of God. While the commands of God regarding holiness are unequivocal, humanity cannot fulfill these commands on its own. Keswick asserts, however, that what God has commanded humanity to do, he also enables it to do. Humanity fails to obey the command of God, however, because it continues to insist on its independence. This failing is not only the failing of humanity in general, but is also the reason for the perceived impotence of the church. The church, like the rest of the world, has sought to fulfill the law of God on its own. The church, like the rest of the world, has failed.

The Keswick secret to victorious living is based on a vibrant and dependent relationship with Jesus Christ by the Holy Spirit. The Christian can only overcome the downward tendency of sin by abandoning all hope of personal victory and relying on the power of the risen and indwelling Christ. This power never becomes the believer's own. Rather, it is the attendant power of Christ himself that equips the believer to overcome sin. As long as the Christian maintains this intimate relationship with Jesus by the Holy Spirit, sin is counteracted.[87] By communicating the holiness of Christ, the Holy Spirit

> sanctifies the believer. He works to counteract the downward pull of sin. He does not eradicate the susceptibility to sin, nor does He displace human responsibility to believe and to choose. Rather, the Spirit exercises a counter-force, enabling the surrendered and trusting believer to resist successfully the spiritually downward pull of his or her natural disposition. Keswick does not teach the perfectibility of human beings prior to the eternal state, but it does teach the possibility of consistent success in resisting the temptation to violate the known will of God.[88]

The impact of the Keswick movement traveled beyond the shores of Great Britain. Through various channels, Keswick soteriology found a home in America shortly after its initial emergence in England's Lake

---

87. In summing up the view of Evan Hopkins, an early Keswick participant and to some degree a Keswick spokesperson, David Bebbington has this to say: "There was sin in the believer until the moment of death, but the Holy Spirit kept the sinful tendencies under control. . . . The result was victory" (Bebbington, *Holiness in Nineteenth-Century England*, 83).

88. McQuilkin, "Keswick Perspective," 155.

District. Major players in this American adoption of Keswick included the revivalists who are the focus of this study. Without the influence of Gordon, and more particularly, Moody and Pierson, Keswick would not have found the audience it did in North America.[89] Although the extent of their associations with Keswick is the subject of debate, the associations themselves are undeniable. The revivalists were Keswick in both association and belief.

D. L. Moody's Keswick ties are well known. Not only did he send his regards to the precursory Brighton meeting, he preached at Keswick in 1892.[90] Furthermore, he encouraged the spread of the Keswick emphasis in America by inviting speakers with connections to Keswick to the annual summer meetings at Northfield.[91] David Bundy credits these latter meetings with "[transporting] the . . . spiritual expression of Keswick back" to America,[92] and James F. Findlay, Jr., notes the "considerable resemblances" between English holiness meetings and those summer conferences held at Northfield.[93]

A. T. Pierson's association with Keswick is even more explicit and thorough. He was introduced to the movement in the persons of Andrew Murray and H. W. Webb-Peploe at Moody's Northfield Conferences.[94] Pierson not only endorsed Keswick theology but actively and knowingly propagated it in both Great Britain and North America. Pierson, like Moody, was also a participant at Keswick, speaking there "in 1897, 1898, and six Conventions after."[95] On more than one occasion, he defended

---

89. Melvin Dieter has argued that the influence of Keswick "has remained a vital factor in American Evangelical life . . . , particularly through Dwight L. Moody, as it reinforced his own earlier contacts with the movement. Adoniram J. Gordon and Arthur T. Pierson, both active in the evangelical student movements at the turn of the century introduced the 'Spirit-filled life' into these groups" (Dieter, *Holiness Revival*, 158).

90. Gundry, *Love Them In*, 159–60.

91. Ibid., 159; Findlay, *Dwight L. Moody*, 342, 407; Sandeen, *Roots of Fundamentalism*, 176, 179.

92. Bundy, "Keswick," 146.

93. Findlay, *Dwight L. Moody*, 342.

94. Robert, "Arthur Tappan Pierson," 331.

95. Pollock, *Keswick Story*, 117. "Beginning in 1897, Pierson spoke at the convention nearly every year" (Robert, "Arthur Tappan Pierson," 332). An example of Pierson's direct and influential involvement in the Keswick Convention may be found in the inclusion of one of his sermons, "The Inbreathed Spirit," in a compendium of some of Keswick's best messages. See Stevenson, *Keswick's Authentic Voice*, 453–60.

Keswick theology, identifying it as one of "The Forward Movements of the Last Half Century" and equating its unfolding significance with that of Pentecost itself![96]

Unlike those of Moody and Pierson, the Keswick connections of A. J. Gordon, were not so explicit, but he was nevertheless profoundly affected by the movement. He never spoke at Keswick, but was deeply affected by Moody's 1877 Boston meetings[97] and later became a regular participant in the Northfield conferences.[98] So great was his commitment to Northfield that Moody personally invited him to direct the Northfield conferences in his absence in 1892 and 1893.[99] Gordon's name is regularly cited as one of the American purveyors of Keswick theology, often in connection with both Moody and Pierson.[100]

These three not only maintained personal connections and associations with Keswick, but they also referred to Keswick's twofold message about the degree and timing of sanctification in their messages. In addition, they all articulated a soteriology in which sin was seen to be incidental to human nature, though destined to remain a continuing tendency that while not eradicated, could be "overcome" through the continuing work of Christ by the Holy Spirit. For all, this work of sanctification was distinct in time and nature from the work of justification/conversion.

A. J. Gordon's Keswick Theology

A. J. Gordon's commitment to a Keswick soteriology was strong and found throughout his writings. He believed the work of sanctification is distinct from justification/conversion in both nature and time. First, the

96. Two examples of Pierson's Keswick vindications are *The Keswick Movement in Precept and Practice*, published in 1903, and "Spiritual Movements of the Half Century—Keswick Teaching and Methods," an article that appeared in *Missionary Review of the World* in December of 1897 See Robert, "Arthur Tappan Pierson," 332; Pierson, *Forward Movements*, 24.

97. Gordon, *Adoniram Judson Gordon*, 95.

98. Ibid., 173. David Bundy notes that Moody invited both Gordon and Pierson, "both prominent Keswick speakers," to speak at his conferences (Bundy "Keswick," 148–50).

99. Shelley, "A. J. Gordon," 110; Gordon, *Adoniram Judson Gordon*, 157.

100. Dieter, *Holiness Revival*, 158, 248; Bundy, "Keswick," 148–50; Waldvogel, "Overcoming Life," 2, 26; Smith, *Called unto Holiness*, 25; Faupel, *Everlasting Gospel*, 69; Dayton, *Theological Roots*, 105.

nature of sanctification is linked to the power of the Spirit. Justification/ conversion may bring the presence of the Spirit into the life of the believer, but, for Gordon, sanctification is an enduement with power in the life of the believer, something "beyond and above what [was] received in conversion."[101] He wrote, "[A] careful reading of the Acts of the Apostles would seem to indicate that this experience is something quite distinct from justification/conversion, being no less than an investment of the believer with a special divine energy and efficiency for carrying on God's work."[102] Both are works of Christ through the Spirit, but Scripture describes their purpose as different and distinct and, therefore, so must the church.[103] "Christ for us [in justification/conversion], appropriated by faith is the source of life; Christ within us through the indwelling of the Holy Spirit is the source of more abundant life; the one fact assures our salvation; the other enables us to glorify God in the salvation of others."[104] He called this second work of the Spirit the "Sealing of the Spirit." It is "a *special* enduement of the Spirit subsequent to that regeneration of the Spirit which takes place when one believes."[105]

Second, Gordon insisted that this work of sanctification, "this second travail," is distinct and subsequent to the work of justification/ conversion, though they may occur so closely together as to appear to constitute a single experience.

> Now the Scriptures seem to teach that there is a second stage in spiritual development, distinct and separate from conversion; sometimes widely separated in time from it, and sometimes almost contemporaneous with it—a stage to which we rise by a special renewal of the Holy Ghost, and not merely by the process of gradual growth. We shall be especially careful not to dogmatize here.[106]

On another occasion he wrote, "To some this anointing has come almost simultaneously with conversion; to many it has come at a consid-

---

101. Gordon, *Holy Spirit in Missions*, 205.

102. Gordon, *Twofold Life*, 76.

103. Ibid., i–ii.

104. Ibid., 9–10.

105. Ibid., 71 (emphasis added).

106. Ibid., 12.

erable period afterward."[107] It is this former possibility that has led to the conflation and confusion of the two, and the spiritually impoverished condition of those in the church. Yet one logically and necessarily precedes the other. Justification, by which we are accounted righteous, prepares us for sanctification, by which the righteousness of Christ is imparted to us for the purpose of carrying on the work of the gospel.[108] The latter cannot take place apart from the preparatory work of the former. Gordon believed that many of those in the church remained "merely saved" because they were either content with a minimal faith or because they confused Christ's righteousness accounted with Christ's righteousness imparted.

Gordon took pains to point out that, in his opinion, the draw of sin will remain throughout one's lifetime. The work of sanctification does not involve the removal of the "lust of the flesh," but its subjection or repression.[109] Separating him from a purely Wesleyan or Palmerian soteriology was his conviction that both entire sanctification and the eradication of the fallen nature were not to be expected or fully achieved in this life.[110] Yet although perfection is not attainable in this life, the believer can still become progressively more and more sanctified. As a progression, sanctification does not move randomly forward but seeks a particular (and ultimately) eschatological goal: not simply a standard but a *someone*—Jesus Christ—with whom the believer will be fully joined at his return. When union with Christ is fully and finally realized in the eschaton, the sanctification of the believer will and can be complete, but even then, only "in Him."[111] What the believer to that time has gained progressively will then be fulfilled instantaneously,[112] when "the unveiled manifestation of God will bring the full perfection of his saints."[113] Whatever progress the believer might make in sanctification

107. Ibid., 190.

108. Ibid., 129–31.

109. Gordon, *In Christ*, 97; Gordon, *Twofold Life*, iv.

110. Though sinning may no longer happen, it is not because the sinful nature has been eradicated (Gordon, *Ministry of the Holy Spirit*, 118). It should be noted that Gordon believed it was better to overstate the possibilities of perfection than to understate them (Gordon, *Ministry of the Holy Spirit*, 117).

111. Gordon, *Ministry of the Holy Spirit*, 167–68.

112. Ibid.,125.

113. Ibid., 124; Russell, "Adoniram Judson Gordon," 69.

will be incomplete and only an earnest or pledge of what will come in the eschaton.[114] Still, the sanctification of the believer never occurs apart from the life-giving indwelling Christ.

> Attachment to Christ is the true secret of detachment from sin; death cannot stand before life; therefore, let us live in the Spirit, breathing in His divine life as we inhale the atmosphere by which we are nourish and the faults and frailties and sins of our fleshly nature will inevitably be subdued and expelled.[115]

This incompleteness should not hinder the quest for sanctification but rather enhance it. This "glory begun in us," rather than defeating believers, should develop in them a longing for that eschatological event of which the current situation is a real, though limited, representation.[116]

For Gordon, the believer's sanctification is "at once both complete and incomplete."[117] This seemingly contradictory statement merely differentiates between the divine and human aspects of sanctification. Humanity cannot improve upon the work of God in sanctification. To the extent that the believer's sanctification finds its content in the person of Jesus Christ, it is complete. It is incomplete, however, with respect to the fulfillment of the secured work of Christ in the believer.[118] As a gift of grace, then, "sanctification is conferred on each Christian as soon as he/she believes. But it is a gift yet *held on deposit* . . . to be appropriated through daily communion and gradual apprehension."[119]

A. T. PIERSON'S KESWICK THEOLOGY

A. T. Pierson, for his part, unequivocally denied the necessity of the ongoing dominion of sin in the life of the believer. His clearest statement on the matter occurs in the introduction to *Shall We Continue In Sin*: "continuance in sin is to be regarded by every true child of God as both

---

114. Gordon, *Ministry of the Holy Spirit*, 119. At times, Gordon can sound rather hostile to the idea of perfection: e. g., "Such wild dreams as that of perfection in the flesh would be little entertained if men kept clearly in view the distinction between what we are in Christ and what we are in ourselves" (Gordon, *In Christ*, 174–75).

115. Gordon, *Holy Spirit in Missions*, 225–26.

116. Ibid., 119–20; Gordon, *Yet Speaking*, 20.

117. Gordon, *In Christ*, 167.

118. Ibid.

119. Ibid., 170 (emphasis original).

needless and wrong. [Scripture does not teach the] doctrine of sinless-ness . . . but of not continuing in sin. Being without sin, and not going on in sin, are two quite different things."[120] Romans chapters 6, 7, and 8 address this problem explicitly. Chapter 6 asks whether the continuance in sin is either necessary or normative for the believer. The answer is an utter "God forbid!" Chapter 7 describes the unnecessary and frustrating vacillations of those who are children of God, yet who have not yet experienced "the Spirit of God [becoming] to [them] a living, present indwelling and inworking Spirit of power and holiness."[121] To experi-ence this latter event is to experience salvation in its present fullness.[122]

A large part of the reason for the continuing failure of so many Christians in relation to sin, according to Pierson, is the very expecta-tion that falling into sin is inevitable. Such a notion is a self-fulfilling prophecy, for "[one's] expectation has everything to do with [one's] ac-tual life. If [one expects] to sin [one] will sin, and if [one expects] not to sin, because [one reckons oneself] no longer under sin's mastery, but under God's [one] will find that expectation itself a security."[123] In fact, he went on to say that such a defeatist attitude is in itself sin because it affords to the enemies of God more power than it affords to the God who has himself said that he will overcome his enemies.[124]

Pierson wrote often about the cessation of sin and the duty of the consecrated Christian to reject sin. Yet he did not deny the enduring principle of sin, that constant downward tendency toward sinful ac-tion. The deliverance that he and Keswick definitely and unmistakably promoted is "a possible and practical deliverance from continuance in known sin;" and so "it is not necessary to be under the dominion of any lust of body or mind, to live a life of doubt and despondency, or to have interrupted communion with God."[125] Though Pierson talked about the

---

120. Pierson, *Vital Union with Christ*, 8.

121. Ibid., 90.

122. Pierson, like his contemporaries, uses the term "salvation" and its cognates in at least two ways. At times, he uses them as synonyms for justification/conversion, that inaugural work of God in the larger work of redemption. However, he also uses them to designate the larger work of redemption. Context is the primary hermeneutical tool for determining the way that Pierson is using these terms in a given instance.

123. Pierson, *Vital Union with Christ*, 55.

124. Ibid.

125. Pierson, *Forward Movements*, 48.

eradication of the presence of sin, he did not believe that it would be achieved in the believer's lifetime.[126] Rather than removing the problem that sin presents by its continual draw on humanity, the work of God in sanctification provides the consecrated believer with the *power* to overcome sin, the same power that, conversely, enables the believer to please God. No such empowering of the believer takes place in the work of justification, which is primarily an objective and abstract phenomenon. Sanctification, however, is at its heart an enduement of power in the impotent.[127] This power enables believers to live holy lives.

> The struggles of the unbeliever against sin are comparatively fruitless and hopeless, and the efforts even of the regenerate man are unsuccessful, so long as he attempts to vanquish sin by his own resolve or power. But the believer must remember that in the resurrection of Christ he receives life, and life stands for vitality, ability, energy, power.[128]

Moreover, this power has an objective. It is "power over sin" so that the believer may live a life that is pleasing to God. Without it, the Christian can only live a life marked by frustration in relation to sin. Yet Pierson was also convinced that this God-given power in the life of the believer makes continuance in sin no longer necessary.[129] Furthermore, the change of character that comes about in sanctification is not only advantageous, it is indispensable for salvation. Justification, though good in and of itself, does not secure salvation. Against the claim that justification without personal reform is sufficient for salvation, Pierson argued that

> while some people say that Christianity teaches that a man is saved irrespective of character, we utterly deny . . . any such teaching in Christianity. The glory of this Gospel is that it teaches us that when Jesus Christ bestows forgiveness He sends the Holy Spirit to regenerate the heart, and renew the heart, and renew the life, and transform or transfigure the character, so that at the last we shall be presented spotless, blameless, undefiled in the presence of the infinite glory.[130]

126. MacLean, *Dr. Pierson*, 96.

127. Pierson, *Vital Union with Christ*, 90; Pierson, *Forward Movements*, 33.

128. Pierson, *Vital Union with Christ*, 34.

129. Ibid., 8.

130. MacLean, *Dr. Pierson*, 172.

Still, the indwelling Christ does not dispense this power primarily to enable believers to live holy lives, as indispensable as this is. No, he has a second and even higher purpose: empowerment for service. The object of this power is not primarily the Christian, but those with whom the Christian comes into contact. It is a power to minister effectively. Nor is it intended for just any ministry: "[it] is, specifically, *power in connection with witnessing*."[131] It is a power to boldly and effectively proclaim the gospel, for "The one supreme qualification of Christ's witness is this: that THEY BE ENDUED AND ENDOWED WITH POWER BY THE HOLY SPIRIT."[132]

Not only is sanctification distinct in nature from justification/conversion; it also occurs at a distinct moment by a distinct movement of faith as well.[133] For Pierson, as for Gordon, sanctification, though a necessary aspect of salvation more broadly conceived, is appropriated at a moment subsequent to justification/conversion. This subsequence is itself a part of God's plan, for

> [e]ven after a man has found refuge in Jesus Christ, and after he has gone behind the blood-stained door, and has claimed mercy and grace from God because he takes refuge in Christ, how often his sins come up behind him, his old habits, the remembrance of his past iniquities, and they try to drag him back into the old bondage of slavery; and then God has a second act of compassion ready for the poor sinner.[134]

As justification/conversion is appropriated by an act of faith at a particular moment in time, so too, sanctification must be appropriated in a distinct act of faith in a moment in time. No matter how soon this occurs after one's justification/conversion it always occurs subsequent to it.[135]

D. L. Moody's Keswick Theology

Despite the fact that many, if not most, who attended his many meetings were already Christian converts, D. L. Moody remained true to

---

131. Pierson, *Acts of the Holy Spirit*, 24 (emphasis original).

132. Ibid., 24 (emphasis original).

133. Pierson, *Keswick Movement in Precept and Practice*, 82.

134. MacLean, *Dr. Pierson*, 127.

135. Ibid.

his perceived calling and continued to make evangelism his priority. Though he would readily acknowledge that the majority of his hearers were in need of sanctification, and though he would look back fondly on his own experience of sanctification of 1871, Moody never allowed it to become a hobbyhorse or to distract him from his primary calling.[136] Yet he did, on occasion, speak directly to the issue.

For Moody, as for Pierson and Gordon, sanctification involves a work of the Holy Spirit distinct from justification/conversion. Although the Spirit is present in the life of the converted from the moment of justification/conversion, the work of sanctification is qualitatively different. That is, from the time of justification the Spirit is "in" the believer; but in sanctification the Spirit is now "on" or "upon" the believer.[137] The difference is not, as may be supposed, the residency of the Spirit. Rather, the difference is one of intensity; for in sanctification, the Spirit is not only present (as he has been since conversion), but the Spirit is now powerfully working through the one in whom he is resident.

Moody too believed that power lies at the heart of sanctification. He also believed that the main purpose of this power is ministry and that it manifests itself most clearly in the ability to declare the gospel with "super-human" effectiveness.[138] This ministry of the Spirit allows one to know and express the mind and will of God in a way otherwise impossible. Furthermore, as it is the Spirit's particular task to witness to Christ, so the one in whom the Spirit resides and whom the Spirit controls speaks of Christ with a boldness, accuracy, and effectiveness beyond mere human fortitude, rhetorical ability, charm, or capacity.[139]

Moody regarded power for ministry as being by far the greatest purpose of sanctification. So much so, that one might be tempted to assert that, for Moody, it was the only purpose for sanctification. The increased activity of the Spirit in the life of the believer, he believed, results not only in power for service, however, but also in power for holy living.[140] The power of the Spirit not only enabled one to witness

136. Gundry, *Love Them In*, 160.

137. In a sermon titled "Power *In* and *Upon*," Moody goes into significant detail about the nature of this difference (Moody, *Success in the Christian Life*, 33, 47).

138. It was an experience of sanctification that preceded his meteoric rise to religious stardom (Moody, *Success in the Christian Life*, 11).

139. Moody, *Best of Dwight L. Moody*, 78, 84.

140. "In this wonderful passage (Titus 2:11–13) we see grace in a threefold aspect:

effectively but also empowered one to live a holy life, to resist the downward pull of the old nature.[141] In contrast to those who believed that holiness could only be attained through constant struggling and the exercise of various ascetic disciplines, Moody promoted his way as a "shortcut to holiness."[142] He did not believe that one was able in any way to wholly and finally free oneself from the lure of sin in this life. The ongoing war with the old nature would continue.[143] He did believe, however, that perfection, despite its elusiveness, ought to remain the goal of the believer. Though perfection may lie beyond one's reasonable reach, it still serves as a worthy goal.[144] To strive for anything less is to strive for that which is less than the will of God.

This distinct work of grace in the lives of believers is distinct from conversion not only in nature but also in time.[145] Moody called it a second filling, a second work, and on at least one occasion, a second conversion.[146] It is not only logically subsequent to conversion but experientially subsequent as well. This is most clearly seen in Moody's description of the steps in the larger work of salvation of which this empowerment in its various manifestations is a part.[147]

Significantly, Moody not only described sanctification as being distinct in time from justification/conversion; he also made a chronological distinction between the work of the Spirit in enabling holy living and the work of the Spirit empowering for service. Here Moody's views

---

grace that bringeth salvation; grace for holy living; and grace for service" (Moody, *God's Abundant Grace*, 77).

141. On at least one occasion, Moody stated that sanctification as power for holy living may precede sanctification as power for service, and necessarily so. He does so, noting that in the area of ministry, the most effective subjects are those who also exhibit a life of holiness. See Moody, *Success in the Christian Life,* 56.

142. Shanks, *College Students at Northfield,* 171.

143. Findlay, *Dwight L. Moody,* 245.

144. Shanks, *College of Colleges,* 243.

145. "The Holy Ghost coming upon them with power is distinct and separate from conversion" (Moody, *Glad Tidings,* 287).

146. Findlay, *Dwight L. Moody,* 243.

147. Here are Moody's steps to the Spirit in the life of the believer: 1) Born of the Spirit; 2) Quickened by the Spirit—power; 3) Sanctified by the Spirit—separation from the world, holiness; 4) Guided by the Spirit; 5) Led by the Spirit; 6) Strengthened by the Spirit. See Shanks, *College Students at Northfield,* 172.

are distinct from those of both Pierson and Gordon and, as we shall see, from those of A. B. Simpson.[148]

Simpson and Sanctification

Arguments against Keswick Categorization

Sanctification is undoubtedly the aspect of A. B. Simpson's theology that has received the greatest attention. Yet classifying his position on the matter is no simple task.[149] Three Alliance authors have attempted such a classification. Gerald McGraw has thoroughly examined Simpson's various published statements—sermons, articles, editorials, manuscripts—on the subject. Richard Gilbertson, who focuses on Simpson's doctrine of the baptism of the Holy Spirit, places him within the context of late nineteenth-century evangelical opinion. Samuel Stoesz examines what he considers to be the roots of Simpson's theology of sanctification, and attempts to classify him accordingly. All three of these Alliance authors not only distinguish Simpson's doctrine of sanctification from that of Wesleyanism but go to some length to distinguish Simpson's teaching from that of Keswick. All three authors, to varying degrees, identify his doctrine of sanctification as a tertium quid—neither Wesleyan nor Keswickian.

Gerald McGraw, in attempting to define Simpson's teaching on sanctification, observes that

> Simpson taught that in a crisis subsequent to regeneration one fulfills God's conditions of separation and dedication, whereupon in response to a distinct act of faith, Christ baptizes him with the Holy Spirit. Separation involves spiritual crucifixion and resurrection. Whereas dedication requires full surrender, habitation provides the living Christ to enter and reside. Because Jesus became Spirit-filled, habitation includes receiving the Spirit. Afterward one maintains that commitment, becom-

---

148. "Although Moody did not completely agree with Simpson on sanctification, Simpson had a high respect for the evangelist; and he noted that Moody had emphasized the Holy Spirit's work and made the deeper life a major emphasis of his later ministry. Simpson invited him to minister at the two climactic services at an Alliance convention in Carnegie Hall, where he powerfully preached . . . 'to a vast multitude of people on the Baptism of the Holy Ghost'" (McGraw, "Doctrine of Sanctification," 190–91; see also Simpson, "Great Life Closed," 1).

149. Dayton, *Theological Roots*, 106.

ing progressively conformed to Christ's likeness. This process
leads to the Spirit's fullness. Sanctification results in holiness
and effective service.

Despite similarities, Simpson's sanctification doctrine included
its own distinctives, not duplicating either Keswick or Holiness
soteriology.[150]

To support his argument with respect to Keswick, McGraw points out
that Simpson's teaching on sanctification differs significantly from that
of Daniel Whittle, who has often been regarded as the holiness teacher
who, more than any other, influenced Simpson to seek the initial experience of sanctification.[151] According to McGraw, Whittle had rejected
Wesleyanism in favor of Keswick "suppressionism."[152] Simpson, on the
other hand, reacted "negatively [to] Whittle's suppressionism, preferring
his view of habitation to either eradication or suppression."[153] McGraw
notes that while the term "suppression" was not alien to Simpson's vo-
cabulary in relation to the doctrine of sanctification, "[such] language
is uncharacteristic of Simpson's usual teachings."[154] Simpson, moreover,
had an innate aversion to the self-effort that would, almost necessarily,
accompany such a theology.[155] For him the secret of sanctification is
not the personal striving of suppressionism, but the merit and work of
another—the indwelling Christ.[156]

150. McGraw, "Doctrine of Sanctification," xii.

151. These differences are in part what led McGraw to conclude that in spite of the
testimony of Simpson's official biography, Simpson's roots of his understanding and experience of sanctification are better linked to William Boardman's *The Higher Christian
Life*. See McGraw, "Doctrine of Sanctification," 184–88).

152. McGraw, "Doctrine of Sanctification," 177–78.

153. Ibid.,186.

154. Ibid., 350.

155. "Simpson decried the dependence on self-efforts which appears inevitable in a
suppressionist theology. Simpson taught the necessity of abiding in Christ for victory
in a continuing relationship, but he thought that the Christ life was far preferable to and
more unifying than suppression" (McGraw, "Doctrine of Sanctification," 351).

156. However, one should not be too hasty to equate Keswick teaching with suppressionism, for according to George Marsden, "[w]hile rejecting as too strong the
Wesleyan view of the *eradication* of one's sinful nature, the Keswick teachers rejected
as too weak the more traditional view that one's sinful nature was simply *suppressed* by
Christ's righteousness. This view, they felt, would encourage a life not only of constant
conflict with sin, but also of defeat by sin, and even tolerance of it as normal. They
came to call their own view counteraction" (Marsden, *Fundamentalism and American
Culture*, 77–78, emphasis original).

Richard Gilbertson, like McGraw, distinguishes between Simpson's view of sanctification and those of Keswick and Wesleyanism:

> There have been frequent attempts to categorize Simpson and the C&MA. Often the assertion is made that Simpson held to a Keswick-type view of sanctification. More precisely, Simpson should be seen as having been influenced by Boardman's *Higher Christian Life*, a book which also impacted the Keswick movement. Other than an 1885 invitation to speak at one of their conferences, Simpson had little formal contact with the British Keswick movement. It is true that prominent Keswick leaders such as F. B. Meyer and Charles Inwood spoke in Simpson's conventions. But it was Simpson's policy to invite speakers from a wide spectrum of theological persuasion.[157]

Gilbertson does not, however, clearly define Keswick theology. Instead, he simply follows Edith Blumhofer in asserting that Simpson, rather than following Keswick, belonged to those "Revivalistic Reformed" preachers who "restated orthodox doctrines with a particular reassertion of the need for an 'overcoming' Christian life, and a reaffirmation of the importance of both the personhood and the ministry of the Holy Spirit."[158]

Samuel Stoesz, too, wants to distinguish Simpson from both the Wesleyan doctrine of sanctification and (especially) Keswick. He acknowledges the ambiguous nature of Keswick teaching, noting that "Keswick did not subscribe to any code of doctrine or polity and stressed the Spirit-filled life through the victorious Christ who by the vicarious atonement defeated self and sin in the life of a believer."[159] It was a dynamic movement, whose emphases changed over time. Although he admits that some of the key themes of early Keswick thought resembled those of Simpson, Stoesz contends that these similarities eventually disappeared[160] as Keswick aligned itself more closely with

---

157. Gilbertson, *Baptism of the Holy Spirit*, 42.

158. Blumhofer (nee Waldvogel) identifies both A. J. Gordon and D. L. Moody as members of this group. It is noteworthy that both Gordon and Moody are often categorized as being affiliated with Keswick. A. T. Pierson self-identified with Keswick (Waldvogel, "Overcoming Life," 1).

159. Stoesz, *Understanding My Church*, 95.

160. Stoesz, *Sanctification*, 18.

"suppressionism," a teaching that Simpson steadfastly opposed.[161] Because of Keswick's theological ambiguity, "[h]istorians with no Alliance background have confused roots of Alliance doctrine with Keswick or holiness teaching."[162] Though both his contention about this confusion and his own isolationist position are open to challenge, Stoesz is correct in noting that many scholars have called Simpson a Keswickian.

Reasons for the Confusion

At least one reason for this confusion can be found in Simpson's apparent and often indiscriminate use of the terminology of particular traditions. Though he was sure to distance himself from what he perceived to be extreme views, he never explicitly identified himself with any one group. He regularly borrowed terms, phrases, concepts, and illustrations from many streams of thought. Although he was not ignorant of their connotations, he did not use them with discriminating precision either. What he may have meant by a particular word or expression may or may not have been what others may have meant by it. Therefore one must seek to understand both the usual sense in which he used a particular term, and the particular context in which he used it.

In addition, scholars tend either to exaggerate or to discount the influence of Simpson's Presbyterian heritage. To approach Simpson's writings from either extreme tends both to preclude close examination of his thought and to bias the outcome of a particular investigation. In regard to Simpson's Reformed heritage, two things must be held in balance: First, he never indicates explicitly that he has rejected his own theological heritage in toto. In fact, in his later writings he mentions its profound and lasting influence on his life and ministry. Second, although a number of factors contributed to his resignation from his Presbyterian charge, some of them involved theological doctrines as fundamental as soteriology. Although Reformed thought would always

---

161. "The adherents of 'suppressionism' held that Spirit-filling but not sanctification was an experience distinct from justification/conversion. This view was represented in Moody and Whittle. The carnal nature remained after the Spirit-filling but was suppressed by the believer's walk in the Spirit. This doctrine, first promoted by a Brethren movement in England, influenced Moody and was spread in America by what was known as the Prophetic Conference movement" (Stoesz, *Sanctification.*, 18).

162. Stoesz, *Sanctification*, 35.

influence his life and teaching, he made a decisive and final break with it at several points. Hence it is not surprising that (as we shall see) Simpson's doctrine of sanctification includes aspects that have affinities with Reformed thought and those that are more clearly distinct.

The Wesleyan Simpson?

At first glance, Simpson's theology could easily appear to be Wesleyan. Simpson was not afraid to associate himself with either Wesleyans or Wesleyan organizations. As was noted in the opening chapter, many of the leaders of the early C&MA had significant Wesleyan pedigrees. George Pardington, the first Alliance theologian, was the son of a Methodist minister and was educated at Drew Theological School, a decidedly Methodist institution. Paul Rader, Simpson's successor, was, like Pardington, the son of a Methodist minister. Simpson freely quoted from and endorsed the teachings of John Wesley, and many of Charles Wesley's hymns were sung at Alliance meetings and were reproduced in Alliance hymnals and other Alliance publications.

As far as sanctification itself is concerned, Simpson's teachings appear to reveal a strong Wesleyan influence. To begin with, Simpson regularly used Wesleyan terminology. Although he clearly rejected the idea of eradication, he frequently used the term "entire" with reference to sanctification. However, such usages often involved a redefinition; for by "entire," he did not mean that the sanctified person had reached a final or independent state, but that sanctification affects and should affect the whole of one's life. If "total depravity" referred to the pervasive stain of sin in the whole of the human condition, then "entire sanctification" was its corollary.

Simpson also broke with his Reformed heritage as far as his hamartology is concerned. What makes his hamartology peculiarly Arminian and therefore Wesleyan was his identification of motive as the root of the problem of sin. For Simpson, sin is inextricably bound up with intent. Reformed hamartology usually defines sin as any shortcoming on the part of humanity with respect to the statutes and character of God. For Simpson, however, sin involves not simply a shortcoming or an inability, but rather a lack of love for God and for one's fellows. He also identified the root of sin as independence,[163] but the essential idea

163. Simpson, *Self Life and the Christ Life*, 32.

remains unchanged, or as he himself bluntly put it, "[t]he absence of love is the fatal source of all sin."[164] Indeed, although "Selfishness is the Essential Principle of Sin,"[165] this "selfishness" consists of a lack of love for God and neighbor, the antithesis of the heart of the law.[166] In defining sin in this way, Simpson must have realized the parallels between his doctrine and that of Wesley.[167]

Furthermore, Simpson did not believe that the Christian could avoid a lifelong struggle with sin. While he did not affirm either the actual annihilation of the sinful nature or the possibility of attaining "Perfect Love," he was convinced that the power of the resurrected Christ would more than enable the believer to consider the sin nature a vanquished foe and to behave as though it were.

> Again, the resurrection of Christ is the power that sanctifies us. It enables us to count our old life, our former self, annihilated, so that we are no longer the same person in the eyes of God, or of ourselves; and we may with confidence repudiate ourselves and refuse either to obey or rear our former evil nature. Indeed, it is the risen Christ Himself who comes to dwell within us, and becomes in us the power of this new life and victorious obedience. It is not merely the fact of the resurrection, but the fellowship of the Risen One that brings us our victory and our power. We have learned the meaning of the sublime paradox, "I am crucified with Christ; nevertheless, I live; yet not I, but Christ lives in me." This is the only true and lasting sanctification, the indwelling life of Christ, the Risen One, in the believing and obedient soul.[168]

Thus, although Simpson gives the positive indwelling of the resurrected Christ instead of the negative eradication of the sin nature as the reason for sanctified living, the results he expects are decidedly Wesleyan.

---

164. Simpson, *Gospel of John*, 141.

165. Ibid., 202.

166. Simpson, *Gospel of Matthew*, 206, 244.

167. It should be noted that Simpson did not consider salvation to be merely a ceasing of selfishness. Although he agreed with Wesley that selfishness lies at the heart of sin, he believed that salvation involves not simply a reformation of character but a resurrection of life centered in the indwelling of Jesus Christ (Simpson, *Old Faith and the New Gospels*, 71–73).

168. Simpson, *Self Life and the Christ Life*, 24–25.

Like Wesley, Simpson believed that sanctification is not only a work distinct in nature from justification/conversion,[169] but that the experience of sanctification occurs subsequent to justification as well. He did not deny that justification/conversion and sanctification could occur so close together as to appear simultaneous, but he argued that this was rarely the case. Moreover, such subsequence is not only experiential, it is also logical; for justification/conversion, although a good and complete work in itself, prepares believers for sanctification by putting them in a place where God can make them holy. "Justification brings us peace *with* God," Simpson wrote; "sanctification, the peace of God."[170] The former is the inaugural event that prepares for the latter.[171]

Furthermore, Simpson believed that sanctification is received through a step of faith distinct from the believer's step of faith taken in conversion. Those who long for sanctification may gain it, but it is not a wholly passive attainment; neither is it automatically consequential to justification/conversion. Sanctification comes as a gift of God and, as with all gifts of grace, must be received by faith. When it is, it becomes as sure as justification/conversion.[172] Yet it must, like justification/conversion, be taken by an identifiable act of faith involving a necessary,[173] absolute, and determined "surrender to Him in everything,"[174] a yielding of claim over self, and a yielding to Christ. Speaking unequivocally about the necessity of this subsequent, distinct event, and opposing any conception of sanctification as a mere evolution of character consequential to justification/conversion, Simpson contended that the New Testament

> tells us of a crisis as distinct as conversion, and a new experience as marked and radical as regeneration. There is a crisis up to which we must come and through which we must pass in death and resurrection, and exchange the human for the divine, and our poor imperfect struggling for God's victorious life. We do not grow into sanctification. Christian progress really grows out

169. Simpson, "Timely Spiritual Watch Words," 65.

170. Simpson, *Wholly Sanctified*, 5 (emphasis original).

171. "It is the germ of the seed, but it is not the summer fullness of the plant" (Simpson, *Fourfold Gospel*, 25).

172. Simpson, *Larger Christian Life*, 5–6.

173. Simpson, *Fourfold Gospel*, 35.

174. Ibid., 35.

of sanctification. There must be a definite and divine beginning before there can be a wholesome growth.[175]

On a number of occasions, Simpson taught a chronology of sanctification and a methodology for receiving sanctification that, at first sight at least, were remarkably similar to those of the noted nineteenth-century Methodist Phoebe Palmer. He not only used phrases and terms that were remarkably similar to hers but, like her, also declared that entering into sanctification involves a simple and sure act of faith. Moreover, both Palmer[176] and Simpson[177] believed the prerequisites for sanctification to be humility, entire consecration, faith, and confession. Simpson set forth his four steps to sanctification in the following way: first, we need to be aware of our need for sanctification before we will ever seek it; second, we must take a step of faith in order to "come to Jesus as [our] Sanctifier"; third, we must make a decisive and memorable decision of surrender to Jesus in everything; finally, "[we] must believe that He receives the consecration we make."[178] Not only are the two sets of steps remarkably similar, but they both also promote a fideistic rationality according to which the believer embraces the promises of God, fulfills their requirements, and in spite of possible evidence to the contrary, steps out in faith as though the promise has been fulfilled.

Though McGraw has argued that "consecration" need not necessarily precede sanctification in Simpson's mind, a full and unhesitating consecration of self still must occur if one is to be sanctified.[179] If this were done, then, like Palmer, Simpson believed that sanctification would necessarily follow. One need not wallow in insecurity following full consecration. Rather, one should step out in faith assured that God

175. Simpson, *Earnests of the Coming Age*, 20–21.

176. Palmer, *Selected Writings*, 121.

177. Nevertheless, Simpson still held to a progressive understanding of sanctification, whereas Palmer believed that sanctification is received in some kind of terminal and complete form. Yet the strong resemblances between their views can be seen from the following (characteristic) quotation from Simpson: "Christian holiness is not a slow and painful attainment, but a free gift of God through Jesus Christ, a glorious and present obtainment, received in Christ Himself, received by faith, and retained by abiding in Him. From this we grow into maturity and expansion and full development, but we do not grow into it, we go into it and grow out from it into all the fullness of the station of Christ" (Simpson, "Distinctive Teachings," 2).

178. Simpson, *Fourfold Gospel*, 35.

179. McGraw, "Doctrine of Sanctification," 305–6.

is able to and will always make good on his promise in response to this step of faith.[180]

> The next step is to believe that the sacrifice is accepted, that the covenant is confirmed, that the Lord accepts and enters the offered temple, that the Holy Ghost possesses our spirit and body, and that Christ is henceforth by right our all in all, on whom we may lean with assurance and rest, and know that He will never fail us.
>
> These two words are expressed perfectly in Rom. vi. by the words YIELD and RECKON. So let us yield and reckon.[181]

The Keswick Simpson

Many scholars believe that A. B. Simpson's doctrine of sanctification either echoes or anticipates that of Keswick.[182] This is not a wholly unfounded conclusion. Simpson associated himself both with Keswick and with leaders with Keswick ties such as Moody, Gordon, and Pierson. He regularly invited such leaders to speak at Alliance meetings and teach at the Missionary Training Institute, and promoted their print and personal ministries in his periodicals. Though it may have been Simpson's habit to invite teachers of various theological stripes to share his various platforms, it would be an overstatement to assert that he and they had little in common, especially since many of the talks that such men gave addressed the Deeper Christian Life in some way.

Simpson was also prone to use Keswick terminology and illustrations in his own teaching on sanctification. He used terms, phrases, and illustrations associated with Keswick and, indeed, were almost inextricably linked with it. For example, he used the characteristically Keswick term "tendency"[183] to describe of the continuing attraction of sin in the lives of those who have entered into an experience of sanctification.

180. Simpson, *Wholly Sanctified*, 10.

181. Simpson, *Foundation Truths Respecting Sanctification*, 10–11 (emphasis original). This step of faith is found also in Simpson's understanding of justification/conversion and of healing. See Simpson, *Fourfold Gospel*, 42–44.

182. Among those scholars of note who identify Simpson with Keswick are Dayton, *Theological Roots*, 106–7; Bundy, "Keswick," 177; Smith, *Called unto Holiness*, 25; Anderson, *Vision of the Disinherited*, 41; Faupel, *Everlasting Gospel*, 249; and Menzies, "Non-Wesleyan Origins of the Pentecostal Movement," 87.

183. Barabas, *So Great Salvation*, 47–51.

Indeed this terminology even accords with his stress (throughout his writings) on the necessity of abiding in Christ[184]

McGraw, Gilbertson, and Stoesz all contend that Simpson should not be classified as a supporter of Keswick. Nor did Simpson consider the Alliance teaching on sanctification to be either Keswickian or Wesleyan. In responding to just such a question of classification, Simpson wrote the following "clarification" in an editorial in *The Christian and Missionary Alliance*:

> A correspondent recently inquired regarding the standpoint of Alliance teaching with respect to sanctification whether we held the Wesleyan view, or what is commonly known as Keswick teaching. *We believe that the Alliance teaching on the subject is neither Wesleyan nor, strictly speaking, an echo of even the excellent teaching given at the meetings annually held at Keswick.* While speaking in greatest appreciation of other teachers and of all who endeavor to hold up the true Scriptural standard of life, yet we believe that the point of view from which the subject of personal holiness is regarded by the teachers and workers in the Christian Alliance is what we might term the "Christ Life," rather than even the sanctified life. There is always a little danger of seeing our experience more than the source of that experience, the Person and work of the Lord Jesus, we have ever been led to rise above all our experiences and recognize our new and resurrection life wholly in Him. At the same time we believe and teach that this will lead to the very highest kind of Christian life; higher than our best experiences, higher than Adamic perfection, for it is the life of Jesus, the second Adam, the Son of God, "manifested in our mortal flesh."[185]

Stoesz contends that the reason why Simpson belongs to neither camp lies in the fact that he was so profoundly influenced by the writings of W. E. Boardman,[186] whose own understanding of sanctification differed from that of Keswick in two essential ways: 1) in his emphasis on the "indwelling of Christ's fullness in the believer" as the source of

---

184. Simpson, *Earnests of the Coming Age*, 47, 80.

185. Simpson, editorial in *Christian and Missionary Alliance*, June 3, 1899, 8 (emphasis added).

186. "In no other organization or agency has Boardman's view of sanctification been more fully preserved than in the C&MA. Thus, to understand Boardman is to more fully understand Simpson" (Stoesz, *Sanctification*, 36).

sanctification,[187] and 2) in his rejection of what he considered to be Keswick's overemphasis of power for service at the expense of power for holy living.

Stoesz believes that Keswick theology departed rather quickly and in significant ways from its earliest emphases, including its christocentricity. The culprit behind this loss of focus was the inappropriate wedding of Higher Life themes and dispensational eschatology. For reasons he does not clearly identify, Stoesz claims that with the arrival of dispensationalism, the "Higher Life" spirituality that gave birth to Keswick was soon swallowed up and eventually even considered a "sentimental heresy."[188] In thus losing its "Higher Life" emphasis, the Keswick movement became alienated from the Holiness movement that gave it birth; and as it moved away from Boardman and the "Higher Christian Life" movement Simpson found it less and less attractive.

According to Stoesz, Simpson also found unpalatable a propensity within Keswick to overemphasize "power for service" at the expense of the equally important, if not more foundational, "power for being."[189] He maintains that Boardman, and therefore Simpson, maintained a proper focus on Christ as the authentic object of human affections and interest, because for both men, to focus on the "power for service," or on anything other than Christ would have led to an imbalanced spirituality. Not that Simpson disparaged "power for service"; indeed, it was key to both his eschatology and his theology of ministry. Rather, he simply did not want to give it undue emphasis, since it is from power for being, or "power for holy living," that power for service flows.

> While empowering for service was an important dimension for this age, to Simpson it was a secondary one. The principal task of the Holy Spirit was to present Christ in His fullness and sufficiency and to impart the benefits of union with Him to believers in communal body-life. The Holy Spirit was given to the church on the day of Pentecost to help them embody Christ to

187. Stoesz, *Sanctification*, 42.

188. "[In] dispensational thought, the indwelling of Christ's fullness in the believer, so central in Boardman and Simpson, is virtually lost; indeed, dispensational leaders considered this emphasis a 'sentimental heresy'" (Stoesz, *Sanctification*, 42).

189. Ibid., 106.

the world, not in any way to glorify man or to magnify individual achievement.[190]

In describing Simpson's doctrine of sanctification, Stoesz emphasizes that Simpson did not develop his thinking "*de novo*," for his christocentrism, the themes of "the all sufficiency of Christ" or "Christ Himself," could be "found . . . in Boardman and the early Keswick movement."[191] Stoesz argues that it is incorrect to identify Simpson with Keswick, because at the heart of Simpson's doctrine of sanctification (indeed at the heart of all Simpson's theology) lies this radical Christ-centeredness, which Keswick had lost very early on, and which is best attributed to the influence of Boardman.[192]

The similarity between the views of Simpson and Boardman, according to Stoesz, comes from their common stress on "the incarnational significance of Christ for our sanctification and union with Him as an affirmation of orthodox doctrine and the focus of evangelical dynamic."[193] Though they certainly have this in common, Stoesz's larger argument is only sustainable if, among other things, his analysis of Keswick doctrine is wholly accurate. This, however, is not the case; for the Keswick movement is much more heterogeneous in nature than Stoesz allows, and as was noted earlier, defies precise definition.

KESWICK SPOKESMAN: HANDLEY C. G. MOULE

Handley C. G. Moule (1841–1920), Fellow of St. Catherine's College, and Norrisian Professor of Divinity, Cambridge, and perhaps Keswick's greatest theological spokesperson, [194] shared much of Simpson's theol-

190. Ibid.

191. Ibid., 18.

192. Though he does not document his claim, Stoesz says that many of the key slogans that Simpson used to describe his theology "originated with Boardman": "Christ Himself," "Jesus Only," "the all-sufficiency of Christ," "Christ's fullness," and even "Christ as Savior, Sanctifier, and Healer" (ibid., 35–36).

193. Ibid., 51.

194. "The adherence of Dr. Moule to the Keswick platform was a great accession of strength, for it brought into the movement one who had long been highly respected as a trusted Evangelical scholar and theologian. *Keswick has had other great scholars, but there is no doubt that Dr. Moule was its greatest*; and his books, though necessarily appealing to a far wider sphere than that represented by Keswick, have done effective service to the Keswick movement" (Barabas, *So Great Salvation*, 175, emphasis added; see also Pollock, *Keswick Story*, 72).

ogy of sanctification, especially with respect to those things that Stoesz identifies as deficiencies in Keswick teaching. Significantly, Stoesz designates Moule as being among those who "ministered one time or another at Simpson's Gospel Tabernacle in New York City."[195]

In good Keswick fashion, Moule maintained that sin is a persistent presence in the life of the believer. Yet sin need not control the believer in the same way that it does unbelievers. Though redeemed humanity is no longer under the necessary "kingship of sin, the Christian is 'not yet exempted from sin's presence' in its members."[196] The Christian, then, is at one and the same time not *in sin*, though sin continues to be *in him or her*. This being so, believers cannot live in some sort of sanctified independence. Humanity needs "every moment the conquering counteraction of the Spirit."[197] If sanctification is to be attained, it can only come about through the incessant empowering of God.

Moule taught that all blessings from the indwelling Jesus Christ are received by acts of faith.

> As by faith we enter the justified state, we so far owe to faith all the holy motives that state brings to bear on our acts and habits. But also faith is exercised at whatever moment the Christian for any purpose definitely trusts his Lord's word and power. It is precisely the same faculty as that exercised in the act of receiving remission and acceptance, and its exercise is *quite as simple* as then; but it now takes another direction, And this direction of faith figures very largely in the Scripture in the matter of the Christian's victory over sin, or deliverance from it. . . . It is clearly indicated that for the man in living contact with Christ the true secret for internal moral purity is Christ . . . living and overcoming within, by the Holy Spirit who effects His presence there. . . . And our part is to believe.[198]

Like Simpson, he did not identify the length of time that must occur between the step of faith leading to justification/conversion and the step of faith leading to sanctification, yet subsequence is implicit in the

---

195. Stoesz, *Understanding My Church*, 95.

196. Moule, *Outlines of Christian Doctrine*, 195.

197. Ibid.

198. Ibid., 191 (emphasis original).

terms "then" and "now." Elsewhere in his writings Moule explicitly identifies sanctification as a postconversion event.[199]

It is not that Moule disparaged justification. Indeed, he understood
that sanctification was not possible apart from it.

> [Justification] gives [the believer] *a new power* with which to
> live the grateful life; a power residing not in Justification itself,
> but in what it opens up. It is the gate though which he passes to
> the fountain; it is the wall which ramparts the fountain, the roof
> which shields him as he drinks. The fountain is his justifying
> Lord's exalted Life, His risen Life, poured into the man's being
> by the Spirit who makes Head and member one.[200]

It is not that the gift of sanctification lies beyond the grasp of believers
at conversion, but that many converts do not perceive the riches and enabling power that the indwelling Christ has placed at their disposal. The
crisis that leads to sanctification involves, in some way, a new awareness
and consequent dependence upon the indwelling Christ for all the challenges of the Christian life, for

> [e]very true entrance on acceptance is a true entrance on spiri-
> tual life and power, in its fullness, because it is an entrance
> into Christ. The man decisively accepted in Christ is the man
> also fully endowed in Christ, and needing only to discover his
> wealth. And no man who . . . in believing so as to receive the re-
> mission of sins, has really seen at all "WHOM he has believed,"
> can be quite in the dark both as to the immediate call to obey
> His Redeemer, and the immediately given new willingness and
> power to obey. But time inevitably discloses spiritual need and
> personal weakness, and there come in the man's life occasions,
> often very definite, of developed insight into and use of spiritual
> resources in Christ. (emphasis original)[201]

Moule was sure to note, however, that the entrance by faith into sanctification, as significant as it is, is not the terminus. Rather, it is only
the beginning of a process, and it is here that yet another distinction
between the faith that results in justification/conversion and sanctification arises.

---

199. Moule, *Thoughts on Christian Sanctity*, 85.

200. Moule, *Epistle to the Romans*, 161–62 (emphasis original).

201. Moule, *Outlines of Christian Doctrine*, 198.

> In . . . justification the real crisis is an entrance, *from the law's point of view*, into acceptance of the person. In . . . sanctification it is an entrance, *from the Christian's point of view*, on realization of inner peace and strength. The first case is in its nature one and single: an admission, an incorporation. The second is in its nature progressive and developing: The discovery, advancing with the occasion for it, of the greatness of the resources of Christ for life. The latter *may*, not *must*, thus include one great crisis in consciousness, one particular spiritual act. It is much more certain to include many starting-points, critical developments, marked advances. The act of self-surrendering faith in the power of Christ for inward cleansing of the will and affections may be, and often indeed it is, *as it were* a new conversion, a new "effectual calling."[202] (emphasis original)

Moule's definition of sanctification identifies sanctified humanity's newly discovered resource for overcoming sin "in Christ."[203] Union with Christ by the agency of the Holy Spirit is the beginning and end,[204] or the "solar truth,"[205] of the matter of sanctification. The secret of the Christian's sanctity is "the Lord himself—in His infinite but personal Being, outside mine, though the source and base of mine still—as able to deal with me."[206] For Moule, it is "the Lord Jesus Christ Himself as the secret of all Christian holiness."[207] The Christian's "secret" of success in sanctification, as in all endeavors, is the presence, indwelling, and enabling of Jesus Christ. Sanctification is not merely the engagement of a latent resident ability, for if one is to be sanctified, then one must take "the Lord Jesus Christ as [one's] sanctification."[208] Jesus Christ is the all-sufficient one, the source of all spiritual blessing and victory. This is the testimony of all of Scripture:

> the Psalms bear inexhaustible witness to a secret of victory which is in fact the man's committal of himself, for victory, to Jehovah. . . . So with the conflict of the Christian under temptation. His secret is to "put on the Lord Jesus Christ" (Rom. xiii.

202. Moule, *Outlines of Christian Doctrine*, 199 (emphasis original).
203. Ibid.,191.
204. Moule, *Thoughts on Christian Sanctity*, 89.
205. Moule, *Thoughts on Union with Christ*, 10.
206 Moule, *Thoughts on Christian Sanctity*, 38.
207. Ibid., 45.
208. Ibid., 97.

14), who is, in effect, "the whole armour, the panoply of God" (Eph. vi. 11). "In Him" alone, as vantage ground and fortress, His follower is "strong" (Eph. vi. 10) against the power of evil. "In Him, enabling," the Christian "has strength for all things (Phil. iv. 13) which are to be borne or done in the will of God.[209]

Perhaps nowhere in his writings does Moule more clearly identify the power of sanctification with the power of the indwelling Christ than in the following passage:

> [the] glorious . . . method illustrated here for triumphant resistance to [the] tendency [of the lure of the flesh is] is to penetrate through the spiritual principle upon a cold naturalistic programme of activity and probity. It is to penetrate through the spiritual principle to the Crucified and Living Lord who is its heart and power; it is to bury self with Him, and to arm the will with Him.[210]

Moule believed that spiritual victory comes from finding

> in Him our power and victory, and to "Put Him on," in a personal act which, while all by grace, is yet in itself our own. And how is this done? It is by the "committal of the keeping of our souls unto Him" (1 Pet. iv. 19), not vaguely, but definitely and with purpose, in view of each and every temptation.[211]

He found not only the secret to sanctification in this vital union with Christ, but indeed all of the blessings of God, as can be seen from the following extract from a sermon titled "The Secret of the Presence":

> But the inmost glory of the Gospel, the mysterious central brightness of its message—what is it? It is the giving by God of Himself to man. It is man's union and then communion, with none other than God in Christ. . . . Here, and no lower, from our point of sight, lies the final cause of all the saving process. It was in order that God, with infinite rightness, and with all the willingness of eternal love, might give Himself to man and dwell in man and walk in him and shine out from him, in measure here, hereafter perfectly.[212]

---

209. Moule, *Outlines of Christian Doctrine*, 192.

210. Moule, *Epistle to the Romans*, 367.

211. Ibid., 367–68.

212. Moule, *Old Gospel for the New Age*, 46.

It is only in light of the presence of Christ in organic union with the believer that one may speak of perfection at any level. It is in this light and only in this light that Moule would venture to assert the possibility of perfection.[213] The secret to this obtainment remains

> the Wonder-Worker Himself, trusted, welcomed in, summoned by the soul, to be the conquering and liberating Presence in its great need and in its depths.
>
> We shall never do it of ourselves. At the center of things, man is powerless to be his own transfigurer; he can as soon run, he can as soon soar, from his own shadow. But his Maker and his Redeemer, as man yields himself to God, can lift him from that shadow into light, and set him free indeed. What is needed—the Person, "dwelling in the heart by faith," so to make His chamber clean.[214]

Moule expands on this thought in a passage that echoes, to some degree, Simpson's famous sermon *Himself*, with its emphasis on the blessing of Christ rather than the blessings that attend his presence:

> Manifold are His gifts, His works. Vast indeed is the importance to our life and peace of clear views of what He is. It is blessed to know that indeed it is He, not only it; that He is no mere gale of power, no mysterious "somewhat" of effluence and influence, but the personal Friend and Lord, coming to His temples, to bless them with His own loving gifts of life, of purity, of power.[215]

---

213. One such instance is the following: "Then let us affirm it to ourselves again. There is such a thing, according to the Holy Scriptures, as heart purity; that is to say, there is such a thing as a state of the human heart, in which the man, the genuine man, the person of the present day and of modern circumstances, entirely loves the will of God, and entirely seeks to do it. There is such a thing as a human heart which, habitually, and with the joy of a steadfast sympathy, not only approves of virtue, which is conscience, but rejoices in it, as at once its liberty and its law; or rather, not in it but in Him, of whom virtue is but as the sunshine to the sun. And such joy and sympathy is purity of heart. There is such a thing as will, mind, and affection, united, not divided against the tempter and for the will of God. There is such a thing as an internal *No* to the siren-call of evil which is entirely true, for it is but the other side of a *Yes* which 'out of a pure heart fervently' responds to the call of Christ" (Moule, *Old Gospel for the New Age*, 234–35). Even here, Moule is sure to qualify his assertion by insisting on the necessity of being found veiled in Christ.

214. Moule, *Old Gospel for the New Age*, 239.

215. Ibid., 185.

Moule defined the message of Keswick in this same christocentric way. Quoting Robert McCheyne, he wrote that the heart of the Keswick message is "Christ for us is all our righteousness before a holy God; Christ in us is all our strength in an ungodly world."[216] He went on to say that this same message was the message of all true Keswick teachers, for they upheld the message "that there was just one divine secret for heart-whole obedience, with all its rest and power, and that secret is the trusted Christ Himself, deep within the heart."[217] Significantly, he admitted to the influence of Walter Marshall's *Gospel Mystery of Sanctification* on his own doctrine of the centrality and all-sufficiency of Christ. [218] On occasion he quoted Marshall, as in the following passage from *Outlines of Christian Doctrine*: "A full view of [sanctification] is vitally connected with the doctrine of our Union with Christ as the Second Man, in whom Manhood, perfected and glorified, is personally united to Godhead, and who, thus constituted the Head of His people, is for them the fountain of all grace and virtue, to be revived from Him by faith in Him."[219] In the conclusion to his book *Thoughts on Christian Sanctity*, Moule exhorted his readers never to separate the idea of the indwelling Christ from the doctrine and pursuit of sanctification: "Yes, let us remember it well. Our strength against temptation, our ability for true obedience resides in nothing less, nothing else, than living union and contact with Jesus Christ our Head. That union and contact is immediate, spiritual."[220]

One must be careful not to assume that Keswickian statements about spiritual power refer only to service and not to holy living. For example, Moule has this to say about the indwelling Christ: "From Him equally we derive both gifts of the New Covenant; acceptance, and spiritual power to do the will of God."[221] In this context "power" evidently pertains to personal holiness and not to some type of supernatural and superhuman talent or ability.

216. Moule, *Christ and the Christian*, 16.

217. Ibid., 19–20.

218. It was this book and author that also played a key role in Simpson's own conversion.

219. Moule, *Outlines of Christian Doctrine*, 193.

220. Moule, *Thoughts on Christian Sanctity*, 104.

221. Moule, *Outlines of Christian Doctrine*, 193.

What is of particular interest to the argument at hand is that Moule, a renowned Keswick speaker, teacher, and apologist very rarely referred to the power derived from sanctification as some supernatural intensification of practical skill. The inverse is true, for if the teachings of Moule, Keswick's foremost theological spokesman, are imbalanced, it is on the side of "power for holy living," not "power for effective service."

Conclusion

"Simpson's exposition of sanctification . . . is difficult to classify."[222] Yet it is clear that Simpson, in keeping with his christocentrism, sought to avoid emphasizing "power for service" at the expense of "power for holy living," as Stoesz has proposed. But the example of Keswick statesman Handley Moule shows that these emphases do not necessarily disqualify Simpson from being categorized as a Keswickian. Admittedly, the teachings of Moule and Simpson are not identical, yet their soteriologies are remarkably similar. For example, Simpson's doctrine of the "Christ life" is virtually interchangeable with Moule's understanding of the Christian life; for both men believed that the secret of the sanctified life is found in personal union and communion with the person of Jesus Christ, who does not merely provide sanctification but is himself the Sanctifier. Finally both Simpson and Moule stress sanctification as "power for holy living," although they do not minimize its derivative, "power for service." Certainly neither man gives evidence of the imbalance that Stoesz warns against (although others within the Keswick movement certainly do). Stoesz accurately describes Simpson's theology of sanctification, but his overly narrow characterization of Keswick prevents him from seeing that Simpson, despite the latter's own protestations, fits within the (rather flexible) Keswick mold.

---

222. Dayton, *Theological Roots*, 106.

"Breathing Out and Breathing In"

Jesus, breathe Thy Spirit on me,
Teach me how to breathe Thee in,
Help me pour into Thy bosom
All my life of self and sin.
I am breathing out my own life,
That I may be filled with Thine;
Letting go my strength and weakness,
Breathing in Thy life divine.

Breathing out my sinful nature,
Thou hast borne it all for me;
Breathing in Thy cleansing fullness,
Finding all my life in Thee.
I am breathing out my sorrow,
On Thy kind and gentle breast;
Breathing in Thy joy and comfort,
Breathing in Thy peace and rest.

I am breathing out my longings,
In Thy list'ning loving ear,
I am breathing in Thy answers,
Stilling every doubt and fear.
I am breathing every moment,
Drawing all my life from Thee;
Breath by breath I live upon Thee,
Blessed Spirit, breathe in me.[223]

223. Simpson, "Breathing Out and Breathing In," in *Hymns of the Christian Life*, 251.

4

Christ, Our Healer

THE CURRENT AGE HAS SEEN THE RISE TO PROMINENCE, AND TO SOME
degree the rise to infamy, of televangelists, some of whom have spec-
tacular ministries of healing. Many of them have proven to be frauds,
and the negative publicity generated by the very public moral downfall
of others has almost irretrievably colored the public's perception of any
type of Christian healing ministry, particularly those of a miraculous
bent. Yet this has not always been the case. In the latter part of the nineteenth century, for example, the church began to renew its interest in
holistic salvation, i.e., the redemption of both body and soul. The manifestations of this increasing spiritual concern about bodily health took
many, varied, and sometimes irreconcilable forms, as can be seen from
some of the terms that were used to describe it: "The Social Gospel,"
"Faith Healing," "Mind Cure," "Homeopathy," and "Water Cure."

A. B. Simpson was not unaffected by this movement of renewal, nor
were D. L. Moody, A. T. Pierson, and A. J. Gordon, for it touched anyone
who moved in the religious circles of the time. In fact, Simpson and
Gordon became leading spokesmen for the divine-healing movement,[1]
though they did not speak with altogether original voices. Most of their
emphases, and even their apologetic for the ministry of healing, can
be found in the teachings of both their mentors and their contemporaries. Pierson and Moody, although they supported the movement in
practice, never made it a central aspect of their own ministries. Moody
even appeared at times to resist it. Ultimately, however, the differences

---

1. Nancy Hardesty identifies Simpson as a pivotal figure in the divine healing
Movement and considers him to be partly responsible for the emigration of the prac-
tice and doctrine of divine healing from Europe to North America (Hardesty, *Faith
Cure*, 94).

that did arise among the four men were those of emphasis and not of substance.

Historical Roots of the Divine Healing Movement

As has been implied above, the divine-healing movement of the latter part of the nineteenth century did not appear ex nihilo, for the ministry itself has been practiced throughout the history of the church.[2] divine healing also has a long history in North America. One of the earliest practitioners was the noted Quaker George Fox (1624–1691), who practiced healing prayer as but "one part of a total ministry."[3] The Quakers believed that these manifestations of miraculous healing continued to occur in their fellowship because the ministry of Jesus Christ had never changed. As miraculous healings were part of Jesus's earthly ministry, so too, are they part of his heavenly ministry.[4] The Shakers or, more properly, "The United Society of Believers in Christ's Second Appearing" were another early American sect who practised healing. Ann Lee (1736–1784), their charismatic leader, believed that an effective ministry of healing was one of the signs of an authentic church in any age. The Shakers began by taking a radical approach to divine healing that left no place for physicians or the use of medicines.[5] Other groups that practiced healing ministries were John Noyes and the Oneida Perfectionists and Joseph Smith's Church of Jesus Christ of Latter-day Saints.

Ellen G. White's Seventh-Day Adventists and Mary Baker Eddy's Church of Christ, Scientist went beyond any of these groups in that they held the doctrine of miraculous healing as a central tenet not only of

2. Morton Kelsey has surveyed the history of the doctrine and practice of healing in church history and has shown how healing, though receiving different levels of attention in different eras, was a continuing focus throughout the church's existence. Strangely, however, he almost completely overlooks the late nineteenth-century divine healing movement. See Kelsey, *Healing and Christianity*.

3. Chappell, "Divine Healing Movement in America," 7. Though Fox only visited America once (1672–1673), his influence on America would remain strong through his organization, the "Religious Society of Friends," or as they are more popularly called, the Quakers.

4. It should not be assumed, however, that the Quakers refused to use medicines, physicians, or physical remedies. See Chappell, "Divine Healing Movement in America," 7–8.

5. Chappell, "Divine Healing Movement in America," 11.

their faith but also of their practice.[6] Although White (1827–1915) and Adventism would later become known for promoting health via a strict dietary regimen, White earlier in her career placed a greater emphasis on miraculous healing.[7] She believed that sickness and disease were satanic and spiritual in origin, and that Christians therefore ought to overcome them through faith in God instead of idolatrously placing their faith in physicians.[8] A spiritual problem, though it manifested itself physically, must be treated by a spiritual remedy that God alone could provide.

The teaching of Mary Baker Eddy (1821–1910) was as distinct from that of the aforementioned groups as it was popular. The other proponents of divine healing considered the problem of sickness, though an intrusion into the created order remained, to be a "real" phenomenon. Eddy's best-selling *Science and Health, with Key to the Scriptures*, by contrast declares that sickness ultimately has no real existence. To be healed is to be released from captivity to the illusion of sickness. Spirit, and Spirit alone, is the end and extent of all being, divine or otherwise. Matter, then, is not real.[9] Consequently, physicality and any physical ailments are not real either. To experience healing, then, is not to have something about physical being rectified; it is rather to realize and reject the illusory, delusive, and unreal character of material being.[10]

The European Influence

Despite the relatively long and popular history of healing belief in North America, most scholars of the nineteenth-century divine-healing movement agree that its theological pedigree is more precisely European than American. In fact, "no direct or organic connection between these early [American] groups and the later divine healing Movement can be established, . . . Ironically, it was the divine healing phenomenon in Europe which was to play a more vital and direct role in influencing the

6. Chappell notes that for the most part, prior to the late-nineteenth century, divine healing was never a "dominating motif with any of the religious groups in America." Chappell, "Divine Healing Movement in America," 26.

7. Numbers and Larson, "Adventist Tradition," 450.

8. Chappell, "Divine Healing Movement in America," 19.

9. "Theology and physics teach that both Spirit and matter are real and good, whereas the fact is that Spirit is good and real, and matter is Spirit's opposite" (Eddy, *Science and Health*, viii).

10. Ibid., 130.

American faith healing movement."[11] To be more precise, the Americans who exerted the greatest formative influence on the divine-healing movement either resided in Europe at the time or affected the movement for reasons other than the position they took on divine healing.

The three Europeans who made the greatest contribution to the movement were Johann Christoph Blumhardt, Dorothea Trudel, and Otto Stockmayer.[12] Before their time, Protestantism had by and large denied the possibility miraculous healing, because of what has been termed "Reformed 'dispensationalism.'"[13] This idea, championed by Luther, Calvin, and much later by Princeton's B. B. Warfield, contends that the miraculous gifts of the church were extinguished with the close of the apostolic age. It does not deny outright the existence of the miraculous. Rather, it asserts that such gifts and wonders had specific and temporally limited purposes: the authentication of the apostles, the authentication of their message, and the establishment of the church. Once they had performed their assigned roles, these preparatory miraculous gifts, by the design of God, passed away. Not until the rise of German Pietism would this opinion be challenged to any great degree.[14]

Johann Christoph Blumhardt (1805–1880) was a German Lutheran Pietist best known for his motto, "Jesus ist Sieger" (Jesus is Victor).[15] He believed that the source of all sickness is sin. Therefore, if one is to be cured, one must treat the sin that underlies the physical manifestation. To do this, one must reattach oneself to the victorious Jesus, who has overcome both sin and sickness not only in his earthly ministry but also in his larger ministry of atonement. Blumhardt deemed the ability to trust God alone apart from "the instrumentality of external means . . . to be the best and more assured way of obtaining healing."[16] Despite his emphasis on the resources of God to secure physical healing, Blumhardt

11. Chappell, "Divine Healing Movement in America," 25–26.

12. The three leading works on the roots of the nineteenth-century divine healing Movement all identify Blumhardt, Trudel, and Stockmayer as seminal figures (Chappell, "Divine Healing Movement in America"; Dayton, *Theological Roots*; and Waldvogel, Overcoming Life).

13. Dayton, "Rise of the Evangelical Healing Movement," 116–17.

14. Donald Dayton identifies Johann Albrecht Bengel as one of the earliest of the German Pietists to challenge this idea. See Dayton, "Rise of the Evangelical Healing Movement," 3.

15. Blumhardt, *Pastor Blumhardt*, 18.

16. Chappell, "Divine Healing Movement in America," 38–39.

did not wholly discard the possibility of human involvement. Indeed, he believed that even the effectiveness of "Jesus the Victor" may be subject to the relative cooperation or resistance of the human will. Consequently, Blumhardt established a retreat facility in Bad Boll, Germany, where the sick could come and focus on spiritual matters, the pursuit of Jesus, and, ultimately, physical healing.

Like Blumhardt, Dorothea Trudel established healing homes, and like him she did not totally dispense with the use of either physicians or medicines—despite her zeal for divine healing and her belief that Christ alone was the true physician. In Trudel's homes "[m]edical remedies [could] be used by patients if they so chose, [but] prayer was believed to be a simpler and more direct means of healing."[17] Moreover, she did not believe that she personally had any gift of healing or that the ultimate secret to health and wholeness could be found in a regimen, no matter how apparently godly. Rather, she "believed that healing was provided in the atonement."[18] The only thing that stood between a believer and healing was his or her ability to accept it. The purpose of her healing homes was not to deliver healing as much as it was to provide a setting where one could be further sanctified and learn to fully trust God to do what he had promised to do.

The third figure, Otto Stockmayer, did more than the either Blumhardt or Trudel to provide a systematic theological defence of the doctrine of divine healing.[19] Stockmayer, like Trudel and Blumhardt, believed bodily healing to be an integral part of the gospel of salvation. However, Stockmayer went one step beyond Trudel in contending that sanctification is not merely a necessary precursor to healing, but rather that healing is part and parcel of sanctification itself: "To Stockmayer, this is the essence of sanctification or Christian Holiness, that man be at the free and absolute disposal of God, both spiritually and bodily."[20] To be set apart to God involves the whole of the human being. Like Trudel, he also believed that provision for divine healing has been made in the atonement, and that sickness had entered creation through the

17. Ibid., 48.

18. Ibid.

19. Stockmayer's influence on Simpson was direct and personal. Simpson identified "Pastor" Stockmayer as one who spoke at the Gospel Tabernacle (Simpson, "Story of Providence," 161).

20. Chappell, "Divine Healing Movement in America," 50.

fall. He took his argument one step further, however, in contending that Isaiah 53:4 ("Surely he has borne our infirmities / and carried our diseases; / yet we accounted him stricken, / struck down by God, and afflicted.") and Matthew 8:16–17 ("That evening they brought to him many who were possessed by demons; and he cast out the spirits with a word, and cured all who were sick. This was to fulfill what had been spoken through the prophet Isaiah, 'He took our infirmities and bore our diseases.'"), ought to be interpreted literally. That is, Stockmayer broke with the conventional metaphorical interpretation of the Isaiah passage that equated "sicknesses" with the spiritual consequences of sin, arguing that Matthew's undeniably physical interpretation of the Isaiah passage made it incumbent on Christians to interpret the "sicknesses" Isaiah refers to as actual physical ailments.[21]

The Holiness Movement

The formative influence of the European healers on the late nineteenth-century American divine-healing movement was matched by that of the Holiness movement. Just as the Europeans provided the theological and practical seed, so the Holiness movement provided the fertile soil that allowed the divine-healing movement to germinate.

John Wesley is known for his own emphasis on health and healing. His book *Primitive Physic* contains an abundance of medical advice and folk remedies. Yet his legacy to the divine-healing movement lies not in his teaching on health and healing *per se* but in his doctrine of sanctification or "Christian Perfection," for

> Wesley's strong sense of the present power of God to restore the fallen creation cast a new light on his concern for physical health (evidenced not only in *Primitive Physic* but also in his work for health care and dispensaries for the poor) and would eventually help raise more insistent questions about the extent to which healing and restoration of health would be included in the benefits of grace to be expected in this life. If, indeed, we might be fully restored spiritually to the full image of God, to what extent might physical restoration also be expected, since disease is ultimately traced to the sin of Adam?[22]

21. Ibid., 51.
22. Dayton, *Theological Roots*, 119.

Wesley's perfectionistic expectations with respect to the soul naturally led to speculation and anticipation with respect to the "perfection" of the body. He and his followers came to believe that the effect and scope of the fall were not limited to the spiritual or theoretical realm. The fall had affected present physical human existence too. If God is truly omnipotent, however, and if one of the purposes of the atonement is to nullify the consequences of the fall, can the results of Christ's death and resurrection be any less powerful and broad than the effects of the fall? Just as it had brought about justification and spiritual renewal, so, too, it seemed to provide the possibility for physical renewal.

This propensity to a somewhat realized eschatology would only be further fuelled by theological developments in nineteenth-century America. Charles Finney's optimism—that faith brings the object of its pursuit, and Phoebe Palmer's idealism that encouraged people to act as though prayer were answered despite any lack of empirical evidence—would both shape the divine-healing movement.[23] Thus, Americans who had already been influenced by the European healing movement began to believe that healing was not only possible but available here and now if one would only step out in faith and claim it.[24]

The North American Divine Healing Movement

CHARLES CULLIS

The undisputed father of the late nineteenth-century American divine-healing movement was Boston homeopathic physician Dr. Charles Cullis.[25] Renowned for his philanthropy he also became widely known

23. This is clearly seen in the ministries of Elizabeth Mix and Carrie Judd Montgomery. See Chappell, "Divine Healing Movement in America," 92–98, 229–50; Judd, *Prayer of Faith*, 15.

24. Referring to these influences, Paul Chappell asserts, "Clearly, it was out of the holiness movement that the American divine healing movement arose" (Chappell, "Divine Healing Movement in America," 80). The connections between the Holiness Movement and the rise of the divine-healing movement are examined in Dayton, *Theological Roots*; and Cunningham, "From Holiness to Healing," 3.

25. "To Dr. Charles Cullis undoubtedly belongs the distinction of having done more than any other man to bring healing by faith to the attention of the church in the last century" (Carter, *"Faith Healing" Reviewed*, 109).

as an advocate of a second work of the Spirit for sanctification[26] and, soon after, as an advocate of divine healing. Following the faith support model of George Müller, he founded a home for incurable consumptives in Boston. He also established a publishing arm for his ministry, the highly successful Willard Tract Repository,[27] and sponsored and taught at many conferences on sanctification and healing.[28] His greatest impact, however, has been as one who drew others into the doctrinal fold, who in turn would propagate the doctrine of healing even more widely than he. Three of the best known of these figures were R. Kelso Carter, A. J. Gordon, and A. B. Simpson.

R. Kelso Carter

Russell Kelso Carter was among Cullis's earliest and most enthusiastic devotees. Though Carter is currently best known for his popular hymn, "Standing on the Promises of God," his earliest fame came as a vociferous proponent of divine healing. Though he was, like Cullis, an energetic conference speaker, his greatest impact came through his writings. In 1884, he published his most popular and influential work, *The Atonement for Sin and Sickness*. This was followed, two and a half decades later, with *"Faith Healing" Reviewed after Twenty Years*, in which he toned down the assertions of his previous writings and, to some extent, renounced the theological assertions that had brought him to his previous viewpoint.[29]

Gordon and Simpson, however, followed Cullis's example unwaveringly. The "Gospel of Healing," as Simpson called it, or "The Ministry of Healing," as Gordon referred to it, would remain a lifelong focus in the ministry of each man.[30]

26. Daniels, *Dr. Cullis and His Work*, 5.

27. "[Cullis's] Willard Tract Repository became a major publisher of Holiness literature in the 1870s and 1880s" (Dayton, *Theological Roots*, 123). See also Cunningham, "Holiness to Healing," 500. Among the titles published by the Willard Tract Repository are three of Cullis's own works: *Faith Cures* (1879), *More Faith Cures* (1881), and *Other Faith Cures* (1885) (Cunningham, "Holiness to Healing," 503).

28. Dayton, *Theological Roots*, 122–24; Cunningham, "Holiness to Healing," 502.

29. At the heart of Carter's retraction is a softening of his former firm endorsement of the doctrine of healing in the atonement and an enumeration of the pastoral difficulties associated with presuming upon the grace of God (Carter, *"Faith Healing" Reviewed*, 69, 92–93, 117).

30. It was Carter's contention, however, that though Simpson and Gordon taught

D. L. MOODY

The place of divine healing in the ministry of D. L. Moody is not easy to determine, for he rarely referred to the doctrine in the course of his revival ministry. Some appear to have taken this relative silence as a sign of disapproval.[31] This view is not wholly without merit or evidence. In the late 1890s, Moody engaged in a debate with his crosstown rival, John Alexander Dowie, founder of Zion City, the Christian Catholic Apostolic Church, and a vociferous proponent of a radical form of divine healing. In this exchange, Dowie wrote that "the last thing Mr. Moody knows much about is divine healing."[32] Moody's responses, which were published in Dowie's magazine *Leaves of Healing*, seem to indicate that he opposed not only Dowie's teaching on the subject but the doctrine of divine healing in general. Since Moody's comments appear in Dowie's publication and are directed particularly at Dowie, however, they do not provide a reliable source from which to determine the full extent of Moody's opinion on divine healing.

Other scholars, such as Stanley Gundry, author of *Love Them In*, and James Findlay, author of *Dwight L. Moody: American Evangelist*, refuse to speculate and therefore make no mention of Moody's views on the doctrine of healing. Still, it does seem strange that they would fail to investigate his opinion on what was at the time such a controversial and popular doctrine, even within Moody's own organizational ranks. Lyle W. Dorsett, author of *A Passion for Souls: The Life of D. L. Moody*, takes a different approach, however. Though he admits the relative silence of Moody on the issue of divine healing, he does not interpret it as antagonism but rather attempts to show Moody's limited support for the doctrine through the testimony of his friends and associates.

Emeline (Emma) Dryer, a highly educated woman whom Moody appointed to found his women's training academy and for whom he had the highest respect,[33] had experienced two miraculous healings

---

one thing, they practiced another. That is, though both Gordon and Simpson endorsed a belief that healing was surely in the atonement, and that it always availed, their practice was more cautious and measured (Carter, *"Faith Healing" Reviewed*, 112–15).

31. C. Allyn Russell has likened Moody's resistance with that of Princeton theologian B. B. Warfield's, the author of *Counterfeit Miracles* (Russell, "Adoniram Judson Gordon," 75).

32. Dowie, "Afternoon Service," 250.

33. This school would grow into what is now known as Moody Bible Institute.

in her own life: first from typhoid and second from an eye disorder. Following the second healing, Dryer began to teach that healing is one of the current ministries of Christ through the Spirit. Moody published her book on the subject, *The Wonders of Prayer*. The book must have made an impression on Moody, because, according to Dryer, he became favorably disposed toward divine healing before his death.[34] Reuben Archer Torrey, a major player in the early Fundamentalist movement, and Moody's choice as the superintendent of his Chicago school and the pastor of his Chicago Avenue Church, was a vocal proponent of divine healing, as can be seen from his work *Divine Healing: Does God Perform Miracles Today?*[35]

Another colleague of Moody's who sat squarely within the divine-healing camp was A. J. Gordon. Dorsett describes Moody's relationship with Gordon as being "extremely close:" the two men worked together, shared each other's platforms, and challenged each other on various doctrinal points.[36] Moody even encouraged his brother-in-law, F. H. Revell, to publish Gordon's *The Ministry of Healing* in 1882.[37]

Dorsett also mentions that Moody "became a friend and admirer"[38] of A. B. Simpson. Indeed, on at least one occasion Moody explicitly endorsed Simpson's ministry of healing to a friend whose wife was ill with tuberculosis. The woman, after being anointed and prayed for by Simpson, was healed and went on to live for fifty-three more years without a recurrence of the tuberculosis that drove her to him.[39]

It is possible that Moody could have associated with such staunch advocates of healing as Simpson and Gordon and still not have embraced the doctrine himself. However, since he both promoted their ministries and encouraged the publication of their books, one may safely assume that Moody also endorsed, at least to some degree, the theology that lay behind them.

34. Dorsett, *Passion for Souls*, 166–67.

35. Torrey, *Divine Healing*.

36. Dorsett, *Passion for Souls*, 251–52, 351.

37. Ibid., 333.

38. Ibid.

39. Ibid., 334.

A. T. PIERSON

Like Moody, A. T. Pierson did not make divine healing a part of his ministry. Yet, he was well-acquainted with the movement and, unlike Moody, spoke and wrote on the subject. In fact, his book *Forward Movements of the Last Half Century* includes a chapter titled "The Divine Healing Movement," in which he summarizes the movement's beliefs and offers his own correctives to what he believed to be its theological and practical weaknesses. Pierson was the movement's congenial yet critical friend.

According to Pierson, humanity is a complex being made up of body, soul, and spirit. Moreover, none of these components stands alone but rather participates in a symbiotic relationship with the others. Thus, if the body is ailing, the ailment affects the health of the balance of one's being.[40] So too physical healing brings both physical and spiritual blessings. It is a more holistic work than it is often considered to be. Pierson sets forth the traditional argument for the ongoing validity of divine healing in the current age as follows: sin is a consequence of fall, the results of "which Christ came to destroy";[41] all healing, medicinal or miraculous, is dependent on the blessing of God; the power to forgive sin and the power to heal are so closely linked that "one is used to confirm and establish the other"; healing was an essential part of the Lord's earthly work and thus is inseparable from the atonement;[42] healing was and continues to be a sign of the presence and authenticity of the gospel; and, finally, the Bible gives no indication that divine healing will ever cease—if the number and frequency of healings have declined, it was not due to some dispensational restriction but due to a lack of faith.[43]

---

40. "Where the body is not normal, a cloud comes over the higher faculties" (Pierson, *Forward Movements*, 37).

41. Pierson, *Forward Movements*, 389.

42. Ibid., 390.

43. Ibid., 391. In a subsequent chapter in the same work, Pierson observes that "Supernatural signs appear to have survived beyond the apostolic age; but we cannot trace them beyond the period of Constantine, when the church lost its separateness, merged with and into the state; when evangelistic activity declined and evangelical faith decayed; and so the conditions of God's special presence among his people no longer existed. If in these days, a new Pentecost should restore primitive faith, worship, unity and activity, new displays of divine power might surpass those of any previous period" (Pierson, *Forward Movements*, 401).

Another aspect of this backsliddenness, and one directly linked to the absence of

Pierson believed that disputes over such matters of doctrine can only be settled on the basis of the testimony of Scripture and trustworthy evidence.[44] As far as the latter is concerned, Pierson could appeal to at least three incontrovertible instances of divine healing. The first was an experience from Pierson's own childhood: God had protected him and the rest of the church he attended from an outbreak of cholera.[45] The second involved his own dramatic healing from an inner ear problem in 1897.[46] The third was the *"unquestionable* cases of God's healing in answer to prayer"[47] that his friend A. J. Gordon had experienced.

Pierson also believed that Scripture supports the doctrine of divine healing. To begin with, it attributes the origin of sickness to the encroachment of sin into the world. Thus sickness is not ultimately a problem of biochemistry and chemical mechanics but rather has deep roots in a primordial, spiritual reality. Thus one must turn to God for the ultimate remedy, for only he can deal with the root cause. Doctors and medicine can only treat symptoms. One must be careful, however, not to assume that sickness serves no purpose in God's economy, for he may use particular instances of sickness for his own ends: e.g., the "fatherly correction" of his children or their perfecting of virtue.[48] Either way, chemical or mechanical remedies are inadequate, or better, categorically inappropriate responses to the problem, for "[s]o far as bodily disease or infirmity is the organic result of sin, a judgment on sin, or a correction for faults, resort to medicine, instead of repentance, evades the whole issue."[49] To pursue these remedies in the face of the chastisement of

---

healings in the church is the church's materialistic and mechanistic view of the world. The church would not be arguing about the possibility of divine healing, "had not materialism and practical atheism so tainted Christian life, that we practically shut God out from our affairs. In modern notions the universe is a clock work, would up somehow, and somehow never running down; the wheels move regularly, and nothing can stop them; there is no intelligence guiding them; blind 'natural law' is the mechanical mainspring. If you get caught and half crushed between the cogs, it is an accident; and all you can hope to do is to get the doctor to bind up your wounds with bandage and healing salve and ointments and set your broken bones" (Pierson, *Forward Movements*, 398).

44. Ibid., 392, 404.
45. MacLean, *Dr. Pierson*, 4.
46. Pierson, *Forward Movements*, 345.
47. Ibid., 393 (emphasis added).
48. Ibid., 394–95.
49. Ibid., 395.

God "would have been a fresh insult to the Lord who was dealing with [that one.]"[50] Many Christians do not experience healing because they fail to realize the ultimate source of sickness and its proper remedy. "Hundreds of cases of bodily infirmity which might be remedied by prayer, holy living and laying hold on God, get no relief, because relief is sought in medical expedients: the cause lying deeper, the remedy fails to reach the seat of the disease."[51]

So despite his warning about taking the doctrine to illegitimate extremes,[52] Pierson certainly believed in divine healing. His confidence was not based on divine healing as an abstract principle but on the power of the indwelling Christ, which not only quickens the believer with respect to regeneration and sanctification but must affect the body as well: "Surely, a body in which the Spirit dwells ought, by virtue of that fact, to be a better body, and feel the thrill of that divine life in better blood, brain, brawn, bone, and nerves! The divine indwelling should have both a purifying and healing effect on even the material temple."[53] Divine healing, and more so, divine life is not an ethereal gift but was the consequence of the indwelling Christ. A body that houses the presence of Christ cannot help but be strengthened by it.

The primary blessing, however, is not health. Health is a mere by-product of the indwelling Christ, the truer and higher blessing.[54] And since sin, not sickness, lies at the root of the problem, so Christ, not the remedy, must take precedence for the Christian. Sin is the problem; Christ is the solution. Divine health comes neither through the infusion

---

50. Ibid., 397.

51 Ibid., 408.

52. "Just here, the 'Faith Cure' school often runs to an extreme. Some say that all sickness is the result of sin; that, as the atonement of Christ avails for sin and all its consequences, of which sickness is one, faith will enable us to escape sickness, and they conclude that all sick persons are sinners, or if not unsaved sinners, unbelieving saints. The fallacy and sophistry of such reasoning are not hard to trace. Sickness is the fruit of sin, but not necessarily the sin of the individual sufferer. As parts of the social organism, none of us are independent of others; and when, at any point, the organism suffers injury, the shock is felt throughout" (Pierson, *Forward Movements*, 400).

53. Pierson, *Forward Movements*, 400.

54. "He is not a means or medium for the reception of blessing, but He *is* Himself the blessing. Not only, therefore, is the blessing in me, but I am in the blessing, because I am in the Blesser Himself" (Pierson, *Believer's Life*, 62).

of some impersonal remedy, "means or [media]."[55] It is a consequence of the power and benevolence of the indwelling Christ himself.

A. J. GORDON

A. J. Gordon was a leading advocate of divine healing in the late nineteenth century, and both his supporters and his detractors regard his book *The Ministry of Healing* as a seminal work in the field. Even B. B. Warfield, the influential author of *Counterfeit Miracles*, lauded him for his clarity and scholarship despite the fact that he himself disagreed with Gordon's arguments.[56] Modern historians recognize the key role that Gordon played in the late nineteenth-century divine-healing movement.[57]

Gordon believed healing to be an integral part of "full salvation" because it has its source in the atoning work of Jesus Christ.[58] He opposed the argument of the Reformed dispensationalists,[59] who contended that the age, and therefore the exercise of such miraculous works, was past, by asserting that the apparent cessation of miracles had not come about by the will of God but through lack of faith. If one presupposed that miracles were not available in this dispensation and, therefore, did not seek them, should one be surprised that they are not manifest?[60] Not surprisingly, Gordon linked this dissolution of faith with the confluence of church and state under the rule of Constantine.[61] He believed that

---

55. Pierson, *Believer's Life*, 62.

56. Warfield applauded Gordon's "straightforward, businesslike style, . . . excellent spirit, . . . great skill in arranging his matter and developing his subject, and . . . [his] persuasive and even ingenious disposition . . . [that enables him] to present his case in the most attractive way" (Warfield, *Counterfeit Miracles*, 159).

57. Some of the church historians who have identified Gordon as a leading exponent of the divine healing movement are Edith Blumhofer, Donald W. Dayton, Paul Chappell, and Gary B. Ferngren. Fergren observes that "[a]mong those who sought to reclaim for the church the ministry of healing that they believed played a significant role in apostolic times were several evangelicals, the most notable of whom were A. B. Simpson (1844–1919) [sic], founder of the Christian and Missionary Alliance, and A. J. Gordon (1836–1895), a nationally prominent Baptist minister in Boston. Both men came to believe in faith healing after they themselves experienced personal healing" (Ferngren, "Evangelical-Fundamentalist Tradition," 491).

58. Waldvogel, Overcoming Life, 124.

59. Dayton, *Theological Roots*, 117.

60. Gordon, *Ministry of Healing*, 2.

61. Ibid., 62–63.

at that point, the church abandoned its primarily heavenly and supernatural orientation and began to see its citizenship as being essentially
earthly. Small wonder, then, that the church would "cease to exhibit the
supernatural gifts of heaven."[62] Gordon also believed that the cessationists denied both the spiritual and the physical promise of salvation.
Moreover, their arguments failed to account for the fact that healings
in response to prayer occurred in Old Testament times. Thus, if such
miracles occurred during the old covenant, how much more should one
expect them under the new.[63]

Gordon also pointed out that miraculous healings had in fact
taken place throughout the history of the church, and especially in connection with movements of renewal.[64] Beginning with Augustine, who
had retracted his own previously cessationist stance, Gordon appealed
to the examples of famous Christians such as Martin Luther, Richard
Baxter, John Albert Bengel, Edward Irving, Thomas Erskine, and Horace
Bushnell, who had either experienced miracles (and especially miracles
of healing) themselves or had defended their continuing legitimacy.[65]

Gordon also argued that the cessationists' principal argument—
that miracles were confined to the apostolic age because they served
primarily as a means of attesting to the authority of the gospel and establishing the church—fails to take into consideration the reality that,
practically speaking, nothing has changed: the gospel was still being
proclaimed in new contexts and still needed miraculous manifestations
to validate its messengers. Since the evangelization of the world will not
be complete until the return of Christ, it follows that the miraculous
manifestations associated with the planting of the church will continue
until the Parousia.[66]

Gordon also believed that that an incipient platonic and un-
Christian anthropology lay behind the cessationists' rejection of divine
healing. It implied a dualistic hierarchy that valued the soul over the
body and considered the soul alone to be worthy of redemption. The
body was at best of peripheral value, and at worst that from which

---

62. Ibid., 64.

63. Gordon, *Ministry of Healing*, 36.

64. Ibid., 65.

65. Ibid., 87–114.

66. Ibid., 117.

humanity needed to be freed. Salvation would thus free the soul from the encumbrances of bodily existence.[67] Hence cessationism, in effect, opposed itself to the full, biblical understanding of salvation, which includes both the resurrection and the glorification of the body. Instead of seeing death and sickness as a product of the fall, it esteemed them as instruments for the chastening of the body and the liberation of the soul.[68] Since it did not have a biblical understanding of the resurrection of the body, it could hardly be expected to affirm the legitimacy of divine healing. Gordon held that the resurrection of the body and divine healing are intimately related. The latter is but a "pledge and foretoken"[69] of the former, just as sanctification is a foretaste of the holiness believers shall experience. In believing in the salvation of the soul but scorning physical healing as beneath the ministry of Christ, the cessationists had, in effect, dismissed the idea that salvation redeems humanity in all its created fullness—body and soul. Full salvation, on the contrary, touches the entirety of its object.

Gordon's most powerful argument, however, centered on Christology. The ministry of Christ, like Christ himself, remains the same yesterday, today, and forever: Christ still saves and heals, just as he did during his earthly ministry. Indeed, given the twofold ministry of Jesus and the apostles, to reject one aspect is to reject the other; for if healing, which was so central to the earthly ministry of Jesus, has ceased, what assures us that the rest of his saving work has not also come to an end?

Gordon also believed healing to be central to the purpose of the incarnation. Healing does not flow from the supposedly capricious mercy of God. Rather, it is part and parcel of the work of the atonement itself. Healing, like salvation, flows from the atonement, for Christ's work on the cross was not merely sympathetic, illustrative, or demonstrative. Rather, it was substitutionary in its entirety.[70] Christ took upon himself those things that the encroachment of sin into creation had conferred upon humanity, and released humanity from their bondage. His substitutionary act, moreover, bore not only our spiritual infirmities but our physical infirmities as well. This view squarely opposed the majority

67. Ibid.,193–95.
68. Ibid., 195.
69. Ibid., 52.
70. Ibid., 18.

opinion of the church throughout its history, which had understood the atonement to be remedial only in relation to the spiritual aspect of humanity. He contended that the atonement sought not only a spiritual goal but a physical one as well. On the cross, Christ was not only the sin-bearer, in the sense of carrying away our spiritual infirmities, but he was the sickness-bearer, too.

Gordon derived this expansive view of the scope of the atonement from his reading of Scripture.[71] He refers in particular to Matthew 8:17, which explicitly links the work of the atonement to the removal of sicknesses.[72] Christ, as the second Adam, came to undo completely the work of the first Adam. This recapitulation on the part of the second Adam cannot be less extensive than the work of the first Adam. The work of Christ effectively recovered the losses of Adam.[73]

Healing, however, does not come unconditionally. Its precondition is the reception and indwelling of the person of Jesus Christ.[74] Those who satisfy this condition receive those blessings that attend Christ. Divine healing is thus not for the unregenerate, There is, moreover, a further condition: one must also live in obedience to the will of God. One cannot live outside God's will and not expect that this divine life, even if in some way resident, will be stifled.[75] Finally, one must pray for healing as the will of God. That is, one must, in praying, be convinced that health is the will of God and that God will heal.[76]

71. The second chapter of *The Ministry of Healing*, "The Testimony of Scripture," lays out what Gordon felt was the scriptural warrant for his beliefs.

72. Surprisingly, Gordon does not refer to Isaiah 53, which is the source of the passage from Matthew. As will be seen, Simpson placed much more emphasis on Isaiah, and cited Matthew passage primarily in support of his interpretation of Isaiah. See Gordon, *Ministry of Healing*, 17–18.

73. Gordon, *Ministry of Healing*, 21.

74. "The first requirement, 'If ye abide in me—' is that of intimate and unbroken communion with the Lord. Our justification depends upon our being in Christ. Our power and fellowship depend upon our abiding in Christ. And this last implies the most constant and uninterrupted intimacy of the soul with the Saviour. It is the entering into his life and having his life so entering into us, that the confession of the Apostle becomes realized in us—'I live, yet not I, but Christ liveth in me'" (Gordon, *Ministry of Healing*, 227–28).

75. Gordon, *Ministry of Healing*, 230.

76. Ibid., 232–33.

Simpson and Divine Healing

To understand A. B. Simpson's conception of the "Full Gospel" and the ways in which it relates to his doctrine of divine healing, one must first understand his theology of disease. Simpson, like Gordon, linked the existence of sickness in the world to the intrusion of sin. Sickness and disease are not essential components of the created order. Rather, they are consequences and manifestations of a fallen, corrupted creation. The fall resulted in the imbalance and distortion of creation. Sickness is one indication of this cosmic condition. Though biological factors undoubtedly contribute to sickness, its primal cause is spiritual and diabolical, namely, sin. For Simpson, this association is unquestionably part of the Christian worldview.

Simpson also believed that Satan could use sickness for his diabolical purposes.[77] In the case of Job, "Satan is permitted to test and try God's people, and in so doing has, by divine permission, power over bodies and over diseases and the elements of nature."[78] Sickness, then, can arise either indiscriminately or as the direct result of the work of Satan.[79] Even so, God only allows such diabolical intrusion for "the ultimate good of the sufferer."[80] Somehow, and in some way, God would use this calamity for the betterment of the sufferer.

Despite its diabolical genesis, Simpson believed that God could still make direct use of sickness to carry out his purposes. Sickness can serve as a "check rein"[81] or a potential messenger in the hands of God, for God "has told us distinctly that sickness and suffering are sent when we will not heed His gentle voice, and that, even then, if we will listen, repent, acknowledge our error, learn our lesson and obey His will the trial will

---

77. Simpson, *Gospel of Healing*, 27.

78. Simpson, *Friday Meeting Talks*,1:23.

79. "[Sickness] is sometimes Satan's tormenting attack when we are walking in obedience and service. He has power even to simulate all symptoms. He often attacks . . . after we have given a testimony against him, especially respecting Healing, at other times when in God's special service. At such times we must resist him and he will flee from us. We must not fear him. Especially we must lay him over on Christ and He will conquer. But to know it is Satan is half the battle" (Simpson, *Inquiries and Answers*, 28–29).

80. Simpson, *Friday Meetings Talks*, vol. 2, 23.

81 Ibid., 1:35.

be arrested or removed, and we restored to His love and favor."[82] To seek healing without removing the problem that caused the sickness would be to work against the will and purpose of God.[83] Indeed, "[there] will not be healing for the body till [one has] yielded at this point."[84]

In any case, since the ultimate cause of sickness is not biological; its ultimate cure will not be found in either chemical or mechanical manipulation. Sin, as the manifestation of a spiritual problem, requires a spiritual solution, and one that will provide a suitable foil to the nature of the malignancy. Which is to say that "[f]rom whatever side we look at disease, [whether it is the result of the fall, the direct work of Satan, or the chastening agent of God,] it becomes evident that its remedy must be found in God alone and the gospel of redemption."[85] Ultimately physical remedies are not remedies at all, for they can at best deal only with the symptoms of sickness. The expulsion of sickness, which is ultimately nothing other than a physical manifestation of a deeper spiritual malady, must be effected by spiritual means that address the root problem of sin. The solution is found in the person and work of Jesus Christ alone, and most especially in the atonement.[86]

---

82 Simpson, *Inquiries and Answers*, 6.

83 However, Simpson unrelentingly asserted that one should not confuse sickness, disease, and their great consequences—death—as the great and final sanctifiers. They may serve as means in the hands of God, but they do not themselves sanctify. Rather, God may use them to direct the afflicted to the one who not only sanctifies but heals. Although in the heavenly realm there is no more sickness, no more disease, and death is forever defeated, these truths must not be considered as the fruit of sickness, death, for they originate in God alone, and certainly not in anything that has its genesis in the fall.

84. Simpson, *Fourfold Gospel*, 46.

85. Simpson, *Gospel of Healing*, 27.

86. "If sickness has come into the world through sin, which is conceded, it must be got out of the world through God's great remedy for sin, the cross of Jesus Christ. If sickness is purely a natural condition, it may be met by natural means; but if it be abnormal, and but a stage of death, which has passed upon all because all have sinned, then its divinely appointed remedy is the atonement of Jesus Christ, which God has set over against all the effects of the fall" (Simpson, *Divine Healing in the Atonement*, 3). "The causes of disease and suffering are distinctly traced to the Fall and the sinful state of man. If sickness were part of the natural constitution of things, then we might meet it wholly on natural grounds and by natural means. But if it be part of the curse of sin, it must have its true remedy in the great Redemption. That sickness is the result of the Fall and one of the fruits of sin, no one can surely question" (Simpson, *Gospel of Healing*, 26).

Full Salvation

Simpson denied Mary Baker Eddy's assertion that physicality and, therefore, physical suffering are illusions. The physical, though distinct from the spiritual, is just as real as the spiritual. Humanity, by the creative design of God, is a bipartite (i.e., physical and spiritual) being. Physicality does not originate with the fall even though the fall profoundly affected it. The "Full Gospel" addresses the physical aspects of the fall as much as it does the spiritual aspects. Bipartite beings under the plague of sickness need a physical salvation as much as they need a spiritual salvation,[87] for the fall not only brought spiritual impoverishment and relational separation from God, it had a ravaging effect on the physical as well. Since the ministry of Jesus Christ was the remedy for the fall and for sin, it must necessarily treat both soul and body.[88]

Atonement

JESUS AS SIN BEARER AND SICKNESS BEARER

As noted previously, Simpson held to a penal-substitutionary theory of the atonement. This understanding of salvation fundamentally shaped his doctrine of divine healing, for it implied that Christ took upon himself those things that were rightly and justly the consequences of humanity's sin and made them his own, thereby (by implication) relieving humanity of the necessity of enduring sickness. Scripture supports this interpretation in that "borne' [in Isaiah 53:4] . . . means not mere sympathy or mere relief, but it means substitution, one bearing another's death. Christ literally substituted His body for our body,"[89] and this salvific act comprehends both the physical and the spiritual consequences of sin. He bore not only sin in general but sickness in particular.[90] Since this was so, Simpson asked, "Having borne in His body what our body deserves to bear, why should we bear it, too?"[91] The redeemed human

87. Simpson, *Gospel of Healing*, 12.

88. "Christ is the remedy for the Fall, for sin and therefore for disease which is the result of sin" (Simpson, *Discovery of Divine Healing*, 18).

89. Simpson, *Lord for the Body*, 78.

90. "Christ is the remedy for the Fall, for sin and therefore for disease which is the result of sin" (Simpson, *Discovery of Divine Healing*, 18).

91. Simpson, *Lord for the Body*, 22.

body is no longer obliged to bear disease. Simpson likened this new freedom to the cancellation of a debt:

> If I owe a debt to a man not only am I liable, my house is liable too, and it may be held until my debt is paid. So my body is my house and it is liable for the debt of my soul to God, even if it had not sinned, as it has alas! Disease is sin's mortgage against my house. But, if the debt is paid, the mortgage is discharged, and my house is free. So Christ has paid my debt of sin and released my body. Judgment has no claims upon it. In the Cross of Calvary he bore in His body all my physical liabilities for sin, and therefore He is said to have borne our sickness and carried our pains and by His stripes we are healed.[92]

This notion of sickness bearing was not merely implicit in biblical teaching; it was made explicit in two texts that the church had always considered foundational to understanding the atonement—Isaiah 53 and Matthew 8.

The Case of Isaiah 53 and Matthew 8

The Suffering Servant text, Isaiah 53 (and especially vv. 3–4), is central to Simpson's argument for the provision of bodily healing in the atonement. Simpson was aware, however, that his interpretation of this text was out of step with much of the history of exegesis. Most interpreters had to that point believed that the passage should be understood metaphorically, and that the "sicknesses" mentioned in it should be taken to be spiritual maladies and certainly not physical illnesses. He noted that this theological bias is most clearly seen in some translators' prejudiced choice of the word "griefs" in Isaiah 53:4 to translate a Hebrew word that on more than one hundred other occasions in Scripture is translated as "sicknesses."[93] This unfounded and divergent change in translation, he argued, is a glaring example of the bias of the church on the divine-healing issue: "To strain a passage from its literal or natural meaning simply to prove a passage or doctrine, is unworthy of true exegesis, and will soon smother the possibility of faith in anything on the part of the man or woman who does it."[94] The natural reading of this passage refers

92. Simpson, *Inquiries and Answers*, 1–2.

93. In the Authorized Version. Simpson, *Lord for the Body*, 77.

94. Simpson, *Divine Healing in the Atonement*, 9–10.

to physical healing; to interpret "by his stripes we are healed" in a purely metaphorical sense denies its otherwise-plain physical ramifications. To see it as simply repetition for the sake of emphasis, as was often argued, "[makes] the verse a weak and unworthy tautology."[95]

Simpson also pointed to the significance of "surely" in the text in question, contending that it had the divinely intended purpose of emphasizing the idea of divine healing. It acted as an anticipatory countermeasure to any attempt to dilute or change the meaning of "sicknesses," "infirmities, and "diseases." The "surely" of Isaiah 53:4 "is the strongest possible statement of complete redemption from pain and sickness by Christ's life and death. And these are the very words Matthew quotes afterward, under the inspired guidance of the Holy Spirit (Matthew 8:17), as the explanation of Jesus' universal works of healing."[96]

Simpson also pointed out that Matthew 8:17 clearly dispels a merely spiritual reading of Isaiah 53, for it has to do with the physical healing of Peter's mother-in-law. Therefore, "Matthew 8:17 confirms [the Isaiah passage's] application to physical healing . . . referring to the body alone."[97] Furthermore, in keeping with the inspiration of Scripture, Matthew "is a translation [of Isaiah 53] by the mouth of the Holy Ghost, and leaves no doubt of the meaning of Isaiah."[98] Because the Spirit of God has interpreted Isaiah 53 to refer to physical healing, the Christian has no alternative but to follow suit.

Resurrection

However, according to Simpson, the foundation for the ministry of divine healing is not found in the work of the cross alone. Though Christ made provision for healing through the cross, and though humanity is therefore no longer under any obligation to bear disease, the power that effects healing is the resurrection life of the indwelling Christ. "Divine healing comes to us through the life of Jesus Christ who rose from the

---

95. Simpson, *Divine Healing in the Atonement*, 9. Cf. also Simpson's claim that "[t]o say that the last clause respecting healing means spiritual healing would be to make the sentence a barren repetition of what he had already said in the first part of the verse" (Simpson, *Isaiah*, 354).

96. Simpson, *Gospel of Healing*, 17.

97. Simpson, *Lord for the Body*, 79; Simpson, *Discovery of Divine Healing*, 118.

98. Simpson, *Divine Healing in the Atonement*, 10.

dead in His own body."[99] Divine healing consists of both a removal and an incorporation or, as Simpson would describe it, a "breathing out" as well as a "breathing in."[100] On the cross, Christ took upon himself sin and sickness so that humanity would not need to suffer them any longer—the "breathing out." The power that heals, however, is also the power of the resurrection life of the Christ who resides within the believer—the "breathing in." Yet even these apparently equal actions do not have the same value in relation to divine healing, for

> there is something higher even than the cross. It is the resurrection of our Lord. There the gospel of healing finds the fountain of its deepest life. The death of Christ destroys it—the root of sickness. But it is the life of Jesus that supplies the source of health and life for our redeemed bodies. The body of Christ is the living fountain of all our vital strength.[101]

New Life

The power and perfection of the life of Christ resident in the believer through the agency of the Holy Spirit is that which enlivens and heals.[102] Healing, though, does not involve merely the restoration of the human life to its own natural capacities. It does not bring merely a renewed life or even a perfect human life. Rather, it brings another life, a divine life; that is, "[divine healing] is not an old man made well, but it is a new heart put into his being and new blood into his veins. It is a renewing of life. It is the deeper teaching of the resurrection life."[103] This new

99. Simpson, *Fourfold Gospel*, 48.

100. From the poem "Breathing Out and Breathing In":

I am breathing out my sickness,
Thou hast borne its burden too;
I am breathing in Thy healing,
Ever promised, ever new.
(Simpson, *Millennial Chimes*, 31).

101. Simpson, *Gospel of Healing*, 29.

102. "The Holy Spirit is the great agent in this quickening, and it is not natural energy that is communicated, but resurrection life, even the life of our risen Saviour. It is 'the Spirit that raised up Jesus from the dead' that quickens us, by bringing us into union with the body of our risen Lord and imparting to us His own resurrection life" (Simpson, *Friday Meeting Talks*, 1:52–53; see also Simpson, *Fourfold Gospel*, 48.

103. Simpson, *Lord for the Body*, 44. "That is the meaning of resurrection life. It does not mean that our natural strength is as good as dead. It was crucified with Christ. It

and divine life lifts those in whom it dwells to a quality of physical life beyond the ordinary. It places those who live by it on a higher plane of existence, one that humanity, left to its own capacities and devices, could never hope to attain.[104]

The power of this healing does not originate in some objective and impersonal energy or life force. Healing power is nothing other and nothing less than the resurrection life of Christ himself and is received through union with him. To receive divine healing is not to receive something, though "something" is what many clamor after.[105] Divine healing is the consequence of the full and invigorating residence of Christ himself. It is someone, not something: "[T]he true secret of physical life [is this], 'not I, but Christ [living] in me.'"[106] It is the result of a near-symbiotic relationship so closely integrated "that the very life of His veins is transfused into ours."[107] It is the physical vitality of the resurrected and indwelling Christ that invigorates the physical life of the Christian, and this is "the great, vital, precious principle of physical healing in the name of Jesus."[108] In sum, "divine healing is the result of a personal union with a personal Christ."[109]

With the residence of Christ, the power of his resurrection body becomes that which invigorates the once-frail body of the Christian. It is through the indwelling of Christ in the believer that the Christian receives not only remedial divine healing but ongoing divine health. Divine health thus does not consist in an occasional event but in an ongoing way of life. Simpson believed that Christians were not only to draw rehabilitation from the life of Christ dwelling within but the power for day-to-day living and, more important, their day-to-day min-

---

means that we have taken another kind of life—the life of the risen Son of God. It is not our strength increased, but it is our strength displaced and God's strength given instead" (Simpson, *Lord for the Body*, 33).

104. Ibid., 10.

105. "So many people are wanting the 'thing' to go; wanting 'it,' whatever 'it' is, inside or outside. There are all sorts of 'its.' You want something that will make you feel better. I do not believe that is what God wants. God wants you to get your eye off of those things and place it on Him; and soon you will have so much of Him you will not have time to watch 'it'" (Simpson, *Discovery of Divine Healing*, 85).

106. Simpson, *Friday Meeting Talks*, 2:56.

107. Simpson, *Fourfold Gospel*, 48.

108. Simpson, *Gospel of Healing*, 30.

109. Simpson, *Friday Meeting Talks*, 1:38.

istry as well.[110] This latter blessing, divine health, is even greater than the first, divine healing.[111]

Simpson called the life of the resurrected Christ working in and through believers an "earnest," that is, the "first instalment, the same in kind," of the physical blessing that Christians will experience when they are fully and finally united with Christ at his return. It is "a foretaste of the resurrection" and a "first installment of that full and immortal energy that shall bear us up to meet our Lord and bring us into His perfect likeness."[112] Divine healing is, to a degree, heaven on earth, the relative and present glorification of the believer.

Availability of Divine Healing

While such healing power may not have been manifest to any great degree throughout most of the history of the church, Simpson was convinced of its continuing availability in the present age because of the immutable character and ministry of Christ. Central to God's incarnation in Jesus was Jesus's ministry of healing, and so "[i]f he did not still [heal], He would not be Jesus Christ the same yesterday, and to-day, and for ever (Hebrews 13:8). These healings were not occasional but continual, not exceptional but universal."[113]

All informed Christians concede that divine healing and other miraculous acts have occurred in the history of the church. What they dispute is the extent to which miracles ought to be expected in the present age. Simpson claimed that divine healing has always been available to the church because the indwelling of Christ by the power of the Spirit has always been its sine qua non. Divine healing, therefore, as the natural consequence of this indwelling, was still available. Moreover, Simpson naturally disagreed with those who believed that miracles of healing had ceased because the church no longer needed them, as it had in its formative years, as a means of establishing its authenticity

110. "Healing is in His risen life, which is in us. We have healing not only from Jesus, but in Jesus. It is in His living body, and we receive it as we abide in Him and keep it only as we abide in Him" (Simpson, Fourfold Gospel, 50).

111. Simpson, "Editorial," Living Truths, August 1905, 441. Nancy Hardesty notes that Simpson's claiming of the divine life as a day-to-day supply for health separates him from many proponents of divine healing (Hardesty, Faith Cure, 94).

112. Simpson, Friday Meeting Talks, 1:59.

113. Simpson, Gospel of Healing, 18.

as the people of God. Miracles of healing were indeed essential to the founding of the church, he conceded, but that church age had never ceased, the church was still being established, and so those promised signs and wonders were still valid.[114] There is no biblical reason to think otherwise. Although healings were not as common in Simpson's day as they once had been, their current scarcity was not due to the design of God but to the "church's growing worldliness, corruption, formalism, and unbelief."[115] Such manifestations were not seen, because they were not sought. If the church did not believe they were available, why would it seek them? If the church did not seek them, they would not be found. The disappearance of such phenomena, then, stemmed not from divine dispensational restrictions but from a thorough lack of implementation. If we are to regain this sense of manifest power in the church,

> we must cease to look upon it as an occasional and miraculous instance of answered prayer and divine interposition, and come to recognize it as the "children's bread" and the redemption right of the household of faith. It is part of the Gospel of Jesus Christ and the purchase of his redeeming blood, then it belongs to the child of God through simple faith without the intervention of healers and special gifts and ministries on the part of others.[116]

Rather than declining or ceasing, the miraculous works of the church were actually increasing, Simpson believed that their resurgence served as a twofold sign: as a rebuke to the church's history of unbelief[117] and as an indication of the coming end of the age. Indeed, as the return of Christ drew near, manifestations of the miraculous would increase, for "divine healing is one of the signs of the age. It is a forerunner of Christ's coming. It is God's answer to the infidelity of today."[118] Furthermore, "[t] he age of miracles [is] not past. The Word of God never indicated a hint

114 "If miraculous power was need in the apostolic age to demonstrate the truth of Christianity, it is as much needed still to impress a godless and unbelieving world" (Simpson, "Editorial," *Living Truths*, August 1905, 441); "I see no place in the Bible where we are taught that the miraculous is to cease with the ascension of the Lord" (Simpson, *Lord for the Body*, 11); Simpson, *Gospel of Healing*, 21

115. Simpson, *Gospel of Healing*, 13, 42.

116. Simpson, "Editorial," *Living Truths*, August 1905, 442.

117. Simpson wrote that healing "is one of the ministries of prayer which God is especially honoring in these days. It is doubtless intended as a special rebuke to the unbelief and materialism of this age" (Simpson, *King's Business*, 71).

118. Simpson, *Fourfold Gospel*, 50.

of such a fact. On the contrary, miracles are to be among the signs of the last days."[119] As miracles begin to occur more frequently, they will no longer be met with incredulity. This is especially true of the ministry of healing. When it attains its true place in the church, it will cease to be seen as a wonder and will be regarded instead as a constituted, ongoing privilege for all believers.[120]

Not surprisingly, Simpson's conviction that healing is related to the atonement and the indwelling of the resurrected Christ led him to believe that divine healing and health are available to all and limited only by one's choice to avail oneself of them: "[It] is not the exceptional privilege of a few favored ones, the occasional special and sovereign gift of God where He is pleased to manifest His healing power for some exceptional cause or special end, but . . . it is the heritage of all the children of faith and holy obedience."[121] Although miraculous healings may appear to occur selectively, Simpson believed that their availability was unlimited. This conviction would come to form the basis of his doctrine of divine health.[122]

Natural Means

At first glance, Simpson appears to have sent mixed messages on the relationship between divine healing and natural means. For example, in one of his earliest published pieces he asserts that "divine healing ceases to be a mere privilege. It is the divine prescription for disease, and no obedient Christian can safely ignore it. Any other method of dealing with sickness is unauthorized. This is God's plan."[123] Later in that same

119. Simpson, *Gospel of Healing*, 43.

120. Simpson, "Editorial," *Living Truths*, August 1905, 442.

121. Simpson, *Divine Healing in the Atonement*, 13.

122 At times, however, Simpson did not clearly express his views on who may actually expect to benefit from divine healing. On one occasion he declared it to be "primarily for the children of God who have already come to know Him as their Saviour and Sanctifier" (Simpson, "Editorial," *Living Truths*, August 1905, 443). This stands in contrast to his earlier assertion that "You must be right with God. You must be saved and know that you are saved; and you must be walking in all the light you have. I do not say that you must be sanctified" (Simpson, *Friday Meeting Talks*, 1:100–101).

123. In one of his earliest published pieces on healing, Simpson wrote, "divine healing ceases to be a mere privilege. It is the divine prescription for disease, and no obedient Christian can safely ignore it. Any other method of dealing with sickness is unauthorized. This is God's plan" (Simpson, *Gospel of Healing*, 23).

text, however, he is more guarded in his absolute dismissal of means: "There may be—there always will be—instances where faith cannot be exercised. And if natural means have—as they do have—a limited value, there is ample room for their employment in these cases. But for the trusting and obedient child of God there is a more excellent way that His Word has clearly prescribed."[124] Certainly one who has such faith should not presume to stand for those who are ill, who cannot or will not take that stand on their own.[125] Ultimately, though, medicines and doctors can only deal with the symptoms and not the cause of sickness. The therapeutic character of much that is found in nature, Simpson granted, was there by the providence of God. Yet they were only sufficient for a sinless and unfallen creation.[126] This is no longer the case. If sickness and disease are to be annihilated, it can only come, fully and finally, by spiritual and not natural means. For this reason, means (that are themselves creaturely, physical, and therefore limited) are not sufficient to deal with the problem to the depth and extent required.[127] There is a better way. There is God's way: divine healing. [128]

124. Simpson, *Fourfold Gospel*, 38–39.

125. Simpson, *Inquiries and Answers*, 16–17; Simpson, *King's Business*, 72.

126. Simpson, *Inquiries and Answers*, 4; Simpson, *Discovery of Divine Healing*, 17.

127. Simpson, *Fourfold Gospel*, 39.

128. On one occasion he summarized his view of means in this way: "[There] is in the human body and the natural world a certain *vis medicatrix* [*naturae*] as the doctors call it, that is a certain restorative power which is part of His divine beneficence for a world which He foresaw would be cursed with sin and sorrow. And we do not deny that natural remedies may go a certain length and possess a limited value in relieving and healing the body. But

1. They [are] limited and extremely uncertain.

2. They are not His way for His children.

3. They are not to be combined . . . in the scriptures with divine healing.

    a. They work through natural, this through supernatural channels.

    b. They do not act on the same principles. The one is local and specific treatment, the other is a direct vital touch upon the springs of life.

    c. All Christ's redemption purchases must be free gifts, by grace without works, and so if divine healing be through Christ's blood, it must be a gift of grace alone. We cannot mix our works with it any more than out justification.

    d. He must have all the glory and, if man touch it he will be sure to claim it."

(Simpson, *Inquiries and Answers*, 20–22).

Simpson criticized the use of natural means among Christians partly because he wanted to protect the glory and reputation of Christ. To try to mix natural means and divine healing was to open the door to the possibility of diminishing the credit that was due Christ alone. If Christ is to receive any of the credit, he must receive all of the credit.[129] Human beings naturally tend to give all of the credit to the physical means employed and to disregard or deny any divine intervention. Moreover, while means have a limited effectiveness, divine healing does not come through medicines, natural remedies, or any other means, despite their ultimate source. Medicines may be part of God's providential creative design, but divine healing "is the direct power of the Almighty hand of God himself. 'Himself took our infirmities,' and He is able to carry them without man's help."[130] Ultimately, then, to shore up one's hope in healing, by attempting to employ both means and the provision of Christ, is a manifestation of unbelief.

> In human affairs no one would think of employing two doctors of different schools to treat the same case. In such a case one or the other of the doctors would retire and leave the patient to the other. And yet people profess to go to Christ as their Healer, while, at the same time, they have put their case in human hands and are looking to man for healing.[131]

Simpson identified a number of different ways that people have used to bring the religious to bear on the issues of sickness, death, and disease. Each of these, however, misses the mark to a greater or lesser degree in the sense that each seeks to effect healing, not through the atonement and the resurrection life of the indwelling Christ alone, but by means of one sort or another.[132]

---

129. "[Divine healing] is a gift of grace, as all that Christ's blood has purchased will ever be, and therefore cannot be mixed up with our own works or the use of human means, but must be received wholly in His name, and in such a manner that He shall have all the glory" (Simpson, *Divine Healing in the Atonement*, 13).

130. Simpson, *Fourfold Gospel*, 38.

131. Simpson, *Friday Meeting Talks* 2:35.

132. Among those means that Simpson identified are medical treatment of any type, the metaphysical healing of Christian Science, magnetic healing, spiritualism, prayer cure, faith cure, and willpower. All of these, including prayer cure and faith cure, attempt to make the means employed somehow responsible for the healing received. See Simpson, *Fourfold Gospel*, 38–44.

Divine healing is a gracious work of God and, like justification and regeneration, must be appropriated by faith alone. Since the absence of faith results in the absence of healing, Simpson felt that the resurgence in the number of healings in his day stemmed from a resurgence of that "great lost lever."[133] Faith must be exercised, although in and of itself it does not heal, for it is merely the God-given and God-ordained channel through which healing is received.[134] Hence he insisted on using the term "divine healing" instead of "Faith Healing."

But this faith, too, has a particular face. It does not merely hope that God can heal or believe that God has the power to heal should it be his will. It is, rather, convinced that it is always God's will to heal.[135] It not only thinks such thoughts but acts on them. It steps out in full assurance that what has been asked for has been received, even in spite of appearances.[136] Anything else is not true faith and is therefore inadequate. For the one who seeks healing, "[it] is not enough to believe that [one] may be healed, or to believe in God's power to do this; but [one] must definitely claim the blessing, count upon it, confess it, and commit [oneself] to it by going forth to reckon upon it, and act as if it were a reality."[137] As it sufficed for salvation, so too the exercise of faith was enough to secure healing. The real nature of substitution makes this all possible.

> In the same way, this thought will bring you victory in your body. You may also hand it over to your Lord in full surrender and perfect trust, and believe that your natural life, with all its

133. Simpson, *Inquiries and Answers*, 96.

134. "Divine healing comes to us by faith. It is not the faith that heals; but faith enables us to receive it" (Simpson, *Fourfold Gospel*, 49).

135. "If the Lord Jesus has purchased healing for you in His redemption, it must be God's will for you to have it, for Christ's whole redeeming work was simply the executing of the Father's will" (Simpson, *Gospel of Healing*, 59).

136. "Now, we teach people to believe that they have salvation before they have sensible evidence of it. The greatest battle we have with the enquirer is to get him to believe that Christ saves him according to His Word, before he has any feeling of it. Then why should it not be so all along the line of faith? It is so. This is the very essence of the faith of the Bible. It is defined to be 'the evidence (or conviction) of things not seen'" (Simpson, *Inquiries and Answers*, 24). Here, of course, Simpson's doctrine of healing, like his doctrine of sanctification, bears a clear resemblance to Phoebe Palmer's doctrine of sanctification. See also Simpson, *King's Business*, 106; see also Simpson, *Fourfold Gospel*, 45.

137. Simpson, *Friday Meeting Talks*, 1:35.

strength and weakness, all its abilities, disabilities and liabilities is exchanged for His divine life and strength, born of His resurrection and imparted from His very life, are your redemption rights in Him. And as old infirmities, symptoms, or sufferings appear, you can treat them as foreign to yourself, refuse to fear them, identify yourself with them or obey them, and draw your strength directly from your living Head, from a source outside you, and yet in touch with you—Him in whom you now live and move and have your being—and again, God will make the reckoning true, if it is maintained in bold and persistent faith, and you will find that the morbid conditions will drop away as the withered leaves from the living tree, and your life will spring from hidden fountains and lift you into supernatural strength and blessedness.[138]

Simpson believed that this indissoluble connection between healing and the atonement includes the reality that healing has become a "great redemption right."[139] It is not something that may or may not be the privilege of the believer depending upon the apparent vacillations of God's inscrutable will. Rather, it is "a constituted privilege"[140] and a component of the salvation that a believer may not only hope for but claim. Thus one appropriates it in the same way that one appropriates justification and conversion. This exercise of faith simply engages what God has already provided.

Furthermore, walking in obedience is the "indispensable element" to "[receiving] any . . . blessing of the Gospel."[141] Indeed, "[it] is necessary that we should be walking with Christ in holy obedience and living up to His present will for us"[142] if we hope to be healed. Simpson even gave this belief poetic expression:

> Would you know an antidote for sickness,
> Would you find a balm for every pain,
> You must drink the springs of holy gladness;
> You must keep from every stain.[143]

138 Ibid., 44–45.

139. Simpson, *Gospel of Healing*, 29; Simpson, *Fourfold Gospel*, 47.

140. Simpson, "Editorial," *Living Truths*, August 1905, 442.

141. Simpson, *Divine Healing in the Atonement*, 13.

142. Simpson, *Friday Meeting Talks*, 1:34.

143. From the poem "Look on the Bright Side" in Simpson, *Millennial Chimes*, 13.

Walking in obedience also leads to divine health, for "as we walk in holy and loving obedience, we shall be kept from sickness."[144] Conversely, disobedience can lead to sickness in the sense that the disobedient activity in which one is involved may, by its very nature, result in physical distress. In addition, as was noted earlier, God can use sickness as a "check-rein." That is, if a believer is living outside of the revealed will of God, God may use sickness to bring that person back into line. Regarding such straying, Simpson believed that should we "touch the forbidden fruit, wander out of the sacred circle of His will or spend our strength on self or sin . . . our life will lose its strength like Samson's arm and wither like Jonah's gourd."[145]

Goal of Divine Healing

Despite its obvious intrinsic worth, divine healing is not an end in itself. Its purpose is not merely to bring comfort and ease to the afflicted, but to empower them for more effective ministry and to live full and holy lives.[146] Sickness, disease, and infirmity by their very natures reduce the volume of work that one is able to do. Divine healing and divine health restore human capacity by removing infirmity. Additionally, they lift one to a higher plane of existence and provide supernatural energy that surpasses natural human reserves.[147]

144. Simpson, *Gospel of Healing*, 14.

145. Ibid., 38.

146. "Divine health is a better kind of health than the natural and it will accomplish a better kind of service for Christ. It is not the health that takes us to the ball game, the dance and theater, but the health that takes us to the slums, the alleys and garret. It is not only the divine message, but the messenger endued with divine strength and power" (Simpson, *Lord for the Body*, 9–10). Moreover, "Christ not only saves your souls and prepares you for heaven, but He comes down into this world that He made, and into the everyday life that He has arranged, and will give you a good strong body; not that you may sit and look at it and wonder at it, but that you may get to work for Him with your fingers, your eyes, your ears and your brain, and in your kitchen and workshop, and your parlor and your dining-room, and every bit of your life have 'Holiness to the Lord' written on it, and Jesus in blessed partnership" (Simpson, *Friday Meeting Talks*, 2:23).

147. Divine healing does not, however, ensure that those who experience it will never finally get sick and die, only that they will be sustained and enabled until the completion of the calling of God in their life. "Neither is divine healing physical immortality, but it is fullness of life until the life-work is done, and then receiving our complete resurrection life at the coming of Christ" (Simpson, *Fourfold Gospel*, 44). "The

As far as living a full and holy life is concerned, Simpson regarded humanity as a psychosomatic unity in which the condition of the one part influences the condition of the other. If the body lives in a state of distress, so too will the soul.[148] Although the soul could possibly struggle for sanctification while inhabiting a tortured body, to seek holiness in a renewed and divinely energized body would reap still higher returns. A healthier body would lead to a healthier and more blessed spiritual existence. Divine healing, at least in part, sought to remedy the body for the good of the soul: "Indeed, the spiritual uplift [that comes with being healed] is much the best part of the blessing and is God's stamp of

---

Word places a limit to human life, and all that scriptural faith can claim is sufficiency of health and strength for our life work and within its fair limits" (Simpson, *Gospel of Healing*, 51).

In connection with the idea that divine healing will keep one until one's work is over, and that then, and only then, will death come, Simpson drew an example from the life of Jesus himself, namely the prayer mentioned in Hebrews 5:7: "His Father heard the cry of His Son, and gave Him supernatural strength for His body, sustaining Him and carrying Him through every struggle of the succeeding days, until the last prophetic word had been accomplished, and He could bow His head on the Cross and bid death to come, and yield up His life as a voluntary sacrifice for the sins of the world" (Simpson, *Friday Meeting Talks*, 2:2.

On at least one occasion, Simpson stated that death is not simply the consequence of disease but may come as one's physical body simply wears out from time and use. He thus implied that death is, at least to some degree, natural: "There is no need that we should die of disease. The system might just wear out and pass away as naturally as the apple ripens and fall in the Autumn, or the wheat matures and dies in June. It has simply fulfilled its natural period" (Simpson, *Inquiries and Answers*, 3). On another occasion, he admitted that death is not necessarily the result of the penalty of sin but can also be understood as the gate through which we pass to heaven (see Simpson, *Friday Meeting Talks*, 2:16).

On at least one occasion, he went so far as to speak of the limitations of divine healing, declaring that sometimes it serves to provide one with the ability to endure disease that God has chosen not to remove. In such cases it enables sufferers to serve more effectively than if their diseases had been cured: "Sometimes, in our physical life, when we take the Lord for healing, the physical pain or symptom is not removed, but God gives us such an inflow of vital energy, strength, and vigor that we are able to rise above it, and go on with our work irrespective of the apparent issue" (Simpson, *Friday Meeting Talks*, 1:26). In making this assertion, Simpson suggests that divine healing may not always extinguish sickness and its symptoms. In such cases, divine healing does not seem to involve healing at all but a sort of supernatural sustenance.

148. "A little cloud of sin upon the heart will leave a shadow upon the brain and nerves and a pressure upon the whole frame" (Simpson, *Gospel of Healing*, 36).

its genuineness and sacredness."[149] And it also makes the believer more useful:

> We want the faith that will claim the deliverance of our bodies from disease and suffering. And the faith that brings us this victory also gives our testimony power for others, while the strength and health that God gives will be channels of deeper spiritual blessing to the souls we labor for. A body filled with God is a better channel for spiritual service than one filled with disease.[150]

Simpson summed up his doctrine of divine healing as follows:

> Yes, Jesus has brought this into our practical and physical experience. Himself, the eternal life of God, with perfect body as well as spirit, He becomes by His own direct touch, nay, His constant indwelling, the very life of our life, the strength of our frame, and the vital energy of our physical and spiritual being; so that it is not merely the healing of some petty disorder that we receive, but a new and full and effectual life in all our veins, as much higher and sweeter and stronger than our mere natural and constitutional life, as the new wine of Cana was better than the water from which it was changed. They that have tasted it once need not any argument to prove its reality, or any warning to keep them from going back to the brackish springs of second causes and human needs.[151]

Conclusion

Simpson wrote far more on the doctrine of divine healing than any of the other revivalists being considered in this study. Even so, he does not go beyond what either his contemporaries or his predecessors in the divine-healing movement had already taught. He was, however a more effective apologist for the movement and developed a more extensive theology of healing than any of his contemporaries, with the possible exception of A. J. Gordon. Especially significant in this regard is his extensive development of the doctrine of the life of the indwelling and resurrected Christ far outran that of his contemporaries.

149. Simpson, "Editorial," *Living Truths*, August 1905, 442.

150. Simpson, *King's Business*, 101.

151. Simpson, *Inquiries and Answers*, 106–7.

"Balm in Gilead"

As I sadly look around me
O'er a world of grief and woe,
O the hearts that break with anguish,
O the bitter tears that flow;
And I sometimes almost wonder
Is there none to help or care?
Is there, then, no balm in Gilead?
Is there no Physician there?

There is healing in the Promise,
There is healing in the Blood,
There is strength for all our weakness
In the Risen Son of God;
And the feeblest of His children
All His glorious life may share;
He has better balm than Gilead,
He's the Great Physician there.

O how sad that life should languish
O how sad that hearts should bleed;
Christ has brought a full salvation;
There is help for all our need.
'Tis because they will not trust Him;
Hearts are asking everywhere
Is there, then, no balm in Gilead?
Is there no Physician there?

Would you prove the Great Physician,
You must do what He commands;
Carefully obey His orders,
Lie submissive in His hands.
You must trust without a question,
Cast upon Him every care;
And you'll find there's balm in Gilead,
There's a Great Physician there.[152]

---

152. Simpson, *Millennial Chimes*, 79–80.

5

Christ, Our Coming King

MILLENNIAL HOPE HAS PLAYED AN INTEGRAL ROLE IN THE SHAPING of the American national identity since the beginning of European settlement. Americans have to a greater or lesser degree always anticipated the culmination of history. Some have considered America to be a significant but passive participant in the apocalyptic events associated with the end times; others understood this new nation as the chief player. Many in the latter camp have regarded their land of promise and freedom the harbinger of the millennium or even as the firstfruits of the millennial blessing itself. Both groups have understood the United States to be not merely a land of material opportunity and religious freedom but rather a place where the sincere in faith could come together to live, to work, and to await, if not to build, the long-anticipated and glorious kingdom of God on earth. To some degree, America was incubated in the warmth of millennial expectation and nursed and nurtured on the milk of personal eschatological promise.

The Early Reign of Postmillennial Eschatology

Despite their agreement that America would play a significant role in the unfolding of history, Americans have never had a homogeneous understanding of eschatology. Even its earliest pilgrims held divergent views on the both the subject itself and on America's eschatological function. However, by the nineteenth century, postmillennialism had become the dominant view within mainstream American Protestantism, and it would remain so for the better part of that century.[1] Few if any

1. Dayton, *Prophecy Conference Movement*, 3.

historians would dispute this.[2] Postmillennialists believe that the divinely empowered church, through its various ministries of conversion, will gradually and increasingly create a global climate of *shalom*, preparing the world for Christ's return and reign.[3] Integral to their understanding are a high anthropology[4] and a confidence in both human potential and the church's ability to effect the spiritual and moral conversion of the world.[5]

Jonathan Edwards is often identified as the progenitor of American postmillennial thought.[6] Edwards had "a fully developed and closely reasoned eschatology."[7] He had come to believe that by the gradual progress and dominance of the Christian religion, the millennium

2. "It has become something of a historical cliché to assert that postmillennialism dominated American religious thought throughout much of the nineteenth century" (Moorhead, "Prophecy, Millennialism, and Biblical Interpretation," 291).

3. Although postmillennialists share this vision, they hold differing views on whether this kingdom will last for a literal one thousand years as described in Revelation 20:4.

George Marsden describes postmillennialism in this way: "According to the postmillennialists, the prophecies in the book of Revelation concerning the defeat of the anti-Christ (interpreted as the Pope and other leaders of false religions) were being fulfilled in the present era, and were clearing the way for a golden age. This 'millennium' (the 'one thousand years' of Revelation 20) would be the last epoch of the present historical era. During this time the Holy Spirit would be poured out and the Gospel spread around the world. Christ would return after this millennial age (hence 'postmillennialism') and would bring history to an end" (*Fundamentalism and American Culture*, 49).

4. According to P. Gerard Damsteegt, "The culture in America was becoming more and more democratic with a growing emphasis upon the dignity and worth of man, a concept advocated by Unitarianism, Universalism, the natural rights philosophy, and Jeffersonian individualism." He further argues that this trend, coupled with Methodism's high view of human capacity and the American preoccupation with nation building, made for a culture that believed in the inherent value of human worth, initiative, and possibility (Damsteegt, *Foundations of the Seventh-Day Adventist Message*, 7). Ernest Sandeen, a historian of American premillennialism, believes that postmillennialism reserved "a significant role for man to play in this drama" of setting up the kingdom in anticipation of Christ's return (Sandeen, "Baptists and Millenarianism," 19). Douglas Frank links postmillennial optimism to the Enlightenment and to the seeming success of industrial capitalism (Frank, *Less than Conquerors*, 33, 67–68).

5. By the 1830s, in light of revivals and the turning of America to religion, postmillennialists declared triumphantly that if the church put her mind and energies to it, the millennium could be attained within a matter of a very few years (Weber, *Living in the Shadow*, 14).

6. C. C. Goen identifies Edwards as "America's first major postmillennial thinker" (Goen, "Jonathan Edwards," 163).

7. Goen, "Jonathan Edwards," 151.

would arrive,[8] and that after a short resurgence of ungodliness, Christ would appear.[9] So effective was Edwards's ministry that his fellow Puritans abandoned their premillennial views and became stridently postmillennial.[10] Edwards's ecclesiastical and academic stature was at least partially responsible for the dominance of postmillennialism in the eighteenth and nineteenth centuries.[11]

The Advent of Premillennialism

Postmillennialism's apparent stranglehold on eschatological thought in the early nineteenth century, however, was neither universal nor lasting. Though some of America's earliest immigrants undoubtedly sought to establish the millennial kingdom, premillennialism never lost its voice in either the colonial or postcolonial era.[12] Premillennialism[13] shares with postmillennialism the conviction that the return of Jesus Christ is the zenith of eschatological hope.[14] However, the two eschatologies differ significantly on such issues as the chronology, purposes, consequences, and nature of Christ's return.

To begin with, premillennialism does not share the optimism of postmillennialism. It rejects, for example, the idea that human agency, even in the form of a divinely empowered church, can stem the tide of human depravity and the morally downward spiral of human history. Indeed, the world will not grow better and better, culminating in

8. Weber, *Apocalypses*, 171; Goen, "Jonathan Edwards," 153.

9. Stein, "Editor's Introduction," 24.

10. Weber, *Living in the Shadow*, 13.

11. "Although Jonathan Edwards is not regarded as the founder of a 'school' of theology in the formal sense, most of his ideas were reproduced—albeit in a modified form—by one or another of the New England theologians" (Goen, "Jonathan Edwards," 162).

12. Cotton Mather (1663–1728), a well-known colonial Puritan academic and minister, described his own eschatological beliefs with stark premillennial imagery. See Weber, *Apocalypses*, 170. Donald Dayton notes that Ernest Sandeen and others have determined that a "vital but more subdued strand of premillennialism" was widely held in nineteenth-century America. See Dayton, *Prophecy Conference Movement*, 3.

13. Ernest Sandeen regularly uses the term "millenarianism" to describe this view. See Sandeen, *Roots of Fundamentalism*, 4–5.

14. "In the Christian tradition, all millennial theologies involve the triumph of Christ, the vindication of the suffering saints, and the eventual reign of Christ on the earth" (Sandeen, "Millennialism," 105).

a kingdom fit for the arrival of Jesus Christ, but will instead constantly regress toward moral and societal decay. This downward slide can only be halted by the independent and sudden incursion of Jesus Christ himself. Moreover, not only will human effort fail to attain any type of social or spiritual utopia, but culture[15] and all human institutions—industrial capitalism[16] among them—will be destroyed at the Last Judgment.[17] The world simply cannot not be reformed,[18] and any attempts to reform it are misguided at best. Its decay is sure. Such is the plan of God.

Yet premillennialists still believe in a millennial kingdom; they just believe that it will not come about prior to the return of Christ. According to their pessimistic anthropology, the betterment of the world can only be achieved by the direct intervention of Christ himself: his return, and his return alone, will usher in and establish the millennium. The second coming is, moreover, imminent; it will happen suddenly and soon.[19] Indeed, many late nineteenth-century premillennialists thought that it would occur during their own lifetimes.

Ironically, despite their pessimism with respect to human potential and their disagreement with postmillennialists over the timing of the millennium, some within the late nineteenth-century premillennial camp believed that Christians, by their obedient actions, could bring the return of Christ sooner. They did not think that it was possible to convert the world and create the kingdom on earth; but they did believe that they could help remove the prophesied obstacles to Christ's return and thus "hasten" his appearing. The key, however, was not to convert the world but to evangelize it; for, as the English Presbyterian minister, W. P. Mackay, put it in an address to the Prophecy Conference held at Holy Trinity Church in New York City in 1878, "We have failed simply because we have been aiming at universal conversion and not at universal evangelization. We have been trying to convert patches and not

15. Dayton, *Prophecy Conference Movement*, 5.

16. Frank, *Less than Conquerors*, 33.

17. David Bebbington believes that "A . . . feature of [the] outlook [of premillennialism] was pessimism. The divine programme of history dictated that world affairs were ripening towards the judgments associated with the second coming. In human terms, therefore, the future was bleak. Symptoms of decay were all around" (Bebbington, "Advent Hope," 106).

18. Weber, *Apocalypses*, 172.

19. Blumhofer, *Restoring the Faith*, 16; Sandeen, *Roots of Fundamentalism*, xv.

evangelize the whole. This is not the age of universal conversion; that is the age that is to come."[20]

It must be noted, however, that premillennialists differed among themselves in the way they understood the "signs of the times." Their disagreements centered for the most part on hermeneutics and on the interpretation of the prophetic events recorded in the book of Daniel and the book of Revelation. The historicist wing believes that almost all these prophecies have been playing themselves out throughout the course of history, so the historicists "attempt to match biblical prophecies to contemporary events."[21] For example, they do not consider the antichrist to be some diabolical individual looming on the horizon, for he has already been revealed—in fact, many late nineteenth-century historicists identified this figure with the papacy.[22] Futurists, on the other hand, think that the characters and events described in Daniel and Revelation are all still to be revealed. Near the end of the age, this succession of prophecies will be fulfilled one after another in fairly short order. To return to the example of the antichrist, even today most futurists believe that the being or institution in question has yet to be identified, has yet to be made manifest and has yet to become active.

A Great Reversal and John Nelson Darby

The Civil War and its attendant inhumanity and divisiveness dashed once and for all any dream many American Christians might have had of building the millennial kingdom. If the millennial kingdom were to appear, it would not be through human effort. Consequently Christians of various stripes began to reconsider their eschatological hopes.

The event that most clearly signaled the renaissance of premillennialism in America was the "Believers' Meeting for Bible Study." Formed in the late 1860s by James Inglis and George C. Needham, these annual meetings were held in a variety of locations in the northern United States until they were given a permanent home (from 1883 to 1897) at scenic Niagara-on-the-Lake, Ontario, Canada, and a name: the "Niagara

---

20. West, *Second Coming of Christ*, 459.

21. Dayton, *Prophecy Conference Movement*, 2.

22. Rennie, "Nineteenth Century Roots of Contemporary Prophetic Interpretation," 44; Bebbington, "Advent Hope," 105; Weber, *Living in the Shadow*, 16; Marsden, *Fundamentalism and American Culture*, 49.

Bible Conference."[23] Although these weeklong conferences had not been established to discuss premillennial eschatology, the topic soon became their focus. Like its English forerunner, the Albury Conferences,[24] the Niagara Conferences drew the "Who's Who" of the emerging American premillennialist movement, as well as speakers and guests from Europe. Thousands of people, clergy and laity alike, attended these meetings. In turn, they brought home the message of premillennial eschatology. Soon, the influence of the Niagara Conference moved far beyond the small resort town that hosted it.

While the Niagara Conference may have been "the mother"[25] of the North American premillennial conferences of the late nineteenth century, it was not the only such gathering. A similar congress, the "First American Bible and Prophetic Conference," took place in October

23 *Dictionary of Christianity in America*, s.v. "Niagara Conferences."

24. These meetings, convened at the English Albury Park estate of Henry Drummond, a sometime member of Parliament whom Edward Irving had converted to premillennialism, were held from 1826 to 1830. Their focus was almost exclusively eschatological, for they were designed to be "an extended discussion of prophetic truth" (Sandeen, *Roots of Fundamentalism*, 18). Many if not most of the leading British premillennialists of the day attended the Albury meetings. The convention's lasting value, however, may have been the consensus that was reached regarding premillennial opinion. See ibid., 18–19.

Despite their differences, these leading premillennialists did agree on at least six points common to their respective eschatological convictions. As summarized by Henry Drummond these points are:

1. the cataclysmic end of the age;

2. the restoration of the Jews to Palestine during the time of the judgment;

3. the judgment would fall primarily on Christendom;

4. the millennium would occur after the judgment;

5. Christ would come before the millennium; and

6. the 1,260 years of Daniel 7 and Revelation 13 would be the period from Justinian to the French Revolution, the vials of wrath (Revelation 16) being poured out now, and the Second Advent would be imminent. (Dick, "Millerite Movement 1830–1845," 2–3).

According to Ernest Sandeen, "basic to the whole statement was the assumption that an irreversible deterioration in religion and culture had now reached crisis proportions and that the final act in this era of world history had begun" (Sandeen, *Roots of Fundamentalism*, 22). The world, which had been racing toward its doom, had now almost arrived at it, and so the promised return of Christ was imminent.

25. Sandeen, *Roots of Fundamentalism*, 132.

1878 in New York City's Holy Trinity Episcopal Church. It arose from a growing discontent with what some felt was the lack of focus of the Niagara Conference's predecessors. Six more of these conferences were held in various locations until 1918.[26] The Niagara Conference and the American Bible and Prophetic Conference would together not only serve as catalysts for developing and disseminating premillennial thought, they also served as a focused setting in which new premillennial ideas could receive a hearing and, eventually, find a home.

The teacher most often associated with late nineteenth-century American interest in premillennial thought was not himself American. John Nelson Darby (1800–1882) was a Church of Ireland cleric turned Brethren preacher. His premillennial views, which are collectively known as dispensationalism, initially had an indirect influence on American eschatology. That is, while holding evangelistic meetings in Great Britain, "[prominent] American Protestant leaders, most notably the famous evangelist D. L. Moody, fell under the influence of advocates of [dispensationalism]."[27] These leaders then propagated Darby's theories on their return to America. The popularity of this new teaching led European dispensational leaders, most notably Darby, to travel to America and hold their own meetings, and to present their eschatological doctrines at various prophecy and Bible conferences. Dispensationalism gained its seemingly unshakable foothold in North American evangelical culture primarily through the prophecy conferences that Darby and his associates attended.

The term "dispensationalism" comes from the idea that the history of the interaction between God and human beings can be understood as a series of distinguishable eras or *dispensations*. During each of these dispensations, God has dealt with humanity in various ways (but always graciously) according to the strictures and expectations of the particular covenant that was in force at the time. To interpret Scripture correctly, or to "rightly divide the word of Truth," one must bear in mind which dispensation and covenant were in play during the time of the writing of the biblical passage in question and then apply the proper and corresponding hermeneutic to that passage. The idea of dispensations of grace, though, is neither unique to dispensationalism nor does it serve

26. Weber, *Living in the Shadow*, 28; *Dictionary of Christianity in America*, s.v. "Bible and Prophetic Conference Movement."

27. Dayton, *Prophecy Conference Movement*, 4.

as its distinguishing feature,[28] for at the heart of dispensationalism lies Darby's ecclesiology, and especially his radical separation of Israel and the church.[29] Darby regarded the church as a gracious parenthesis in the program of God, as the "heavenly bride" of God whose existence stemmed from Israel's rejection of the promised Messiah, Jesus Christ. Hence the promises and prophecies of Scripture do not apply to the church (which is a temporary phenomenon) but to the earthly bride, Israel, alone.

Darby was a futurist in regard to the timing of prophecy. Since we live in the church age, a parenthesis in the greater flow of prophetic history, the prophecies of Scripture do not apply to current events.[30] The prophetic chronology, as it were, will not recommence until this parenthesis comes to an end. Prophecy is not now being fulfilled; something must happen to bring this parenthetical era to a close and to start the prophetical clock ticking again.

This critical event may very well be the most distinguishing mark of dispensationalism—the secret and imminent "rapture" of the church.[31] Darby believed, in effect, that Christ would return twice: first to take the church away from the earth, and second to come in judgment and close world history. God must remove the church from the earth before he can turn his attention to the final restoration of Israel. This secret and invisible rapture, or taking away, of the church may happen at any moment. It has no prophetic precursors. All prophecies still to be fulfilled will follow the rapture and the reinstatement of the prophetic timetable. This emphasis on the imminence of the rapture brought to late

28. "The system of dispensations is not primary in Darby's thought; and, furthermore, it is shared by many of Darby's opponents and by literally scores of others, some of whom were not millenarians at all" (Sandeen, *Roots of Fundamentalism*, 68).

29. According to Timothy Weber, this separation of the church and Israel was original and distinctive of Darby. See Weber, "Happily at the Edge of the Abyss," 89.

30. "While Bible prophecy reveals much about past and future dispensations, it is silent on the present one, the Church Age," according to Darby's dispensationalism (Boyer, *When Time Shall Be No More*, 87).

31. Though the rapture is certainly distinctive of dispensationalism, historians disagree about whether this idea and dispensationalism in general originate with Darby. Mark Patterson and Andrew Walker argue that the idea of the secret rapture of the church is found in both Edward Irving and Albury. Ernest Sandeen, noting that the same charges were made during Darby's lifetime in an attempt to discredit him by association, argues that such was clearly not the case. See Patterson and Walker, "Our Unspeakable Comfort," 67; and Sandeen, *Roots of Fundamentalism*, 64.

nineteenth-century American evangelicalism a sense of urgency and earnestness that postmillennialism had not and could not.[32]

D. L. Moody

Premillennial Associations

D. L. Moody was a thoroughgoing premillennialist. Some scholars claim that he was "significantly influenced by the writings of and contacts with the Plymouth Brethren, thus making him the first note-worthy premillennial preacher of revival and evangelism in America"; that he unabashedly advertised his indebtedness to the Plymouth Brethren and "their futurist premillennialism and dispensationalism";[33] and that, "[it] is entirely possible that Moody came under Darby's direct influence in 1868, and certainly no later than 1872."[34] Others contend that even though he may have been influenced by Darby and the Brethren movement, he "never endorsed the details of the new dispensational version of premillennialism."[35] This would accord with the fact that Moody never developed a thoroughgoing and systematic eschatology of any kind.[36] Yet it is nonetheless certain that the eschatology that he did espouse was clearly premillennial, and that it emerged in embryonic form no later than the 1870s.[37]

32. "Although American evangelicals argued about Darby's views on dispensations and the rapture (some rejected them outright; others insisted that end-times prophecies were already being fulfilled; some questioned Darby's radical separation of Israel and the Church), many concurred with his underlying premise that Christ's coming was imminent, and they focused on the significance of that conviction for their everyday lives. Far more powerful at first than Darby's intricate prophetic charts was the simple expectation of Christ's return. In this most basic form, late nineteenth-century premillennialist teaching animated the lives and ministries of hundreds of thousands of evangelicals who, for many reasons, proved receptive to the view that they lived as 'evening light saints' in 'the shadow of the second coming'" (Blumhofer, *Restoring the Faith*, 16–17).

33. Gundry, *Love Them In*, 178, 180.

34. Findlay, *Dwight L. Moody*, 251.

35. Marsden, *Fundamentalism*, 38. Findlay echoes this same observation: "It is questionable whether the evangelist ever became a thorough-going dispensationalist"; though undoubtedly dispensationalisms, both British and North American, nudged Moody toward premillennialism (Findlay, *Dwight L. Moody*, 250–51).

36. Gundry, *Love Them In*, 178.

37. Findlay, *Dwight L. Moody*, 250; Sandeen, *Roots of Fundamentalism*, 173.

Moody's influence on late nineteenth-century evangelicalism cannot be overestimated, and so for him to have embraced a premillennial eschatology of any kind would certainly have increased its popularity. He did, in fact, promote premillennialism. For example, he opened his popular Northfield Conferences to premillennial and dispensational speakers.[38] These conferences, along with other contemporary conferences more directly associated with eschatological themes, provided important and well-attended platforms for a deeper exposition of premillennial eschatology and its underlying hermeneutic.[39]

Moody's own preaching on eschatology was an even more powerful force for premillennialism and, indeed, may have been the catalyst through which American evangelicals first became enamored with premillennial eschatology.[40] His premillennialist sermons may very well have "marked a new departure in evangelistic preaching in America."[41] Moreover, he insisted that if one carefully and thoroughly read the Scriptures, one could not help but adopt the premillennialist point of view. He even went so far as to repudiate postmillennialism explicitly:

> Some people say, "I believe Christ will come on the other side of the millennium." Where do they get it? I can't find it. The Word of God nowhere tells me to watch and wait for signs of the coming of the millennium, (such as the return of the Jews,) but for

38. "During the last two decades of the nineteenth century the unordained Dwight L. Moody was the most influential 'clergyman' in America" (Sandeen, *Roots of Fundamentalism*, 172). As such, his invitations to millenarians to speak at his conferences and his endorsements of their teachings significantly furthered the millenarian movement. Yet Sandeen points out that although the conferences were at first overwhelmingly filled with millenarian speakers, by 1888 they had ceased to be invited. Sandeen feels that this may have been a reaction to the apparent seizure of the conferences by narrow-minded and divisive premillennialists. Premillenialists did not return to the platform until 1893, when A. J. Gordon, himself a premillennialist, took over, at Moody's request, as director of the conferences. See Sandeen, *Roots of Fundamentalism*, 174–175. Moody's handwritten invitation to Gordon is held in the Gordon Collection at Gordon College. See Shelley, "A. J. Gordon," 110.

39. Moody's Chicago Bible Institute went on to become a bastion of dispensational thought for most if not all of the twentieth century, even though it was not strongly dispensationalist in Moody's own lifetime.

40. The topic of the imminence of the premillennial coming of Christ, that increased the sense of urgency for both the preacher and the audience, was usually a topic of Moody's preaching nearer the end of each campaign. See Findlay, *Dwight L. Moody*, 253.

41. Gundry, *Love Them In*, 175.

the coming of the Lord, to be ready at midnight to meet him, like those five wise virgins.[42]

He also expressed his pessimism in regard to the prospects of human moral achievement and the likelihood that human efforts would ever bring about a postmillennial utopia:

> At one time I thought the world would grow better and better until Christ would stay away no longer; but in studying the Bible I don't find any place where God says so, or that Christ is to have a spiritual reign on earth of a thousand years. I find that the world is to grow worse and worse, and that at length there is going to be a separation. The Church is to be translated out of the world. . . . Nowhere in the Scriptures is it claimed that the whole world shall be brought to the feet of Christ in this dispensation.[43]

Categorization

Though Moody was certainly a premillennialist, his premillennialism does not fit nicely into any of the categories that have been discussed above. At times he distinguishes between prophetic events already fulfilled and those still awaiting their realization, sounding much like a historicist.[44] At other times, especially in his teaching on the rapture and on the nature of the church, he comes across as a dispensationalist.

Stanley Gundry insists that Moody spoke neither of the church as a parenthesis in prophetic history nor of two comings of Christ. Instead, he believed that the return of Christ is a unique event for the sole purpose of setting up the kingdom, and that Christ's imminent return is the key to eschatology.[45] Gundry misreads Moody, however, for although Moody did not use phrases such as "parenthesis" to describe the nature of the church, he clearly taught that the

---

42. Moody, "Second Coming of Christ," 26.

43. Ibid., 26–27, 29.

44. "If God did not mean to have us study the prophecies, He would not have put them into the Bible. Some of them are fulfilled, and He is fulfilling the rest, so that if we do not see them all completed in this life, we shall in the world to come. Prophecy, as has been said, is the mold in which history is cast" (Moody, "Second Coming of Christ," 16–17).

45. Gundry, *Love Them In*, 188.

coming of Christ to take His Church to Himself in the clouds, is not the same event as His coming to judge the world at the last day. The deliverance of the Church is one thing, judgment is another. Christ will save His Church, but He will save them finally by taking them out of the world.[46]

Moody's eschatology, then, reveals at least some of the marks of dispensationalism, yet his is clearly not a thoroughgoing futuristic dispensationalism. Though he undoubtedly believed that much biblical prophecy remains to be fulfilled, he also held that at least some of it had already been fulfilled. Though he agreed with the dispensationalists on both the rapture and the nature of the church, even his "any-moment" understanding of the rapture was tempered by his belief in the need to call out the fullness of the Gentile elect beforehand. As Gundry has noted, "[a]lthough [Moody] was clearly a premillennialist and he had obviously been influenced by the dispensationalists, Moody's preaching of the Lord's return would not have been fully satisfactory to his dispensational friends. This is even more characteristic of his preaching in later years."[47]

A. J. Gordon

Premillennial Associations

A. J. Gordon's association with the late nineteenth-century revival of premillennialism is at least as extensive as Moody's. Gordon has been described variously as a one of the "highly respected premillennial pastors of the day,"[48] "a major source of . . . the evangelical premillennial movement,"[49] "a foremost leader in the millenarian prophetic movement,"[50] and "one of the most important premillennialists in American theology."[51] Ernest Sandeen goes so far as to call him a figure of mythic proportions within the premillennial movement.

---

46. Moody, "Second Coming of Christ," 24.

47. Gundry, Love Them In, 190–191.

48. Marsden, Fundamentalism and American Culture, 83.

49. Shelley, "A. J. Gordon," 110.

50. Russell, Adoniram Judson Gordon, 61.

51. Robert, "Legacy of Adoniram Judson Gordon," 178.

The death of A. J. Gordon in 1895 deprived the millenarians of the greatest Baptist leader in the movement's history, but his influence lived on in the *Watchword*, the Boston Missionary Training School, and the Clarendon Street Church, and in the careers of many devoted followers.[52]

Gordon not only attended but was in part responsible for the premillennial flavor of many of the Northfield Conferences that he organized at Moody's request. His clearest and most important contribution to the late nineteenth-century revival of premillennialism, however, was his founding role in the Niagara Bible Conferences, which were the most important vehicle for the dissemination of premillennialist doctrine in the late nineteenth century. He also served as a committee member and keynote speaker at the Prophetic Conference at the Church of the Holy Trinity in New York City in 1878, a meeting heralded as "a series of carefully prepared papers on the pre-Millennial advent of the Lord Jesus Christ and connected truths" and as an opportunity "to participate in such discussions as the topics may suggest."[53] Gordon saw himself as a confirmed premillennialist or, as he would also describe it, a "chiliast."[54] For Gordon, such an eschatological view was not only biblical; it was the faith of the earliest of the church fathers and the Reformers, who, like Gordon, anticipated the imminent return of Jesus Christ and the consequent inauguration of the millennial kingdom.[55]

Premillennial Pessimism

As one might expect, Gordon took a pessimistic view of humankind's ability to reform society. He was certainly not "optimistic about the future of secular society."[56] Instead, he believed that the world was presently wallowing in a sea of despondency from which it could not, through its own efforts and resources, escape. Only the premillennial return of Jesus Christ would establish a kingdom of righteousness, and

---

52. Sandeen, *Roots of Fundamentalism*, 165. The *Watchword* was a "journal to help believers 'looking for that blessed hope, and the glorious appearing of the great God and our Saviour Jesus Christ'" (*Dictionary of Christianity in America*, s. v. "Gordon, A[doniram] J[udson] [1836–1895]").

53. Dayton, *Prophecy Conference Movement*, 12.

54. Gordon, *Ecce Venit*, v, vi.

55. Gordon, *Adoniram Judson Gordon*, 129, 322; Gordon, *Ecce Venit*, 181.

56. Russell, "Adoniram Judson Gordon," 66.

only through this promise could one "patiently endure the present controlling democracy of lists and crowding selfishness and shouldering vanities, with its 'cries and counter-cries of feud and faction.' Even the darkness has its message of cheer: 'The shadows point to the dawn.'"[57] Any apparent societal progress was at best "external and formal,"[58] and but a temporary gilding of an ultimately rotten core.[59] When Christ returns, he will not simply slide easily into a paradisiacal realm prepared for him in advance. Rather, he himself will usher in the millennial age. The present state of affairs, in which the Spirit is working to prepare the church, "will continue until the Lord Jesus returns from heaven, when another order will be ushered in and another dispensational ministry succeed."[60]

Any hope of universal redemption, therefore, must be reserved for the age that follows the return of Jesus Christ and cannot be seen as a cause of the Parousia.[61] Though Gordon granted that people will continue to be converted, and that Christianity will continue to make a positive moral impact on society, he was just as certain that "by neither process as now going on is the millennium destined to be ushered in."[62] He repeatedly denied the legitimacy of postmillennial eschatology, calling it an "interpretation [that] completely deranges the programme of prophecy."[63] He also denied that either experience or Scripture could provide anything close to a basis for belief in a universal conversion leading to a celestial kingdom on earth. Postmillennialism erred in confusing the possibilities of the future age with the possibilities of the present age, thereby "telescoping [the age of the church], the

---

57. Gordon, *Adoniram Judson Gordon*, 319.

58. Ibid., 311.

59. Gordon did not deny that the church has made, and will continue to make some impact for good on the world. Its influence, however, was not comprehensive enough to save the world from its impending doom. Gordon, *Adoniram Judson Gordon*, 312.

60. Gordon, *Ministry of the Spirit*, 15–16

61. Here "universal salvation" refers to the conversion of a representative elect from all peoples of the earth. It does not, however, speak about the moral and spiritual restoration of humanity as a whole. See Gordon, *Ecce Venit*, 56–58.

62. Gordon, *Ecce Venit*, 50.

63. Ibid. 54.

dispensation of grace, with the third age, the millennium that follows the return of Christ and the rapture of the Church."[64]

Categorization

Historicism

Gordon, like Moody, defies easy categorization. Though he held clearly premillennial views, Gordon, too, seemed to use historicist, futurist, and even dispensational terminology. Gordon called the former two types of premillennialists the "historicalists" and the "futurists."[65] He labeled himself as a "historicalist" because he believed that the "Antichrist [had] already come in the bloody and blasphemous system of the papacy, and that the Apocalypse [had] been continuously fulfilling from our Lord's ascension to the present time."[66] The key prophetic event that remains unfulfilled is the calling out of the Gentiles, but this is not to be understood as a global conversion but as a worldwide presentation of the gospel to which the elect will respond, giving rise to a church composed of representatives from all nations. The goal of the church, then, was not cosmic conversion but extensive evangelization.[67] Its task was not to change all, but to tell all. The evangelization of the world, not its conversion, would serve as the necessary precursor to the return of Christ.[68]

64. Ibid., 61.

65. Ibid., vi.

66. Ibid., vi, 112–45. Bruce Shelley states: "Gordon's views of premillennialism, we should note, were not those of that dispensationalism later inscribed in the notes of the *Scofield Reference Bible*. He felt, for example, that the papacy was Antichrist and he evidenced no support for the doctrine of the pre-tribulational rapture of the church" (Shelley, "A J. Gordon," 112). The last part of this statement, as will be shown, is overstated.

67. "[Our] task is not to bring all the world to Christ, our task is unquestionably to bring Christ to all the world" (Gordon, *Holy Spirit in Missions*, 14).

68. "Such an 'out-gathering' of the elect from all nations was a necessary prelude to Jesus' second-coming. Premillennial emphasis on the evangelization of the world, therefore, focused on preaching the gospel to the whole world so that Jesus would return soon" (Robert, "Legacy of Adoniram Judson Gordon," 178). While some supported missionary activity on the basis of democratic and humanitarian sentiment, Gordon's singular emphasis remained that of evangelism as a prelude to the second coming of Christ. See Russell, "Adoniram Judson Gordon," 24.

Because of his personal desire for the return of Christ[69] and his conviction about the relationship between the universal evangelization of the gospel and the Parousia, Gordon came to regard eschatological concerns as the primary motivation for missionary activity. The preaching of the gospel, to the extent that it fulfilled prophecy regarding the outgathering of the Gentiles, was thus not merely a phenomenon that would precede the return of Christ but a tool to be used for its hastening. The sooner the gospel is spread, and the sooner the Gentiles are gathered out, the sooner Christ will return. The relationship between the evangelization of the world and the return of Christ, then, is not merely chronological but causative. Gordon's hymn, "He Shall Reign from Sea to Sea," draws out this connection.

> O Church of Christ, behold at last
> The Promised sign appear,—
> The gospel preached in all the world;
> And lo! the King draws near.
>
> With girded loins make haste!
> Make haste, thy witness to complete,
> That Christ may take His throne and bring
> All nations to His feet.
>
> And thou, O Israel, long in dust,
> Arise and come away!
> See how the sun of righteousness
> Sheds forth the beams of day.
>
> Thy scattered sons are gathering home,
> The fig tree buds again;
> A little while and David's Son
> On David's throne shall reign.
>
> Then sing aloud, O Pilgrim Church,
> Brief conflict yet remains,
> And then Immanuel descends
> To bind thy foe in chains.[70]

---

69. Gordon identifies his primary motivation for missions not as a love for humanity but as a "philo-Christy," a love for Christ. This "constitutes the greatest missionary motive" (Gordon, *Holy Spirit in Missions*, 16).

70. Gordon and Pierson, *Coronation Hymnal*, 356.

The return of Christ remains, in a sense, imminent. This does not mean that it can occur at any moment, because some preconditions remain to be met, yet it will likely come soon and will certainly come suddenly. A. J. Gordon also believed that Christ's imminent return ought to serve as an incentive to holy living and an encouragement to steadfastness in times of trial: "Amid all the disheartenment induced by the abounding iniquity of our times; amid the loss of faith and the waxing cold of love within the church; and amid the out breaking of lawlessness without, causing men's hearts to fail them for fear, and for looking after those things that are coming on the earth,—this is our Lord's inspiring exhortation: 'Look up and lift up your heads, for your redemption draweth nigh.'"[71]

Gordon converted to historicism from futurism because he had become convinced that it was based on a "more obvious and simple interpretation of the Word; and also because it [had] such verifications in fulfilled history and chronology as to compel even some of its strongest opponents to concede that it is a true interpretation if not the complete and final one."[72]

Futurism/Dispensationalism

Yet Gordon's work also includes dispensationalist elements.[73] For example, he draws a distinction between the Jews and the church. However, he does not describe the current dispensation, the church age, as a parenthesis in God's prophetic timetable, after which God will again turn his attention back to the Jews.[74] In rejecting the Messiah, the Jews found themselves "in the shadow of God's averted countenance," but they will eventually, in their own time, repent and return to a place of favor. Their repentance will lead God to resurrect his interest in them, and not the

71. Gordon, *Ecce Venit*, 12.

72. Ibid., vi–vii.

73. C. Allyn Russell mistakenly labels Gordon "a pronounced" and "a confirmed dispensationalist," because Gordon makes reference to different dispensations or epochs of human history. As has been shown, however, dispensationalism is not the only theological system to refer to the dispensations or eras in God's redemptive plan. See Russell, "Adoniram Judson Gordon," 76–77.

74. On at least one occasion Gordon does use the term "parenthesis" to describe the church age, but he does not use it in the dispensational sense. See Gordon, *Holy Spirit in Missions*, 10.

other way around, as in dispensationalism.[75] It is in this context that Gordon discusses that second distinctive of dispensationalism: the rapture. The rapture will take place after the gathering out of the Gentiles, but not (apparently) as a separate and secret event. Rather, it constitutes merely one aspect of Christ's triumphal return to establish his millennial kingdom.[76] It will precede the final restoration of Israel, but not in an almost causative way, as in classic dispensationalism.

However, Gordon believed both historicism and futurism to be acceptable Christian options. To begin with, both positions center their hope in the Lord's "literal, visible, and bodily return to earth."[77] Premillennial hope, whether historicist or futurist, keeps its object, the person and presence of Jesus Christ, secure. Christ will appear in a bodily, visible, and literal form and not, as was the case with other views, merely as a "spiritual apparition," such as his mystical presence in the church.[78] In addition, both views attempt to return the doctrine of Christ's return to its proper place at the heart of Christian theology.[79] The return of Christ "is the axis of a true eschatology; that in which all its doctrines and all its hopes stand together."[80] Eschatology necessarily interprets and informs all other doctrines, and so to overlook or misinterpret eschatology is to pervert all other areas of doctrine.

A. T. Pierson

Premillennial Associations

A. T. Pierson, like A. J. Gordon and D. L. Moody, has been identified as one of the leading figures in the late nineteenth-century premillennial movement. His own conversion from a Presbyterian postmillennialism

---

75. Gordon, *Ecce Venit*, 57.

76. Ibid., 60. Gordon does not wholly deny the possibility of a secret and separate rapture, but neither does he endorse it. A particular doctrine of the rapture should never become a source of division, however; for only the passing of the event itself will finally reveal all of these chronological mysteries. See Gordon, *Ecce Venit*, 211. Yet Gordon remained convinced that the rapture will occur as part and parcel of the final Parousia and not as a separate event. See Gordon, *Holy Spirit in Missions*, 22.

77. Gordon, *Ecce Venit*, 208.

78. Ibid., 208–9.

79. Ibid., vii.

80. Ibid., 209–10.

to premillennialism came as a result of "extensive bible [*sic*] study after a chance meeting with George Müller of Bristol in 1878."[81] He furthered the premillennialist cause through his book *The Coming of the Lord* (published in 1896) and his regular involvement as a speaker at the Niagara conferences.[82]

Premillennial Pessimism

Typical of premillennialism was Pierson's skepticism regarding the future of human history. Despite the church's finest efforts, human history is doomed to end in failure. After almost two thousand years of Christian influence, little real progress had been made, for "[t]hough some seem to think that the world is growing better, the carnal heart hates [God] as it always has, and if He were here on the earth to-day would be ready to crucify Him, as in the days of His flesh."[83] Pierson also debunked the postmillennial idea that despite past and present appearances, the church will ultimately succeed in converting the world. On the contrary, the church will always remain a minority. It will never be, at least numerically, triumphant.[84]

Pierson believed that the drift of the world into debauchery is beyond the church's ability to halt. The church cannot stem the flow of immorality at home, and the sheer number of the unsaved and the geographic distance between them place it beyond the church's reach.

> The church confronts the world, with its thousand million unconverted souls, scattered over fields, continental in breadth, and proves incompetent to reach them with the gospel; while at home, there is a widening gulf between the church and the world, which the church cannot bridge, and meanwhile intemperance, licentiousness and anarchy become more threatening and revolutionary.[85]

81. Robert, "Legacy of Arthur Tappan Pierson," 122; Sandeen, *Roots of Fundamentalism*, 143.

82. *The Coming of the Lord* was first published with the Fleming H. Revell Company in 1896. See Sandeen, *Roots of Fundamentalism*, 143.

83. Pierson, *Coming of the Lord*, 40–41.

84. Citing the noted Presbyterian and Princeton theologian A. A. Hodge. See Pierson, *Coming of the Lord*, 34.

85. Pierson, *Forward Movements*, vii.

A. T. Pierson also rejected the long-held belief that the world is slowly being converted, in favor of a more pessimistic assessment: the world's population is growing so rapidly that Christianity is actually losing ground.[86] Thus the world cannot be changed by human effort but only by the glorious return of the visible, personal, and real Jesus Christ[87] and his establishment of the kingdom. This millennial dawn will occur at the darkest moment, at the morally and religiously lowest point in history.

> [W]hen the crisis is greatest, the danger most extreme, the darkness deepest, and the distress of the church the most overwhelming, [Jesus] will suddenly appear, in the very midst of the troubled waters, walking on the sea in the majesty of God; and immediately when he comes into the ship it will touch the millennial shore, and all the dangers and disasters of church life will be past.[88]

Both this diabolical moment and the consequential return of Jesus Christ are imminent.

Pierson believed the imminent return of Jesus was sure. Jesus would come again because it was the testimony of Scripture and because no one had yet been able to predict with certainty its precise timing.[89] Indeed, Christ's coming "may be very much nearer than most of us think. Some of the most devout students of Scripture have said that it would not at all be surprising if some saints, now living, should never pass through the experience of death but be alive and remain at his coming."[90] Though he would present in his works a number of different theories of imminence, including some based on one style or another of prophetic mathematics,[91] Pierson's own convictions rested on his observation that a number of eschatologically significant phenomena had begun to manifest themselves in his day. These included the revived interest in the pursuit of holiness, the expanding role of women in the

---

86. Pierson, *Greatest Work in the World*, 12.

87. Pierson, *Believer's Life*, 83.

88. Pierson, *Coming of the Lord*, 42–43.

89. Pierson, *Believer's Life*, 83; Pierson, *Coming of the Lord*, 53.

90. Pierson, *Believer's Life*, 89.

91. In *Forward Movements of the Last Half Century*, Pierson outlines twelve "conspicuous" arguments for the impending coming of the King, though he did not personally endorse all of them. See Pierson, *Forward Movements*, 411–20.

church, and the resurgence and success of the missionary enterprise.[92] Not only did Pierson believe that the recuperation of holiness and missionary activity point to the imminent return of Jesus Christ, he also believed that as one's anticipation of the event grew, it would reciprocally serve as a powerful incentive to both holy living[93] and missionary endeavor.[94]

Categorization

HISTORICISM

Pierson's premillennialism, like that of Gordon and Moody, defies easy categorization as either historicist or futurist/dispensationalist, because it seems to possess essential characteristics of both views. Like Gordon, Pierson believed in the imminence of the return of Jesus Christ and, therefore, appears to be a historicist. Yet both Pierson and Gordon

---

92. In regard to developments on the mission front, Pierson noted that the God's evident participation in the work of missions shows that he is preparing for Christ's return. Such evidence includes "the unity and continuity of the work itself, and in the marked fitness between the workers and the work; in the opening of new fields and the provision of new and greater facilities for their occupation; in the raising up of sufficient labourers to carry out the Divine purpose; and in stirring up His people to furnish sufficient means for their equipment and support," and the "unlocking of long-shut gates" (Pierson, *Modern Mission Century*, 23, 24). With respect to the renewed interest in holiness, Pierson observes that those who were entering and involved in the missionary enterprise were "men and women so marvelously fitted for the exact work and field as to show unmistakable foresight and purpose." He also mentions in this connection the establishment of the Keswick meetings (ibid., 25, 70). Finally, "The Victorian era coincides with that of missionary expansion, and especially, of woman's epiphany—her emergence out of her long eclipse" (ibid., 162). As far as women's involvement in mission is concerned, "[w]ho can measure woman's work for the conversion of woman in pagan countries, and in the organization of her own sex in Christian lands for missionary effort. She can especially understand and appreciate the condition of her own sex, and the elevation to which the Gospel has brought herself, and can bring her degraded sisters; and she alone can have access to women in countries where the restrictions of the seraglio, harem, zenana, forbid a man to enter, even a physician" (ibid., 170).

93. Pierson asserted that it was through the belief in the imminent return of Jesus Christ that "I am enabled to live soberly, maintaining my holy equilibrium." Moreover, "In the opinion of the apostle John, there was nothing that helped to the personal purification of character like this blessed hope set on the appearing of Jesus Christ. (1 John 3:2)" (Pierson, *Coming of the Lord*, 58, 61).

94. This point will be explored more thoroughly in paragraphs to follow.

thought that at least one prophetic event awaited fulfillment in the current era—the evangelization of the world. The Lord would not return until this had occurred and the full number of the elect had been received into the church.[95] Contrary to his otherwise general anthropological pessimism, Pierson's optimism about the church's ability to fulfill this mandate of worldwide witness is noteworthy. Not only did he believe that the fulfillment of this task was possible, but even that it was possible in his own lifetime, should the church wholeheartedly embrace its responsibility.[96] Pierson's sanguine view was shared by the Student Volunteer Movement, a missionary organization with whom Pierson was intimately associated, and whose "watchword" was "the evangelization of the world in this generation."[97]

This optimism was based on Pierson's differentiation between the church's responsibility to convert the world, on the one hand, and the church's mandate to evangelize the world, on the other. As noted earlier, Pierson was adamant that the conversion of the world was a task beyond both the church's resources and commission. Neither was it the church's mandate. The church could not and would not transform the moral character of the world, but it could universally proclaim the gospel. The reasonableness and feasibility of this view gave hope and encouragement to the church, whereas the impossibility of the postmillennialists' goal could bring only despair.

> [T]he hope which the Word of God holds up before us, in this dispensation, is not the conversion of the world but its evangelization; and we are simply going forth into the world, as our

95. "According to this view, the church is not called to convert the world but to *bear witness* to the world, until her testimony is borne in all parts of the earth. Then the Lord will come; as soon as this elect body of Christ is fully gathered out from the nations so that Christ's body becomes complete, the Head will appear and the body will be associated with Him in glory" (Pierson, *Coming of the Lord*, 47; emphasis original).

96. To fulfill its task the church needed only "[t]o submit to His authority, to believe in the ability divinely assured, to attempt great things for God and expect great things from God—[these] would insure an era of missions for far eclipsing all hitherto done or attempted that the present activity of the Church would be seen as the winking of an eye or the movement of the little finger, in comparison to the energetic action of the whole body in a race for the prize" (Pierson, *Greatest Work in the World*, 8).

97. Robert, "Legacy of Arthur Tappan Pierson," 120. "The vigorous students of the 1880s and 1890s believed that they would be the ones who would complete the work began by Jesus' disciples nearly 2,000 years before" (Robert, "Origin of the Student Volunteer Watchword," 146).

Savior did, to bear our witness and gather out of mankind those whom the Father hath given to Christ, and incorporate them into the mystical body of Christ. This hope the actual facts so far confirm and fulfil, for this is exactly what is being done. Therefore, our Scripturally warranted hope is not defeated, nor even deferred; our hearts are not made sick and we know that have a Scriptural hope, because we find the confirmation of that Scripturally warranted expectation in our actual experience.[98]

For Pierson, as for Gordon, the relationship between the evangelization of the world and the subsequent return of the Lord was not just chronological. It was, to some degree, causal. The church in going about its work of evangelizing the nations would actually hasten the return of Christ.[99]

Futurism/Dispensationalism

Though he shows traces of a historicist outlook, futurist and dispensationalist aspects of Pierson's eschatology are also present. Pierson's greatest dispensational notoriety is found in his role as one of the seven original editors of *The Scofield Reference Bible*.[100] Pierson enhanced his dispensational pedigree by speaking at various Bible and prophecy conferences that would later become almost exclusive forums for dispensationalism.[101] In contrast to Gordon, he did not equate the antichrist

98. Pierson, *Coming of the Lord*, 79.

99. Dana Lee Robert makes repeated mention of this characteristic of Pierson's eschatology: "Part of the urgency the committee [of which Pierson was a part] felt for world evangelization was that it would hasten 'the day of the Lord.' The sooner the whole world heard the good news of the gospel, the sooner Jesus Christ would return to usher in the millennium. This millennial hope fueled Pierson's passion for systematic world evangelization. William Carey, Alexander Duff, and other missions notables had long envisioned worldwide evangelization, but Arthur Pierson linked the concept of worldwide evangelization with the urgency of premillennialism to formulate a plan for 'the evangelization of the world in this generation'" (Robert, "Legacy of Arthur Tappan Pierson," 147).

100. Yet one should not jump too quickly to the conclusion that Pierson would agree with all or even most of what was found in its editorial comments. As Dana Lee Robert has noted, "*The Scofield Reference Bible* was completely the work of C. I. Scofield. Though he consulted with the editors and asked advice of people as critical as Professor S. R. Driver, he personally wrote each note and the final interpretations were his" (Robert, "Arthur Tappan Pierson," 382).

101. For example, Pierson spoke at the second and third American Bible and Prophetic Conferences, as well as at the International Prophetic Conference in 1901. See Robert, "Arthur Tappan Pierson," 211.

with the office of the papacy. Rather, Pierson still awaited the future manifestation of this prophetic character.[102]

Dana Lee Robert, the leading authority on A. T. Pierson, categorizes his overall eschatology as dispensational.[103] To begin with, Pierson divides earthly history into three major epochs or dispensations, and he interprets the events of each according to rules suited to that particular era.[104] Each of the three dispensations of history aligns with the three offices of Christ—Prophet, Priest and King. The prophetic dispensation stretches from the point of creation to the incarnation. The priestly dispensation extends from the death of Christ until his return, and it is only with his return at "the End" that the world will truly experience the dispensation of the enthroned Christ, and not before.[105] Pierson hypothesized that the message of the kingdom preached by Jesus, John the Baptist, the seventy, and the other early evangelists began with Jesus's victory over Satan in the desert and ceased with the rejection of Jesus as king upon his entry into Jerusalem. From this time on, Scripture only referred to the kingdom as an event in the far distant future.[106] It is for this reason that Pierson considered postmillennialism to be the result of a hermeneutical mistake, for it applied the rules and expectations of the kingly era to that of the current priestly one. It assumed a Jesus who is fully reigning rather than a Jesus who is merely "heir-apparent."[107] However, Pierson's division of history into three distinct dispensations is not enough to make his eschatology dispensational, for as we have already seen, such distinctions are not peculiar to dispensationalism.

Dana Lee Robert also calls Pierson a dispensationalist because he always takes care to distinguish between Israel and the church and never uses the terms interchangeably: "The Church of God never means Israel, and Israel never means the Church of God."[108] The two terms rep-

---

102. Pierson, *Coming of the Lord*, 31.

103. Robert, "Legacy of Arthur Tappan Pierson," 123; Robert, "Arthur Tappan Pierson," 387.

104. Pierson, *Coming of the Lord*, 38.

105. "[T]here is no indication in the Word of God that Christ has *ever yet assumed the kingship*" (Pierson, *Coming of the Lord*, 17, emphasis original); see also Pierson, *Believer's Life*, 91.

106. Pierson, *Coming of the Lord*, 20.

107. Ibid..

108. Ibid., 68.

resent two distinct and eternally separate entities, and so the promises and destiny of one are not those of the other. Though both Israel and the church currently exist as peoples of God, Israel will not return to God's favor until the return of Christ. During his time of millennial reign, the Spirit, who is now poured out upon the church alone, will be poured out on all flesh. Through this divine action, the Jews will be restored. Their restoration, however, will not be according to the Abrahamic covenant, which they have long since broken, but according to the new grace found in Jesus Christ.[109] Yet Pierson almost never discusses the rapture, another feature of dispensationalism, if by *rapture* one means the snatching of the church out of the world by Christ so that he might continue his work in the world: "If Arthur Tappan Pierson believed in the pretribulational rapture, he did not emphasize it,"[110] and he said nothing about it by name.[111] Therefore, it would be correct to identify Pierson as, at most, an "inconsistent dispensationalist."[112]

Pierson remarked on the revival of interest in eschatological matters in his day and on the "general consensus of opinion" that his generation was on the threshold of the age for which Christ had told his disciples "to watch and pray."[113] This proved to be an encouragement to Pierson, who believed not only that the return of Jesus was imminent but that the doctrine concerning this return was eminent: "In the New Testament the coming of the Lord is the one transcendent, eminent event, that rises in dignity and importance over every other event mentioned—even the incarnation of Christ and the coming of the Holy Ghost."[114] Indeed, it is the return of Jesus Christ that "overtops all events that ever took place from the foundation of the world."[115] Therefore, if one wants to understand Christianity, if not the flow of human history,

109. Pierson, *Acts of the Holy Spirit*, 34; Pierson, *Coming of the Lord*, 30. On this very point, Pierson breaks with classic dispensationalism in the Scofield stream, for he did not agree with Scofield that "grace through Jesus Christ was not applied to the Jews" (Robert, "Arthur Tappan Pierson," 390).

110. Robert, "Arthur Tappan Pierson," 393.

111. Ibid., 394.

112. "If Scofield's scheme . . . is taken to be dispensational orthodoxy [as I would argue it is], then Arthur Tappan Pierson was an inconsistent dispensationalist" (Robert, "Arthur Tappan Pierson," 383).

113. Pierson, *Forward Movements*, 409.

114. Pierson, *Coming of the Lord*, 54.

115. Pierson, *Believer's Life*, 83.

one must understand the timing and nature of Christ's return. Pierson considered it "a shame to a Christian disciple to know practically nothing about the Second Coming! To treat it with scornful contempt, or even with indifference!"[116]

Yet as important as this doctrine may have been to Pierson, he, like Gordon, sought to avoid division among premillennialists. Those issues that might divide premillennialists into various camps, though important in their own right, were not reason enough to rend asunder the unity of those who believed in and hoped for the return of Christ, premillennial or otherwise. Pierson's ecclesiology, especially his desire for Christian unity, outweighed the need for eschatological unanimity in his eyes. For this reason,

> [h]e largely kept his controversial premillennialism out of his speeches and articles, [even though] it underlay his mission theory. He did not wish to divide the church over the issue of the second coming of Jesus Christ, [although] he defended the doctrine when attacked or when he was asked to explain his position to fellow premillennialists, such as the Bible students who met yearly for Niagara conferences.[117]

A. B. Simpson

Premillennial Associations

Like the other three subjects of our study, A. B. Simpson has been identified as a significant premillennialist,[118] yet his overt premillennial associations pale in comparison to the associations of the others. Nevertheless, he believed that the resurgence of premillennialism, especially during the late nineteenth century, was part of the gracious restoration of the central tenets of pure Christianity that had been lost over time, especially "during the Middle Ages and only partly recovered by Luther, and since then . . . slowly restored to the Church of God."[119] Part of his intent for The Christian and Missionary Alliance was the further

116 Ibid., 91.

117. Robert, "Legacy of Arthur Tappan Pierson," 122.

118. "Among the leaders of conservative evangelicalism, none was more explicitly premillennial than A. B. Simpson, founder of the Christian and Missionary Alliance" (Hutchison, "Moral Equivalent for Imperialism," 173).

119. Simpson, *Lord for the Body*, 128.

restoration and propagation of premillennialism or, more particularly, "to bear united testimony to . . . Christ's Personal and Pre-millennial coming."[120]

Simpson, however, held that eschatology and the doctrine of Christ's premillennial return were not just ordinary doctrines, even within his own system, but that they fulfilled and shaped all of the other themes of the "Fourfold Gospel" and of theology in general.[121] The high point in God's purpose, from which all other things flow or to which they are leading, is neither creation nor the incarnation, but the future event of Christ's return, millennial reign, and the "consummation of the age."[122] Hence all other events in history find their full meaning only as they contribute to and reflect this highest goal. The day of Christ's return is "the day for which all other days were made, the one event to which all other things are tending."[123] Consequently to understand God's intention for any single historical phenomenon, one must see it through the lens of Christ's return.[124]

As dedicated as he was to this doctrine, and as central as he thought premillennial eschatology was to the overall scheme of the gospel and God's intent for creation, Simpson refused to make it either a test of orthodoxy or, at least initially, a condition of membership in the Christian and Missionary Alliance. Those who dissented could remain in the fold, though they were not to present their views in such a way as to foster dissent or controversy.[125] In keeping with his own certainty about what

120. Simpson, *Christian Alliance Year Book, 1888*, 49.

121. Sawin, "Fourfold Gospel," 6.

122. Simpson, *Earnests of the Coming Age*, 1–3; "That is the goal, that is the outlook, that is the perspective of faith and hope—not the cross, not even the resurrection, not the work of missions, not even the blessed presence of the Master and the power of the Holy Spirit. All these only lead up to that transcendent and eternal hope, that one far off event to which the whole creation moves" (Simpson, *Cross of Christ*, 111).

123. Simpson, *Coming One*, 211.

124. Simpson, *Earnests of the Coming Age*, 3. Kee Ho Sung has noted that eschatology has in fact defined and shaped Simpson's overall theology. See Sung, "Doctrine of the Second Advent," 147.

125. At first, such persons were granted full membership if they affirmed the first three points of the "Fourfold Gospel" and were willing to "give this subject their candid and prayerful consideration" (Christian Alliance, *Christian Alliance Year Book, 1888*, 50). Within ten years, however, such persons were only permitted auxiliary membership. See Simpson, "Editorial," *The Christian and Missionary Alliance*, 12 March 1897, 252.

the Scriptures teach regarding the nature and timing of the eschaton, Simpson called for caution and tolerance with respect to issues about which Scripture is silent[126]

Premillennial Pessimism and the Nature of Christ's Return

Like Moody, Pierson, and Gordon, Simpson bucked the general cultural trend and took a pessimistic view of the world's future. He was, for example, convinced that the universe was withering and not flourishing.[127] The notion of "the growth of a spiritual millennium was unscriptural; the world was becoming worse and worse."[128] Christ would not be greeted at his return by a spiritual utopia.[129] Rather, "when He comes He will find the world and its rulers not waiting to welcome and worship but arrayed against Him in the last dread battle of Armageddon."[130] The church age will always be filled with licentious behavior and sin. Even at its height, sin and apostasy will abound.[131] History gave no hint of a millennial kingdom before Christ's return, only a developing chaos.[132]

If things are to improve, Christ must come to change them. Simpson believed that Revelation 20 describes the coming of the Lord as preceding, introducing, and making possible the millennial kingdom.[133] Christ "the Morning Star shall precede the Millennial dawn."[134] In so saying, he distanced himself from the classic postmillennialism of his Scottish heritage.[135] In addition to rejecting the inherent optimism of postmillennialism, he also refuted what he perceived to be its understanding of the nature of Christ's return. This despite the fact that Simpson had been

126. Simpson, *Fourfold Gospel*, 62; Simpson, "Editorial," *The Christian Alliance and Foreign Missionary Weekly*, 24 January 1896, 84.

127. "The prophetic picture is a very dark one. 'Evil men shall wax and worse'" (Simpson, *Earnests of the Coming Age*, 7).

128. Simpson, "How I Was Led," 298.

129. "[A] holy, happy world will not be waiting to welcome its King" (Simpson, *Fourfold Gospel*, 59).

130. Simpson, *Gospel of Matthew*, 31–32.

131. Simpson, *Coming One*, 26.

132. Simpson, "That Blessed Hope," 166.

133. Simpson, *Fourfold Gospel*, 58.

134. Simpson, *Larger Christian Life*, 11.

135. Interestingly, one of the prizes that Simpson received while in seminary was for a paper that defended this very view. See Simpson, "Simpson Scrapbook," 18

"trained in the Scottish school of theology, and was taught to consider Christ's coming to mean His manifestation to the soul of the believer by the Spirit, His coming at death to the saint, and His coming spiritually by the spread of the Gospel."[136] His premillennial conversion, however, led him to believe that the return of Christ is to be a far more "personal coming"[137] and paradigm-shifting arrival.

Simpson believed that Christ would return personally and bodily, and would not merely enter spiritually or figuratively into the life of the believer, the church, or the world. He used two complementary metaphors for the two advents of Christ. The Christ of the first advent, the incarnation, was the "Lamb of Calvary;" The Christ of the second advent would be the "Lion of Judah." Since these two metaphors are scriptural, complementary, and equative, he insisted that as the first was physical, so the second must be. Therefore, to deny a literal, physical return of Christ is either to deny the physical reality of the incarnation, which is anathema, or to destroy the harmony of Scripture, which is equally untenable. Christ the Lion will return bodily, just as Christ the Lamb had come bodily.[138]

Given his pessimistic outlook on humanity and his belief in Christ's millennial reign, Simpson also believed that Christ will return as a disruptive and conquering figure who will vanquish evil. That is,

> the second advent of the Son of God at the close of time, [will be a time] of judgment and destruction towards the enemies of the Gospel; coming not to convert and purify, but to supersede the governments of the earth, and to be a kingdom more enduring than all the kingdoms of the past.[139]

At his return, Christ will forcibly and even violently remove those who stand in opposition to him, eliminate human government, and establish his kingdom of righteousness.

---

136. Simpson, "How I Was Led," 298.

137. Ibid.; Simpson, *Coming One*, 157.

138. "It will be a literal coming" (Simpson, *Heart Messages*, 199).

139. Simpson based this conclusion, at least in part, on his interpretation of Daniel 2, a passage in which a stone from the heavens smashes the feet of Nebuchadnezzar's multimetaled statue and destroys it. The statue represents the glory of human government, the stone the returning Christ. See Simpson, *Coming One*, 49.

Categorization

Not surprisingly, the categorization of Simpson's eschatology is no simple matter. He explicitly identified himself as a historicist because he believed historicism to be the only biblically consistent view.[140] In keeping with this identification, Simpson declared: "we have always frankly believed and taught that a large portion of the prophecies respecting our Saviour's coming, and the events that are to precede it, have been fulfilled."[141] Among the key apocalyptic figures already manifest was the antichrist. In harmony with a choir of other historicists, Simpson believed that the antichrist had already appeared in the form of the papacy.[142] Furthermore, futurism, as Simpson understood it, was a threat not only to sound doctrine but to the nature of the church's mission as well. Given its long list of yet-unfulfilled prophecies, futurism detracts from the urgency of the church's missionary task and denies the imminence of Christ's return: "Futurism, in [Simpson's] opinion, effectively denied imminency by reason of the sheer number of things yet to happen."[143]

HISTORICISM AND ITS IMPACT ON MISSION STRATEGY

Simpson believed the return of Christ to be imminent. It is not something on the far-off horizon of history separated from the present by a seemingly endless string of unfulfilled prophecies. Rather it is "an ever-impending event"[144] and a swiftly approaching milestone.[145] Simpson's understanding of imminence was based on certain historicist assumptions, and especially on the assumption that the prophetic timetable had continued to run during the church age so that many contemporary events were fulfillments of prophecy and, therefore, pointed to the

---

140. "[T]he historical rather than the futurist view of antichrist, the only view, we are persuaded consistent with Scripture, the facts of ecclesiastical history, and the true testimony of the Church of Christ respecting the vital issues and real perils of to-day" (Simpson, "Editorial Paragraphs," 251).

141. Simpson, "Futurist and Praeterist," 416.

142. On at least one occasion, Simpson also identified the papacy with the beast mentioned in Revelation 13. See Simpson, *Heart Messages*, 207.

143. Pyles, "Missionary Eschatology of A. B. Simpson," 35.

144. Simpson, "That Blessed Hope," 166.

145. Sung, "Doctrine of the Second Advent," 122.

approaching return of Jesus Christ.[146] He identified no fewer than nine such categories of sign:

1. preternatural signs, such as an increase in earthquakes and other natural calamities;[147]

2. "political signs," including the breakup of the great empires, the waging of great wars, the rise of socialism and anarchy, as well as labor unrest;[148]

3. "commercial signs" that included the growing speed and ease of travel, the increase of knowledge, and the advent of electrical power;[149]

4. "moral signs" tied to his social pessimism, including the rise of murder, divorce, and youth crime;[150]

5. "ecclesiastical signs," marked by what he called the "Great Apostasies," the declension of the Christian church, the rejection of the Bible and the cross, and the growth of the liquor traffic;[151]

6. "spiritual signs" that contrasted with the general moral degradation and that he identified as the "increasing light of faith and holiness." Though he thought that the world was approaching a time of unparalleled wickedness, he also believed that there would be an "unequaled godliness, faith, prayer and the outpouring of the

---

146. Though he was not completely immune to calculating the nearness of Christ's return on the basis of chronology, Simpson put greater confidence in his belief that prophesied events would mark the nearness of Christ's return, for "God does not measure time according to our calendars and chronologies in every instance." Instead, "Spiritual conditions rather than mathematical figures measure God's great epochs" (Simpson, *Coming One*, 183). See also Simpson, *Fourfold Gospel*, 62; and Simpson, "Looking For and Hasting Forward," 557.

147. Simpson, *Coming One*, 183.

148. Ibid., 185. Surprisingly, Simpson identified the runaway growth of democracy as a sign of the end and insinuated that democracies are worse than monarchies. See Simpson, *Earnests of the Coming Age*, 8.

149. Simpson, *Coming One*, 186. Though Simpson believed many of these developments to be truly marvelous and described them as glimpses of what humanity will be able to achieve during the millennium, he did not overlook their potential to be used for evil. See Simpson, *Earnests of the Coming Age*, 5.

150. Simpson, *Coming One*, 188; Simpson, *Earnests of the Coming Age*, 7.

151. Simpson, *Coming One*, 189.

Holy Spirit upon those who are willing to walk with God in holy obedience";[152]

7.   "Jewish signs," including the rise of Zionism, a spiritual awakening among the Jewish people, and the cooperation they were receiving from other nations;[153]

8.   "missionary signs," including "the intense missionary movement that [was] stirring the heart of every earnest section of the Church to-day" and leading to "the evangelization of the world in the present generation;"[154] and, finally, in both order and importance;

9.   "chronological signs," by which Simpson meant the various date-setting schemes, many of which seemed to point to the late nineteenth or early twentieth centuries.[155]

Though Simpson was adamant about the imminence of Christ's return, he would normally refuse to describe it as an "at-any-moment" imminence. Rather he believed that two if not three events must take place first, namely, 1) the preparation of the church in its "separation and sanctification" from the world, 2) the preaching of the gospel to all the world, and 3) the return of the Jewish people to Palestine. The first of these was being completed with the reassertion of the sanctified life evident in the Holiness movement of the late nineteenth century.

Simpson believed that the return of the Jewish people to Palestine would occur in his own lifetime. Later in his life, he noted that World War I and the Russian Revolution had freed "one half of the Jewish population of the world" to return to the land of Palestine. He was deeply moved when British forces occupied Jerusalem in 1917. In the

---

152. Simpson, *Coming One*, 190; Simpson, *Wholly Sanctified*, 3. This would also include an increase of instances of and dependence upon Divine Healing. See Simpson, *Earnests of the Coming Age*, 13; "Simpson, therefore, was persuaded that the widespread spiritual movement for personal holiness in his days was one of the most hopeful signs of the imminent coming of the Lord. Later, however, in the last decade of his life, he presumed that this condition was nearly completed" (Sung, "Doctrine of the Second Advent," 115).

153. Simpson, *Coming One*, 191; Simpson, *Earnests of the Coming Age*, 10.

154. Simpson, *Coming One*, 192; Simpson, *Earnests of the Coming Age*, 13–14.

155. Simpson, *Coming One*, 193.

memorial edition of the *Alliance Weekly*, published just over a week after Simpson's death, the editors related this anecdote:

> He was returning from St. Paul on his last extended tour, when in Chicago, he picked up an extra, telling of the capture of Jerusalem. He immediately hurried to his hotel, and falling on his knees by the bedside, burst into tears of joy, because of the culmination of his life-long hope. He wired to New York that he would preach on the great theme of Jerusalem's fall and its meaning. In spite of unutterable weariness, he delivered his marvelous address, which has been an inspiration to thousands.[156]

The capture of Jerusalem apparently indicated to him that the stage was set for the return of the Jews to the land, and that, consequently, the return of Christ himself was also imminent. In an editorial published approximately two weeks after Allenby's forces entered Jerusalem, he wrote that since Israel was no longer being "trodden down," the world stood on the brink of the eschaton.[157]

He was not alone in understanding the return of the Jews to Palestine as a necessary precursor to the return of Christ. In 1891, W. E. B. Blackstone, a noted Chicago land developer and conference speaker, and the author of *Jesus Is Coming*,[158] drafted the "Blackstone Memorial," a document addressed to President Benjamin Harrison, which called for the return of Palestine to the Jewish people.[159] The four hundred who signed this document included a veritable "Who's Who" of American public life, including such notables as J. P. Morgan, J. D. Rockefeller, and Chief Justice Melville W. Fuller. Also among the signatories were D. L. Moody, A. J. Gordon, and A. T. Pierson. Though Simpson's name did not

---

156. "Editorials." *Alliance Weekly*, 8 November 1919, 97–99.

157. "However gradual its progression may be and however slowly its preliminary unfoldings may appear, the fact remains that we have entered a new zone and we are already in the beginning of the end. Surely it becomes us as never before to watch and pray and stand in continual preparedness for the coming of our Lord" (Simpson, "Editorial," *Alliance Weekly*, 22 December 1917, 177.

158. Blackstone was one of the keynote speakers at the founding meetings of what would become the Christian and Missionary Alliance in 1887. He spoke on the return of Jesus Christ and its relationship to the missionary mandate of the church. He regularly published articles in Alliance periodicals, most often on the topics of eschatology and the role of Israel in the end times.

159. This document predated the more famous Balfour Declaration by over twenty-five years.

appear on the list, he certainly would have supported the intentions of the document.

In keeping with his social pessimism, Simpson did not believe that the conversion of the world was either a necessary sign of Christ's return or even an attainable goal. The idea that the world could be converted was inextricably bound up with the optimism of postmillennial eschatology. However, Simpson believed that a careful and critical examination of history would show that the churched portion of the world's population was, in fact, shrinking. The task of conversion, therefore, was neither "possible nor practical."[160] Rather, Simpson, like the rest of the rest of the subjects of this study, believed that the church's job is to evangelize the world, not to convert it. By the evangelization of the world, he meant the primarily verbal presentation of the gospel apart from any subjective response or change on the part of its hearers. The task, then, was not to convert but to communicate: "The witnessing of the Gospel to all nations is the business of the church in the present age,"[161] but universal conversion is neither the hope nor the goal of this work. Still, the presentation of the gospel was not an end in itself but rather a means of identifying and drawing in all the remaining elect so as to fully and finally bring together the church. With this in mind, Simpson saw the goal of the Christian and Missionary Alliance as "not so much to get the whole human race converted as to gather out of the nations a people for His name and to preach the gospel as a witness unto all nations in order that the truth may be God's magnet for drawing from the mass of unbelieving men the souls that are to constitute the Bride of Christ."[162] Moreover, the church, like Christ himself, not only must be authentically human but must also represent the whole of humanity. While Christ represented the whole of humanity as an individual, the bride of Christ, the church, would only do so by being composed of representatives of each and every nation,[163] "every tribe and tongue, . . . of all races and kindreds and tongues of earth."[164] The elect were

160. Pyles, "Missionary Eschatology," 37.

161. Simpson, *Coming One*, 25.

162. Simpson, "Missionary Standpoints of the Alliance," 205.

163. "God wants us to bring the representatives of earthly tongues, and when this shall have been done, then, He tells us, the end shall come. The Bride of the Lamb, like the Son of man, must represent humanity as a whole" (Simpson, *Coming One*, 222).

164. Simpson, *Coming One*, 25.

"universal in scope, [even if] limited in numbers."[165] Therefore, the church's mission is to fan out across the world and bring in these representatives, for until this aspect of the evangelistic task is complete, Christ will not return. This task of the evangelization of the world, like the return of the Jews to Palestine, needs to be fulfilled before the second advent will occur. As Simpson put it, "[until] the whole number of His elect shall have thus been called and gathered home, His coming would seem to be delayed."[166] Christ will not return until the church, in this representative form, is complete: "When this is done and all who will accept Jesus as Savior have been called, converted and fully trained, the time for the next stage will have come."[167]

Simpson's goals of evangelizing the world, drawing out the elect, and completing the church all gained their impetus from Matthew 24:14: "And this gospel of the kingdom shall be preached in all the world for a witness unto all nations; and then shall the end come" (KJV). He interpreted this verse to mean that "above everything else the preaching of the gospel as a witness in all the world will *hasten the coming of the Lord Jesus Christ* and the age of the Blessing for which the Church is waiting and the faith and hope of God's children have looked forward."[168] The church is not to wait passively for the return of Jesus Christ, but, given the causal and not merely chronological relationship between world evangelization and Christ's return (Matt 24:14), must actively pursue it. In fact, the evangelization of the world and the consequent preparation of the bride was the "Lord's own appointed way of hastening His second coming."[169]

According to Simpson, the Lord's second coming depends on the completion of two different kinds of tasks: those that the Lord himself must accomplish, and those that he has left for his people to complete.[170] He believed that the tasks under the exclusive control of the Lord had

---

165. Ibid., 222.

166. Ibid.

167. Simpson, *Fourfold Gospel*, 61.

168. Simpson, "Motives to Missions," 349 (emphasis added).

169. Simpson, "New Missionary Alliance," 366.

170. "Indeed it is in a measure true that the Lord's people have quite as much to do with hastening His coming as the Lord Himself, by fulfilling the conditions and completing the preparations which He Himself has prescribed" (Simpson, *Coming One*, 183).

all been completed. That of worldwide evangelization, however, was the church's responsibility and was "the great unfulfilled condition of the Lord's return."[171] Therefore, the current "business . . . of the Holy Spirit, and the Church through which He operates"[172] must be its completion. Put more poetically,

> The Master's coming draweth near,
> The Son of man will soon appear,
> His kingdom is at hand.
> *But ere that glorious day can be,*
> *The Gospel of the Kingdom we*
> *Must preach in every land.*[173]

And,

> Soon may our King appear, Haste Bright Millennial Year;
> *We live to bring it near*; Thy kingdom come, Thy kingdom come.[174]

So Christ now waits for humanity to complete its mission.[175] Simpson took great encouragement from this doctrine. Accelerated modes of travel and the opening borders of the late nineteenth century in combination with his somewhat-anomalous residual optimism regarding human ability, led Simpson to believe that the "evangelization of the world in the present generation,"[176] and, therefore, the return of Christ in his generation, were entirely possible.

This view of the relationship between world evangelization and the second advent deeply influenced Simpson's mission strategy. Since only a truly international church would hasten Christ's return,[177] rather than addressing those fields that already possessed an evangelical witness, The Christian and Missionary Alliance focused its attention on neglected and yet-unoccupied mission fields. To work in those areas where an evangelical witness already existed was a redundant use of

171. Simpson, *Gospel in All Lands*, 60.

172. Simpson, *Acts*, 20.

173. Simpson, *Coming One*, 228 (emphasis added).

174. Simpson, "Thy Kingdom Come," 138 (emphasis added).

175. Simpson, "Looking For and Hasting Forward," 557.

176. Simpson, *Coming One*, 193.

177. "When you see the bride arrayed in her wedding robes, you know the Bridegroom must be near" (Simpson, *Coming One*, 203).

resources and, as such, would only delay the return of Christ. The more efficiently this task of the completion of the bride could be accomplished, the sooner Christ would return.[178]

Like Pierson, Simpson believed premillennialism (with its stress on the feasibility of the goal and on evangelization instead of universal conversion) to be the theology most suited to the accomplishment of the missionary task. Postmillennialism, by contrast, had an impossible and impractical goal that always remained out of reach.[179] It could lead only to pessimism and, ultimately, to the abandonment of the missionary enterprise. On the other hand, "[missionaries] are cheered by the blessed thought that their task is not to convert the whole human race but to evangelize the nations and give every man a chance to be saved if he will."[180]

The proper longing of the Christian heart to commune ever more deeply with Christ also serves as an incentive to missionary involvement. This longing can only find its satisfaction in the eschaton, when the believer's intimacy with Christ will be unmediated and complete. Thus those who truly longed for deeper communion with Christ would involve themselves in evangelization in order to bring their relationship with him to perfection. If it was the means of hastening Christ's return, and if his return meant even deeper communion with him, then the truly pious would make this task their priority:

> If we long to see Him, if we long to clasp again the hands that we touched so long ago, if we long for the fulness of our salvation, and the glory of the new creation, let us send forth the gospel into every land and carry the invitation to the Wedding Feast to every creature.[181]

Simpson made hastening Christ's return one of the distinctives of his theology, and just after his death some of his followers claimed that it was unique to him.[182] However, the very same doctrine was the

---

178. "When this is done, and all who will accept Jesus as Savior have been called, converted and fully trained, the time for the next stage will have come" (Simpson, *Fourfold Gospel*, 61).

179. Simpson, "Christ's Coming the Key," 229.

180. Simpson, *Fourfold Gospel*, 62.

181. Simpson, *Heart Messages*, 213–14.

182. In the memorial edition of *The Christian Alliance Weekly*, which came out immediately after Simpson's death, the editor, Walter Turnbull, observed that "he was the

catalyst for a number of other late nineteenth-century figures and agencies, including the other subjects of this study. Dana L. Robert notes that

> [p]rominent missions leaders such as A. T. Pierson, A. J. Gordon, A. B. Simpson, and others felt that they were living during a "crisis of missions": the Holy Spirit in the late nineteenth century was opening the world to Christianity in preparation for the Second Coming of Jesus Christ. It seemed probable that their generation would be the one to preach the gospel from one end of the world to another in fulfillment of Matthew 24:14, "And this gospel of the kingdom shall be preached in all the world for a witness unto all nations and then shall the end come."[183]

Futurism/Dispensationalism

Simpson regularly used language and categories associated with futurism and more particularly with dispensationalism. Some may be tempted to identify him as a dispensationalist because he used the term "dispensation" and because he believed that the seven churches of Revelation can be interpreted figuratively to refer to distinct eras.[184] He even went so far as to say that to exegete Scripture properly, one cannot overlook the determinative role of rightly understanding the dispensations.[185] As has been shown, however, this trait in and of itself does not constitute adequate grounds for such a categorization. Though clearly part of the dispensational schema, dispensations themselves neither are particular to dispensationalism nor serve as the system's sine qua non.

However, Simpson's understanding of the relationship between the church and Israel may be attributed to the direct influence of dispensational theology. Indeed, he broke with his Presbyterian heritage in contending that the church neither supersedes Israel as the particular

---

only great teacher we know who linked the evangelization of the world as a necessary preparation for Christ's return with the study of Bible prophecy" (Turnbull, "Editorial," 8 November 1919, 99). Probably based on Turnbull's assertion, Charles Nienkirchen identifies Simpson as "the only nineteenth-century leader to assert the evangelization of the world as a precondition to Christ's second advent" (Nienkirchen, *A. B. Simpson*, 23).

183. Robert, "Crisis of Missions," 31–32.

184. Simpson, "How I Was Led," 298.

185 Simpson, "Christ's Coming the Key to All Questions of the Age," 228.

people of God nor exists as one confluent entity. Rather, the two terms represent two distinct and eternal peoples of God, each with its own particular destiny and attendant divine promises.[186] Simpson makes a particularly sharp distinction between the two concepts in his defense of the rapture—a distinctly dispensational doctrine, if not the sine qua non of the entire system. Simpson himself believed that there will actually be two comings of Christ at the close of history: the Parousia and the Epiphaneia.[187] The rapture will occur at the time of the Parousia, when Jesus will come secretly in "a visitation in the air."[188] However, he will not at this time present himself majestically to the world and introduce the millennial kingdom. Rather, he will secretly receive the church to himself and remove it from the earth.[189] First, the dead in Christ will be resurrected and enter into his presence. Immediately thereafter will occur "the Rapture of the Saints," or the snatching up of Christians still alive on earth at Christ's return.[190] At the Second Coming, the Epiphaneia, Christ will appear "to the entire world . . . as King and Judge."[191] The Epiphaneia (or Epiphany), and not the Parousia, will be the public and majestic advent of Christ when he will usher in the millennial kingdom.

The interlude between these two advents is an era Simpson and most dispensationalists describe as the Great Tribulation. Following the Parousia, on the heavenly plane where the church is assembled with

186. "There are a number of important points which we should clearly understand in order to follow intelligently these prophetic Scriptures. The first is the distinction between the times of the Gentiles and the times of the chosen people" (Simpson, *Coming One*, 40).

187. "The two principal Greek words used to describe the coming of the Lord Jesus are Parousia and Epiphaneia. The first literally means presence, and the second appearing or manifestation. They have come to be recognized as describing the two aspects of the Lord's return" (Simpson, *Coming One*, 133). See also Simpson, *Heart Messages*, 203.

188. Simpson, *Heart Messages*, 204.

189. "[T]his coming [is] secret." "[T]he thief does not send out a public announcement of his coming, but the first public evidence of his visit is seen after he has gone. So the world will not know that the Lord has come until it wakes some morning to find that all the best people have disappeared" (Simpson, *Coming One*, 133, 134).

190. Ibid., 128, 140.

191. On at least one occasion, Simpson did speak of Jesus's return as being at "any hour." It must be noted, however, that this was an anomaly, and when he did speak of the return of Jesus in this way it was in reference to the rapture, in contrast to the Epiphany and the inauguration of the kingdom. See Simpson, *Fourfold Gospel*, 64.

Christ will occur the consummation of the relationship of the church and Christ, the "beatific joy which the Lord Himself described as the Marriage of the King's Son."[192] Meanwhile, on the earthly plane, the rapture will inaugurate a seven year period during which the grace of God will be removed from the earth.[193] Without the church to restrain the influence of Satan, sin will reach its full potential.[194] It will be "the time when the Antichrist shall reign and all the world shall be under the arbitrary and cruel sway of the last and worst form of human government represented by the Beast."[195]

Although the church will escape this time of terror, Israel, which had rejected Jesus, will not. The Parousia will bring the church age to an end, and God will turn his attention to the salvation of Israel.[196] Israel's full-scale conversion will begin with their political restoration[197] and be brought to completion after the Tribulation at the Epiphaneia: "[When Jesus] appears on earth again there will be no member of the Hebrew race that can lawfully dispute His title, that He is alive to-day, and that [He is] the only living heir to David's throne."[198] That is, when Jesus is manifest in all of his glory and majesty, the Jews will no longer doubt but turn in faith to him. Thus Israel too, though at a different time and through different means, will see Jesus as Lord and be saved through him.

It must be noted that Simpson expressed uncertainty whether the church in its entirety would escape the Great Tribulation. Franklin Pyles has described this wavering, which he asserts occurs only twice—in a sermon on the ten virgins of Matthew 25 and in *The Holy Spirit*—as a "certain . . . fleeting fancy."[199] In *The Coming One*, published in 1912,

192. Simpson, *Coming One*, 141.

193. Contrary to many dispensationalists, Simpson did not equate the tribulation with the pouring out of the seven vials of wrath in Revelation. In keeping (for the most part) with his claim to be a historicist, he believed that the events represented by this image had already occurred, and that they were intended as a preparation for the Parousia. See Simpson, *Heart Messages*, 206–7.

194. Simpson, *Coming One*, 122–126.

195. Ibid., 126.

196. Ibid., 40, 43.

197. "Israel's political restoration will be followed by their conversion to Christ" (Sung, "Doctrine of the Second Advent," 112).

198. Simpson, *Gospel of Matthew*, 3.

199. Pyles, "Missionary Eschatology," 31.

Simpson confidently asserts that the church as a whole will escape the tribulation.[200] Yet as early as 1886, he had wondered whether all who were part of the church and were still alive at the time of the Parousia would be transported with Christ. Simpson tentatively concluded that only those who had experienced both regeneration and sanctification would be raptured by Christ.

> That is why we want divine holiness, that we may be present at the coming of Christ. Beloved, I don't know much about this subject, but I do know that there is an important difference between the holy and those not sanctified. I don't know what becomes of the unsanctified, but I don't think they will go in to the marriage supper of the Lamb.[201]

If they will not attend the marriage supper, then the unsanctified might conceivably have to undergo the Great Tribulation. In any event, having passed through this time of testing, they will be fully redeemed.[202] Though this belief never became a guiding theme of Simpson's theology, and though he may have softened on this issue later in his ministry, he did not totally abandon it, as Pyles claims. For example, in *The Coming One*, published in 1912, Simpson appears to qualify his belief in the rapture of the whole church:

> The Parable of the Ten Virgins in the 25th chapter of Matthew gives us a far-off vision of the Marriage Supper of the Lamb, and suggests with solemn warning the danger that some may miss their place in that blessed company. Surely there must be a difference between the saintly souls that have been "washed and made white and tried," and the men and women who have found their happiness in the things of the world, and would not understand the Rapture of the Bridegroom's love. Are these earth-stained souls, even if saved at last, to have the same place as John of Patmos, and Bernard of Cluny, with Monica and Mary

---

200. "[The church will] escape it, they are caught up in His first coming and are before the throne and before the Lamb with white robes and palms in their hands" (Simpson, *Coming One*, 129).

201. Simpson, "Lord's Second Coming," 170.

202. "I would not make holiness a term of salvation. We are saved by believing in Jesus. But I believe if we are not sanctified we shall not go in when Jesus comes. When he comes back to complete his millennial reign, I think they will be with Him. But they may have come through an ordeal by fire" (Simpson, "Lord's Second Coming," 171).

of Bethany? Surely, the question is enough to make us pause and ask our hearts if it is worth while to run the risk.[203]

Moreover, on at least one occasion, Simpson makes the same assertion in a different context. One such instance occurs in *The Love Life of the Lord* (1891), an exposition of the Song of Solomon:

> Who is meant by this little sister that hath no breasts, or, in other words, who with the years of a woman is still in form a child? Of course it is a type of some class of persons who shall be on earth at the time of the Lord's coming, and who shall be related to the real bride of the Lamb by a bond of sisterhood, but yet shall be different from her in perfection and spiritual maturity, and one who shall be of doubtful purity in the judgment of the Lord, for it must be remembered it was He who asked the question whether she be a wall or a door; that is, a separated one or a loose and lax woman open to every evil influence. What is more natural than to suppose that she represents that portion of the church of Christ which shall not be prepared for the Lord's coming, and which through the fault of its members willingly remains unsanctified.[204]

Apparently Simpson's belief in a partial rapture was something more than a "fleeting fancy."

Despite his pastoral concern for the unsanctified, Simpson refused to make dogmatic assertions about their destiny but chose rather to emphasize the certain reward that would accrue to the sanctified: "I don't know what will become of the unsanctified, but I am sure there will be a difference somehow. But those who are watching and waiting and walking with Jesus, ah!, there is no doubt of what is coming to them."[205] Indeed, the sanctified will meet the Lord at the Parousia, escape the tribulation, and attend the marriage feast of the Lamb.

This view of a partial rapture, with its attendant bifurcation of the eschatological destiny of the church along lines of sanctification, is not, however, exclusive to Simpson. Indeed, its most notable exponent was Robert Govett, fellow of Worcester College, Oxford. Though he never expected his doctrine to become popular,[206] Govett believed

---

203. Simpson, *Coming One*, 142–43.

204. Simpson, *Love Life of the Lord*, 203–4.

205. Simpson, "Lord's Second Coming," 170.

206. Govett, *Entrance*, v.

that though justification is adequate to save in an ultimate sense, it is not enough to entitle one to the reward of reigning with Christ in his kingdom through the millennium. Those who will share Christ's reign will do so on the basis of their actual behavior and not their regenerative standing alone.[207] All the regenerate will participate in the eternal life that will follow the millennium, but not all will participate in the life of the kingdom itself.[208]

Although both Simpson and Govett agreed that the sanctified will receive privileges in the eschaton that the unsanctified will not, they differed considerably in the particulars of their beliefs. Govett believed that the unsanctified will not participate at all in the millennial kingdom, but Simpson only asserted that the unsanctified may not escape the Great Tribulation. The actual millennial kingdom, according to Simpson, will begin with the whole of the church being brought together with Christ. The unsanctified will not take part in either the rapture or the first grand reunion with Christ, but they will participate fully in the millennial kingdom from the beginning. Another point of difference was Govett's belief that admittance to the millennial kingdom is a reward for righteous deeds. Simpson did not deny the importance of deeds, but he regarded them as being simply consequential to a more determinative experience of Christ through the agency of the baptism of the Holy Spirit. As was noted in a previous chapter, the heart of sanctification for Simpson lies in the nature of one's relation to Christ. Govett's language of achievement and reward is thus somewhat foreign to him.

Simpson believed that the Parousia will usher in the Great Tribulation, and that the Epiphaneia will inaugurate the millennial kingdom. Only the Epiphaneia will be "public and visible to all the world."[209] This one-thousand-year reign, as prophesied in Revelation 20:4, will take place on the earth. The personal, visible, enduring presence of Jesus Christ will result in the "most glorious and complete evangelization earth has ever seen,"[210] including the conversion of the Jews. Moreover, the world will be "brought into subjugation to Christ, and ostensibly at

---

207. Govett, *Entrance*, 2.

208. "'Will all believers reign with Christ?' By no means. The kingdom of the thousand years is never said to belong to those who only believe" (Govett, *Govett on Revelation*, vol. 2, 233).

209. Simpson, *Coming One*, 151.

210. Simpson, *Fourfold Gospel*, 62.

least, shall be righteous and obedient."[211] As a result, it will be a place of "righteousness and peace," where "wickedness and war [have been] abolished."[212] The millennium itself will be "a state and time of exalted glory and happiness."[213] This state of bliss will come about because of the presence of Christ and his kingdom of holiness and righteousness, and the consequent absence of Satan[214] (who has been bound) and of the diabolical social structures that have oppressed humanity and have led it astray.[215] For Simpson, the presence of Christ lies at the heart of the eschaton. His presence coupled with the absence of Satan is all that is needed "to make a heaven."[216] Simpson believed that the personal and visible return of Jesus Christ alone is the focal point of eschatology and the eschaton. All the other benefits are merely consequential. Therefore, those eschatologies that focus on events, dates, and the perfection of society instead of on the personal and visible return of Jesus Christ miss the mark.

This does not mean that Simpson did not look forward eagerly to the consequences of Christ's advent. Foremost among the blessings that he anticipated was the fulfillment of those things that the church was only able to have imperfectly, yet still blessedly, in the previous age: "Not only will we have the presence of the Lord Jesus, but our own state will be as glorious as His. We shall be like Him."[217] This perfection will consist not merely in attaining one's greatest potential but in divine transformation. It will involve both a quantitative and a qualitative change: "God's highest thought is [neither] self-improvement [for the individual] nor the best possible result of natural character and human

211. Simpson, *Coming One*, 156.

212. Ibid.

213. Simpson, *Fourfold Gospel*, 58.

214. Simpson, *Coming One*, 153.

215. "Not only will Satan be cast out, but the great systems of evil through which he has governed men. These include first, the forms of human government which have oppressed the world since the days of Egypt; second, the forms of false religion that have worshipped Satan in the name of God, and sanctioned every enormity and evil under the guise of the good. Three especially of these have been the curse of the ages, viz.: Romanism, Mohammedanism, and Paganism" (Simpson, *Coming One*, 154–55).

216. Simpson, *Coming One*, 158.

217. Ibid., 159.

culture, but a new creation, a regeneration so complete that old things pass away and all things are made new." [218]

Primary among these benefits will be the perfection of what God's people had already experienced in sanctification and Divine Healing. These two blessings are only imperfect "earnests" of the fullness of what will be experienced in the final resurrection. In the realm of the physical, "[w]e shall bear the image of His resurrection body. We shall have His marvelous beauty, and His mighty powers." [219] Furthermore, "[we] shall know no pain or weakness; we shall feel our being thrill with the pulses of His glorious life and the Rapture and ecstacy of eternal health and strength." [220] The frailties and limitations of believers' current physical existence will be overcome, but more important, their "spiritual and intellectual nature shall be conformed to His likeness. [They] shall be holy as He is holy." [221]

Conclusion

Following his conversion from Presbyterian postmillennial optimism, Simpson remained a consistent premillennialist. As such, he had the same eschatological convictions as a rapidly growing number of American evangelicals. As has been shown, not only was his premillennialism common, but many of the distinctive beliefs of his particular kind of premillennialism were not atypical either. In fact, like Simpson, his contemporaries D. L. Moody, A. J. Gordon, and A. T. Pierson believed in the imminence of Christ's return, rejected postmillennial optimism regarding the prospects of human achievement, distinguished between Israel and the church, taught that the church would be raptured, and regarded the evangelization of the world as both a preferential goal to the conversion of the world and a means of hastening Christ's return. Furthermore, their premillennial eschatology included traces of dispensationalism, and all four were at once inconsistent historicists and inconsistent dispensationalists. Even where Simpson deviated from Moody, Gordon, and Pierson (most notably on the doctrine of the

218. Ibid., 214.
219. Ibid., 160.
220. Ibid.
221. Ibid.

partial rapture of the church), he did not venture into wholly unex-plored territory even though he differed significantly with Govett.

"Thy Kingdom Come"

O Christ, My Lord and King,
This is the prayer I bring,
This is the song I sing:
Thy Kingdom come, Thy Kingdom come.

Help me to work and pray,
Help me to live each day
That all I do may say,
Thy Kingdom come, Thy Kingdom come.

Upon my heart's high throne,
Rule Thou, and Thou alone;
Let me be all Thine own!
Thy Kingdom come, Thy Kingdom come.

Through all the earth abroad,
Wherever man has trod;
Send forth Thy Word, O God—
Thy Kingdom come, Thy Kingdom come.

Soon may our King appear!
Haste bright millennial year!
We live to bring it near.
Thy Kingdom come, Thy Kingdom come.[222]

222. Simpson, "Thy Kingdom Come," in *Hymns of the Christian Life*, 472.

6

Conclusion:
The Heart of the Gospel

A. E. Thompson, who was A. B. Simpson's authorized biographer, lionizes him as "[a] Modern Prophet" and a "Great Teacher"[1] who had been divinely equipped and invigorated for this vocation and who was "more than a great pulpiteer, evangelist, and pastor. . . . [He] was lifted into the circle of those to whom are committed the oracles of God."[2] Some within The Christian and Missionary Alliance assume that this hagiographical portrait has no basis in fact and dismiss Simpson as an insignificant figure within American religious life. As is often the case in such instances, however, the truth may very well lie somewhere between these two extremes.

Simpson's "oracles" were not wholly original. Each of the doctrines he adopted and championed, and even his expressions of these doctrines, already existed and were gaining popularity within contemporary evangelicalism. He neither conjured them *ex nihilo* nor received these oracles directly from heaven. He merely followed, developed, and further popularized contemporary theological trends and teaching. His contribution, therefore, was not as a theological innovator.

---

1. "A Modern Prophet" is the chapter in which the term "Great Teacher" is found. See Thompson, *Life of A. B. Simpson*, 201.

2. Thompson, *Life of A. B. Simpson*, 195. A little later, Thompson, furthering Simpson's elevation over his peers, recounts an anecdote in which D. L. Moody, while in New York, is to have told A. T. Pierson about having just heard Simpson preach: "Pierson, I have just been down to hear A. B. Simpson preach. No one gets at my heart like that man" (quoted in Thompson, *Life of A. B. Simpson*, 200).

Simpson's contribution, however, lies in his bringing together these four christological tenets into one larger gestalt and naming it the "Fourfold Gospel."[3] He believed that most people of his day, Christian or not, were not experiencing the holistic ministry of Christ epitomized in this novel doctrinal formulation. The Christ of his gospel brings not only a salvation that includes regeneration and justification, but also some less-predictable essential elements (sanctification and divine healing) and promises their fulfilment and perfection at Christ's premillennial return. Simpson believed that the great majority of Christians were either settling for a "half-salvation"[4] of regeneration alone or believed that no further benefits of Christ's work are necessary to humanity in the present age. Simpson was convinced, however, that the saving ministry of Jesus, by the design of God and the eternal nature of Christ, was as far-reaching, profound, and effectual as the fall,[5] and so not to pursue salvation to its fullest extent would be to fall short God's will for humanity.

However, these four tenets (regeneration/justification, sanctification, divine healing, and premillennial eschatology) composed not only Simpson's "Fourfold Gospel" but the doctrinal heart of the gospel of other leading evangelicals as well. To be sure, Simpson used his own particular language to explicate his gospel, and he also gave each tenet a unique emphasis. Nevertheless, D. L. Moody, A. J. Gordon, and A. T. Pierson gave all four of Simpson's emphases pride of place in their messages and ministries, and all three men defined them much as Simpson had.

Significantly, Simpson, Moody, Gordon, and Pierson were leading (if not *the* leading) evangelicals in the four great American cities of the day, respectively: New York, Chicago, Boston, and Philadelphia. The Fourfold Gospel, then, was peculiar neither to one man nor to one region; neither did it develop in isolation. The combined stature and popularity of the four revivalists enabled this particular doctrinal formulation to reach and influence thousands if not millions of late nineteenth-century Americans. The Fourfold Gospel, then, was not a

3. As John Sawin notes, Simpson claimed that the title "Fourfold Gospel" was given to him by divine inspiration, and that others near him credited him with so naming the *gestalt*.

4. See Sawin, "Fourfold Gospel," 3. See also Hardesty, *Faith Cure*, 92.

5. Simpson, "Himself," in *Hymns of the Christian Life*, 248.

theology of the margins. It was popular American evangelical theology.[6] Consequently, the Fourfold Gospel serves a determinative role in identifying the extent to which other theologies of that era were truly part of the evangelical mainstream. The degree and extent to which a given theology conforms to the Fourfold Gospel is the degree and extent to which it may be identified as a thoroughgoing late nineteenth-century evangelical theology.[7]

Since the Fourfold Gospel is paradigmatic, late nineteenth-century evangelical orthodoxy cannot be interpreted simply as Reformed orthodoxy. Indeed, Simpson, in developing his theology, broke with his own Presbyterian heritage, and though the break was not exhaustive, it was definitive. As has been shown above, each aspect of the Fourfold Gospel is distinct from its historic Reformed counterpart. On more than one occasion, a figure no less than Reformed stalwart and Princeton Theological Seminary professor B. B. Warfield questioned Simpson's theology and Reformed identity. He not only criticized Simpson's understanding of both sanctification and healing, he also challenged the foundation of all of Simpson's theology—his mystic christocentrism.[8] Warfield completed his criticism of the Fourfold Gospel by denying the legitimacy of Simpson's eschatology.[9] In criticizing Simpson, however, he also criticized Moody, Gordon,[10] and Pierson. Ironically, in accurate-

---

6. Simpson, *Gospel of Healing*, 29.

7. Simpson and the early Alliance leadership understood it as such. When challenged that their teachings fell outside of the purview of evangelical orthodoxy, they responded that to subscribe to the Fourfold Gospel was to subscribe to evangelical theology. While the Alliance understood itself to be evangelical in its teaching and practices on issues beyond the particular realm of the Fourfold Gospel, it believed that the Fourfold Gospel itself was thoroughly evangelical, too. "[The] principles [of the C&MA], in all other respects *also*, are thoroughly evangelical" (Simpson, "Is the Christian Alliance an Evangelical Body?" 274; emphasis added).

8. Of particular significance in this respect is the hotly debated issue of the relationship of Pentecostalism to mainstream evangelicalism. As recent scholarship as shown, Pentecostalism finds its theological roots in the Fourfold Gospel, and so it can legitimately consider itself part of mainstream evangelicalism. Donald Dayton, more than any other single author, has identified Pentecostalism's debt to late nineteenth-century evangelical theology and refers to Simpson as a key theological contributor to the development of the Pentecostal movement.

9. In faint praise, Warfield notes that all Simpson does is to take the doctrine of Charles G. Trumbull to its logical conclusion. See Warfield, *Perfectionism*, 2:597–600.

10. Warfield, *Selected Shorter Writings*, 355.

ly distinguishing his own position from that of the revivalists, Warfield inadvertently placed himself and the Princeton Theology beyond the borders of turn-of-the-century evangelical theology.[11]

Thus Simpson and the Fourfold Gospel rather than Warfield and Princetonian orthodoxy are the standard by which late nineteenth-century evangelicalism (and, perhaps, even late nineteenth-century American popular culture, religious and otherwise) ought to be identified and understood. Hence Simpson, given his representative role, must be taken seriously as a pivotal and defining figure of late nineteenth-century evangelicalism and evangelical theology. The Fourfold Gospel, far from being heterodox and idiosyncratic, needs to be understood as the heart of the gospel.

11. Warfield criticizes Gordon directly on the issue of healing. In fact, Gordon is the main target of Warfield's attack in his chapter "Faith-Healing" in *Counterfeit Miracles*. See Warfield, *Counterfeit Miracles*, 157–96. In this same chapter, Warfield identifies Simpson as a man of integrity in a movement prone to be less than virtuous. Yet Warfield does not refrain from calling Simpson's theology of healing spurious. See Warfield, *Counterfeit Miracles*, 195.

"Jesus Only"

Jesus only is our message,
Jesus all our theme shall be;
We will lift up Jesus ever,
Jesus only will we see.

Jesus only, Jesus ever,
Jesus all in all we sing,
Saviour, Sanctifier, and Healer,
Glorious Lord and coming King.

Jesus only is our Saviour,
All our guilt He bore away,
All our righteousness He gives us,
All our strength from day to day.

Jesus is our Sanctifier,
Cleansing us from self and sin,
And with all His Spirit's fullness,
Filling all our hearts within.

Jesus only is our Healer,
All our sicknesses He bear,
And His risen life and fullness,
All His members still may share.

Jesus only is our Power,
He the gift of Pentecost;
Jesus, breathe Thy power upon us,
Fill us with the Holy Ghost.

And for Jesus we are waiting,
Listening for the advent call;
But 'twill still be Jesus only,
Jesus ever, all in all.[1213]

12. With respect to Warfield's critique of Simpson's theology, Mark Ellingsen's erroneous claim that Simpson received his education at Princeton is ironic. See Ellingsen, *Evangelical Movement*, 142.

13. Simpson, "Jesus Only," in *Hymns of the Christian Life*, 398.

Bibliography

Anderson, Robert Mapes. *Vision of the Disinherited: the Making of American Pente-costalism*. New York: Oxford University Press, 1979.

Barabas, Steven. *So Great Salvation: The History and Message of the Keswick Convention*. Westwood, NJ: Revell, 1952.

Bebbington, David. "The Advent Hope in British Evangelicalism since 1800." *Scottish Journal of Religious Studies* 9 (Autumn 1988) 103–14.

———. *Holiness in Nineteenth-Century England*. Carlisle, UK: Paternoster, 2000.

Blumhardt, Johann Christoph. *Pastor Blumhardt: Selections from His Life and Ministry*. New York: Christian Alliance, 1902.

Blumhofer, Edith L. *Aimee Semple McPherson: Everybody's Sister*. Grand Rapids: Eerdmans, 1993.

———. *Restoring the Faith: The Assemblies of God, Pentecostalism, and American Culture*. Urbana: University of Illinois Press, 1993.

Boardman, Mary. *Life and Labours of the Rev. W. E. Boardman*. London: Bemrose & Sons, 1886.

Boardman, W. E. *The Higher Christian Life*. 1858. Reprint, The Higher Christian Life series. New York: Garland, 1984.

Boyer, Paul. *When Time Shall Be No More: Prophecy Belief in Modern American Culture*. Studies in Cultural History. Cambridge, MA: Belknap, 1992.

Brumback, Carl. *Suddenly . . . From Heaven: A History of the Assemblies of God*. Springfield, MO: Gospel Publishing House, 1961.

Bundy, David D. "Keswick: A Bibliographic Introduction to the Higher Life Movements." In *The Higher Christian Life: A Bibliographical Overview*, with a preface by Donald W. Dayton, 111–94. 1975. Reprint, The Higher Christian Life series. New York: Garland, 1985.

———. "Keswick and the Experience of Evangelical Piety." In *Modern Christian Revivals*, edited by Edith L. Blumhofer and Randall Balmer, 118–44. Urbana: University of Illinois Press, 1993.

Campbell, Reginald J. *The New Theology*. London: George Bell & Sons, 1907.

Carpenter, Joel A. "Propagating the Faith Once Delivered: The Fundamentalist Missionary Enterprise, 1920–1945." In *Earthen Vessels: American Evangelicals and Foreign Missions, 1880–1980*, edited by Joel A. Carpenter and Wilbert R. Schenk, 92–132. Grand Rapids: Eerdmans, 1990.

Carpenter, Joel A., and Wilbert R. Schenk, editors. *Earthen Vessels: American Evangelicals and Foreign Missions, 1880–1980*. Grand Rapids: Eerdmans, 1990.

Carter, R. Kelso. *"Faith Healing" Reviewed after Twenty Years*. Boston: Christian Witness, 1897.

Chappell, Paul Gale. "The Divine Healing Movement in America." PhD diss., Drew University, 1983.

Charlottetown Guardian, 23 November 1914.

The Christian Alliance. *The Christian Alliance Yearbook (1888)*. Nyack, NY: Word, Work, and World Publishing, 1888.

The Christian and Missionary Alliance. *Annual Report of the Christian and Missionary Alliance (Reorganized) New Constitution and Principles (1912)*. New York: Christian and Missionary Alliance, 1913.

The Christian and Missionary Alliance in Canada, "Statistics." Online: http://cmalliance.ca/statisticsp88.php.

Committee for Christian Education & Publications. *The Confession of Faith; Together with the Larger Catechism and the Shorter Catechism with Scripture Proofs*. 3d edition. Atlanta: Committee for Christian Education & Publications, 1990.

"Constitution of the Evangelical Missionary Alliance (1887) A New Missionary Alliance." *Word, Work, and World* (August/September 1887) 40–41.

Cox, Harvey. *Fire from Heaven: The Rise of Pentecostal Spirituality and the Reshaping of Religion in the Twenty-first Century*. Reading, MA: Addison-Wesley, 1995.

Cunningham, Raymond J. "From Holiness to Healing: The Faith Cure in America 1872–1892." *Church History* 43 (1974) 499–513.

Dahms, John. "'The Social Interest and Concern of A. B. Simpson" in *Birth of a Vision: Essays on the Ministry and Thought of Albert B. Simpson, Founder of the Christian and Missionary Alliance*, edited by David F. Hartzfeld and Charles Nienkirchen, 49–74. Beaverlodge, AB: His Dominion, 1986.

Damsteegt, P. Gerard. *Foundations of the Seventh-Day Adventist Message and Mission*. Grand Rapids: Eerdmans, 1977.

Daniels, W. H. *Dr. Cullis and His Work*. 1885. Reprint, The Higher Christian Life series. New York: Garland, 1985.

Dayton, Donald W. *Discovering an Evangelical Heritage*. New York: Harper & Row, 1976.

———. "Preface." In *The Higher Christian Life: A Bibliographical Overview*, vii–x. 1975. Reprint, The Higher Christian Life series. New York: Garland, 1985.

———. "Presidential Address: The Wesleyan Option for the Poor." *Wesleyan Theological Journal* 26 (1991) 7–22.

———. "The Rise of the Evangelical Healing Movement." *Pneuma* 1 (Spring 1982) 1–18.

———. *Theological Roots of Pentecostalism*. Foreword by Martin E. Marty. Studies in Evangelicalism 5. Metuchen, NJ: Scarecrow, 1987.

———. "Whither Evangelicalism?" In *Sanctification & Liberation: Liberation Theologies in Light of the Wesleyan Tradition*, edited by Theodore Runyon, 142–63. Nashville: Abingdon, 1981.

———, editor. *The Prophecy Conference Movement*. Vol. 1. New York: Garland, 1988.

Dick, Everett N. "The Millerite Movement 1830–1845." In *Adventism in America: A History*, edited by Gary Land, 1–35. Grand Rapids: Eerdmans, 1986.

Dieter, Melvin Easterday. *The Holiness Revival of the Nineteenth Century*. 2nd edition. Studies in Evangelicalism 1. Lanham, MD: Scarecrow, 1996.

Dorsett, Lyle W. *A Passion for Souls: the Life of D. L. Moody*. Chicago: Moody, 1997.

Dowie, John Alexander. "Afternoon Service, Jan. 24, 1897: Repentance!" *Leaves of Healing* 3:16 (1897) 248–54.

Eddy, Mary Baker G. *Science and Health with a Key to the Scriptures.* Boston: The First Church of Christ, Scientist, 1994.

"Editorials." *Alliance Weekly* (8 November 1919) 97–99.

Edwards, Jonathan. *A Faithful Narrative of the Surprising Work of God.* N.d. Reprint, Grand Rapids: Baker, 1979.

Ellingsen, Mark. *The Evangelical Movement: Growth, Impact, Controversy, Dialog.* Minneapolis: Augsburg, 1988.

Evearitt, Daniel J. *Body and Soul: Evangelism and the Social Concern of A. B. Simpson.* Camp Hill, PA: Christian Publications, 1994.

———. "The Social Gospel vs. Personal Salvation: A Late Nineteenth-Century Case Study—Walter Rauschenbusch and A. B. Simpson." In *Alliance Academic Review 1997,* edited by Elio Cuccaro, 1–18. Camp Hill, PA: Christian Publications, 1997.

Faupel, David W. "The American Pentecostal Movement: A Bibliographic Essay." In *The Higher Christian Life: A Bibliographical Overview.* 57–110. 1975. Reprint, The Higher Christian Life series. New York: Garland, 1985.

———. *The Everlasting Gospel: The Significance of Eschatology in the Development of Pentecostal Thought.* Sheffield: Sheffield Academic, 1996.

Ferngren, Gary B. "The Evangelical-Fundamentalist Tradition." In *Caring and Curing: Health and Medicine in the Western Religious Traditions,* edited by Ronald L. Numbers and Darrel W. Amundsen, 486–513. New York: Macmillan, 1986.

Findlay, James F. *Dwight L. Moody: American Evangelist, 1837–1899.* Chicago: University of Chicago Press, 1969.

Finney, Charles G. *Finney's Systematic Theology (1878).* Compiled and edited by Dennis Carroll, Bill Nicely, and L. G. Parkhurst, Jr. New expanded edition. Minneapolis: Bethany House, 1994.

———. *Revivals of Religion.* Edited by William Henry Harding. 3rd revised edition. London: Oliphants, 1928.

Frank, Douglas W. *Less than Conquerors: How Evangelicals Entered the Twentieth Century.* Grand Rapids: Eerdmans, 1986.

Fraser, Brian J. *Church, College, and Clergy: A History of Theological Education at Knox College, Toronto, 1844–1994.* McGill-Queens Studies in the History of Religion 20. Montreal: McGill-Queen's University Press, 1995.

Gilbertson, Richard. *The Baptism of the Holy Spirit: The Views of A. B. Simpson and His Contemporaries.* Camp Hill, PA: Christian Publications, 1993.

Goen, C. C. "Jonathan Edwards: A New Departure in Eschatology." In *Critical Essays on Jonathan Edwards,* edited by William J. Scheick, 25–40. Critical Essays on American Literature. Boston: Hall, 1980.

Goff, James R. Jr. *Fields White Unto Harvest: Charles F. Parham and the Missionary Origins of Pentecostalism.* Fayetteville: University of Arkansas Press, 1988.

Gordon, A. J. *A. J. Gordon,* introduction by Nathan R. Wood. Great Pulpit Masters 8. New York: Revell, 1951.

———. *Ecce Venit.* London: Hodder & Stoughton, 1890.

———. *Grace and Glory: Sermons For the Life That Now Is and That Which Is to Come.* Chicago: Revell, 1880.

———. *The Holy Spirit in Missions.* London: Hodder & Stoughton, 1893.

———. *In Christ, or, The Believer's Union with His Lord.* New York, Revell, 1880.

———. *Ministry of Healing: Miracles of Cure In All Ages.* New York: Christian Alliance Publishing, 1882.

———. *The Ministry of the Spirit.* New York: Revell, 1894.

———. *The Twofold Life, or, Christ's Work for Us and Christ's Work in Us.* 2nd edition. New York: Revell, 1884.

———. *Yet Speaking: A Collection of Addresses.* London: James Nisbet, 1897.

Gordon, A. J., and Arthur T. Pierson, editors. *The Coronation Hymnal: A Selection of Hymns and Songs.* Philadelphia: American Baptist Publication Society, 1894.

Gordon, Ernest B. *Adoniram Judson Gordon: A Biography.* 1896. Reprint, The Higher Christian Life series. New York: Garland, 1984.

Govett, Robert. *Entrance into the Kingdom, or, Reward according to Works.* Miami Springs, FL: Conley & Schoettle, 1978.

———. *Govett on Revelation.* Vol. 2. N.p., 1861. Reprint, Original title *The Apocalypse: Expounded by Scripture* by Matheetees (pseudonym for Robert Govett). Miami Springs, FL: Conley & Schoettle, 1981.

Gundry, Stanley N. *Love Them In: The Proclamation Theology of D. L. Moody.* Chicago: Moody, 1976.

Hardesty, Nancy A. *Faith Cure: Divine Healing in the Holiness and Pentecostal Movements.* Peabody, MA: Hendrickson, 2003.

Hardman, Keith J. *Seasons of Refreshing: Evangelism and Revivals in America.* Grand Rapids: Baker, 1994.

Harford, C. F. *The Keswick Convention, Its Message, Its Method, and Its Men.* London: Marshall Brothers, n.d.

Hartzfeld, David F., and Charles Nienkirchen, editors. *Birth of a Vision: Essays on the Ministry and Thought of Albert B. Simpson, Founder of the Christian and Missionary Alliance.* Beaverlodge, AB: His Dominion, 1986.

Hicks, John Mark. "What Did Christ's Sacrifice Accomplish: Atonement in Early Restorationist Thought." Paper presented at the annual meeting of the Society of Biblical Literature. Chicago, Illinois, November 1994.

Howard, Ivan. "Wesley versus Phoebe Palmer: An Extended Controversy." *Wesleyan Theological Journal* 6 (1971) 31–40.

Hutchison, William R. "A Moral Equivalent for Imperialism: Americans and the Promotion of 'Christian Civilization,' 1880–1910." In *Missionary Ideologies in the Imperialist Era: 1880–1920,* edited by Torben Christenson and William R. Hutchison, 167–78. Århus, Denmark: Aros, 1982.

Hymns of the Christian Life: A Book of Worship in Song Emphasizing Evangelism, Missions, and the Deeper Life. Revised and enlarged edition. Harrisburg, PA: Christian Publications, 1978.

Jones, Charles Edwin. *A Guide to the Study of the Holiness Movement.* ATLA Bibliography Series 1. Metuchen, NJ: American Theological Library Association and Scarecrow, 1974.

———. *Perfectionist Persuasion: The Holiness Movement and American Methodism, 1867–1936.* ATLA Monograph Series 5. Metuchen, NJ: Scarecrow, 1974.

Jordan, Philip D. *The Evangelical Alliance for the United States of America, 1847–1900: Ecumenism, Identity and the Religion of the Republic.* Studies in American Religion 7. New York: Mellen, 1982.

Judd, Carrie F. *Prayer of Faith.* New York: Revell, 1880.

Kane, J. Herbert. *Understanding Christian Missions*. Grand Rapids: Baker, 1974.

Kelsey, Morton T. *Healing and Christianity: In Ancient Thought and Modern Times*. New York: Harper & Row, 1973.

Kinlaw, Dennis. "Foreword." In *Birth of a Vision: Essays on the Ministry and Thought of Albert B. Simpson, Founder of the Christian and Missionary Alliance*, edited by David F. Hartzfeld and Charles Nienkirchen, ix–xi. Beaverlodge, AL: His Dominion, 1986.

Kostlevy, William. *Holiness Manuscripts: A Guide to Sources Documenting the Wesleyan Holiness Movement in the United States and Canada*. ATLA Bibliography Series 34. Metuchen, NJ: American Theological Library Association and Scarecrow, 1994.

LaBerge, Agnes N. O. *What Hath God Wrought*. n.d. Reprint, The Higher Christian Life series. New York: Garland, 1985.

Latourette, Kenneth Scott. *The Great Century: Europe and the United States*. Vol. 4, *A History of the Expansion of Christianity*. Grand Rapids: Zondervan, 1970.

Long, Kathryn Teresa. *The Revival of 1857–58: Interpreting an American Religious Awakening*. Religion in America Series. New York: Oxford University Press, 1998.

MacLean, J. Kennedy, editor. *Dr. Pierson and His Mission*. London: Marshall Brothers, n.d.

Magnuson, Norris. *Salvation in the Slums: Evangelical Social Work, 1865–1920*. Grand Rapids: Baker, 1977.

Marsden, George M. *Fundamentalism and American Culture: The Shaping of Twentieth-Century Evangelicalism: 1870–1925*. New York: Oxford University Press, 1980.

Matthews, Douglas K. "Approximating the Millennium: Toward a Coherent Premillennial Theology of Social Transformation." PhD diss., Baylor University, 1992.

McGraw, Gerald E. "The Doctrine of Sanctification in the Published Writings of Albert Benjamin Simpson." PhD diss., New York University, 1986.

McKaig, Charles Donald. "The Educational Philosophy of A. B. Simpson, Founder of the Christian and Missionary Alliance." PhD diss., New York University, 1948.

McLoughlin, William G. *Modern Revivalism: Charles Grandison Finney to Billy Graham*. New York: Ronald Press, 1959.

———. *Revivals, Awakenings, and Reform: An Essay on Religion and Social Change in America, 1607–1977*. Chicago History of American Religion. Chicago: University of Chicago Press, 1978.

McPherson, Aimee Semple. *Aimee Semple McPherson: The Story of My Life*. Edited by Raymond L. Cox. Waco, TX: Word, 1973.

McQuilkin J. Robertson. "The Keswick Perspective." In *Five Views on Sanctification* by Melvin E. Dieter et al., 151–95. Grand Rapids: Academie, 1987.

Menzies, William. "Non-Wesleyan Origins of the Pentecostal Movement." In *Aspects of Charismatic-Pentecostal Origins*, edited by Vinson Synan, 81–98. Plainfield, NJ: Logos International, 1975.

Minus, Paul M. *Walter Rauschenbusch, American Reformer*. New York: Macmillan, 1988.

Moberg, David. *Inasmuch: Christian Social Responsibility in the Twentieth Century.* Grand Rapids: Eerdmans, 1965.

Moody, Dwight Lyman. *The Best of D. L. Moody.* Edited by Ralph Turnbull. Grand Rapids: Baker, 1990.

———. *Glad Tidings. Comprising Sermons and Prayer-Meeting Talks, Delivered at the New York Hippodrome.* New York: E. B. Treat, 1877.

———. *God's Abundant Grace.* Updated edition. Originally published as *God's Sovereign Grace.* 1891. Reprint, Chicago: Moody, 1998.

———. *Notes from My Bible: From Genesis to Revelation.* Chicago, Revell, 1895.

———. "The Second Coming of Christ." In *The Second Coming of Christ,* Harriet Beecher Stowe, et al., 16–32. Chicago: Moody, n.d.

———. *Sovereign Grace: Its Source, Its Nature, Its Effects, and Other Addresses.* London: Marshall, Morgan, & Scott, 1900.

———. *Success in the Christian Life.* Grand Rapids: Baker, 1972.

———. "There Is No Difference." *Fundamentalist Journal* 8 (1989) 47.

Moody, Dwight Lyman, and Charles F. Goss. *Echoes from the Pulpit and Platform, or, Living Truths for Head and Heart.* Hartford, CT: Worthington, 1900.

Moorhead, James H. "Prophecy, Millennialism, and Biblical Interpretation in Nineteenth-Century America." In *Biblical Hermeneutics in Historical Perspective: Studies in Honor of Karlfried Froehlich on His Sixtieth Birthday,* edited by Mark S. Burrows and Paul Rorem, 291–302. Grand Rapids: Eerdmans, 1991.

Moule, H. C. G. *Christ and the Christian: Words Spoken at Keswick.* London: Marshall Brothers, n.d.

———. *The Epistle to the Romans.* London: Pickering & Inglis, n.d.

———. *The Old Gospel for the New Age and Other Sermons.* Chicago: Revell, 1901.

———. *Outlines of Christian Doctrine.* New York: Thomas Whittaker, 1889.

———. *Thoughts on Christian Sanctity.* London: Seeley, 1885.

———. *Thoughts on Union with Christ.* London: Seeley, 1890.

Nienkirchen, Charles. *A. B. Simpson and the Pentecostal Movement: A Study in Continuity, Crisis, and Change.* Peabody, MA: Hendrickson, 1992.

Niklaus, Robert L., et al. *All for Jesus: God at Work in the Christian and Missionary Alliance Over One Hundred Years.* Camp Hill, PA: Christian Publications, 1986.

Numbers, Ronald L., and David R. Larson. "The Adventist Tradition." In *Caring and Curing: Health and Medicine in the Western Religious Traditions,* edited by Ronald L. Numbers and Darrel W. Amundsen, 447–67. New York: Macmillan, 1986.

Oden, Thomas C., editor. *Phoebe Palmer: Selected Writings.* Sources of American Spirituality. New York: Paulist, 1988.

———. "Introduction." In *Phoebe Palmer: Selected Writings,* 1–29, edited by Thomas C. Oden. Sources of American Spirituality. New York: Paulist, 1988.

Orr, J. Edwin. *The Event of the Century: The 1857–1858 Awakening.* Edited by Richard Owen Roberts. Wheaton, IL: International Awakening Press, 1989.

Palmer, Phoebe. *The Devotional Writings of Phoebe Palmer.* 1867. Reprint, The Higher Christian Life series. New York: Garland, 1985.

———, editor. *Pioneer Experiences, or, The Gift of Power Received by Faith.* 1868. Reprint, The Higher Christian Life series. New York: Garland, 1984.

Pardington, G. P. *Twenty-five Wonderful Years, 1889–1914: A Popular Sketch of the Christian and Missionary Alliance.* 1914. Reprint, The Higher Christian Life series. New York: Garland, 1984.

Park, Myung Soo. "Concepts of Holiness in American Evangelicalism: 1835–1915." PhD diss., Boston University, 1992.

Patterson, Mark, and Andrew Walker. "'Our Unspeakable Comfort': Irving, Albury, and the Origins of the Pretribulational Rapture." *Fides et Historia* 36 (Winter/Spring 1999) 66–81.

Pearse, Mark Guy. "Preface." In *Life and Labours of the Rev. W. E. Boardman*, by Mary Boardman, v–viii. London: Bemrose & Sons, 1886.

Pierson, Arthur T. *The Acts of the Holy Spirit.* New York: Revell, 1895. Reprint. Harrisburg, PA: Christian Publications, 1980.

———. *The Believer's Life; Its Past, Present, and Future Tenses.* London: Pickering & Inglis, 1900.

———. *The Coming of the Lord.* Chicago: Revell, 1896.

———. *Forward Movements of the Last Half Century.* 1905. Reprint, The Higher Christian Life series. New York: Garland, 1984.

———. *George Müller of Bristol and His Witness to a Prayer-Hearing God.* New York: Revell, 1899.

———. *The Greatest Work in the World, or, The Evangelization of All Peoples in the Present Century.* New York: Revell, 1891.

———. *God and Missions Today.* Chicago: Moody, 1955.

———. *The Heart of the Gospel: Twelve Sermons Delivered at the Metropolitan Tabernacle in the Autumn of 1891.* 2nd edition. London: Passmore and Alabaster, 1892.

———. *In Christ Jesus, or, The Sphere of the Believer's Life.* Los Angeles: Horton, 1898.

———. *The Keswick Movement in Precept and Practice.* New York: Funk & Wagnalls, 1903.

———. *The Modern Mission Century Viewed as a Cycle of Divine Working: A Review of the Missions of the Nineteenth century with Reference to the Superintending Providence of God.* New York: Baker & Taylor, 1901.

———. *Vital Union with Christ.* Grand Rapids: Zondervan, 1961.

Pollock, John Charles. *The Keswick Story: The Authorized History of the Keswick Convention.* London: Hodder & Stoughton, 1964.

Pyles, Franklin Arthur. "The Missionary Eschatology of A. B. Simpson." In *Birth of a Vision: Essays on the Ministry and Thought of Albert B. Simpson, Founder of the Christian and Missionary Alliance*, edited by David F. Hartzfeld and Charles Nienkirchen, 29–48. Beaverlodge, AB: His Dominion, 1986.

Randall, Ian M. "Spiritual Renewal and Social Reform: Attempts to Develop Social Awareness in the Early Keswick Movement." *Vox Evangelica* 23 (1993) 67–86.

Randall, Ian M., and David Hilborn. *One Body in Christ: The History and Significance of the Evangelical Alliance.* Carlisle, UK: Paternoster, 2001.

Reid, Darrel Robert. "'Jesus Only': the Early Life and Presbyterian Ministry of Albert Benjamin Simpson, 1843–1881." PhD diss., Queen's University, 1994.

Rennie, Ian. "Nineteenth Century Roots of Contemporary Prophetic Interpretation." In *Handbook of Biblical Prophecy*, edited by Carl E. Armerding and W. Ward Gasque, 41–59. Grand Rapids: Baker, 1977.

Rivard, Eugene. "Rediscovering the Music of A. B. Simpson." In *Birth of a Vision: Essays on the Ministry and Thought of Albert B. Simpson, Founder of the Christian and Missionary Alliance*, edited by David F. Hartzfeld and Charles Nienkirchen, 75–106. Beaverlodge, AB: His Dominion, 1986.

Robert, Dana Lee. "Arthur Tappan Pierson and Forward Movements of Late Nineteenth-Century Evangelicalism." PhD diss., Yale University, 1984.

———. "The Crisis of Missions: Premillennial Mission Theory and the Origins of Independent Evangelical Missions." In *Earthen Vessels: American Evangelicals and Foreign Missions, 1880–1980*, edited by Joel A. Carpenter and Wilbert R. Schenk, 29–49. Grand Rapids: Eerdmans, 1990.

———. "The Legacy of Adoniram Judson Gordon." *International Bulletin of Missionary Research* 11 (1987) 176–81.

———. "The Legacy of Arthur Tappan Pierson." *International Bulletin of Missionary Research* 8 (1984) 120–24.

———. *Occupy Until I Come: A. T. Pierson and the Evangelization of the World*. Grand Rapids: Eerdmans, 2003.

———. "The Origin of the Student Volunteer Watchword: 'The Evangelization of the World in This Generation.'" *International Bulletin of Missionary Research* (1986) 146–49.

Robertson, Darrel M. *The Chicago Revival, 1876: Society and Revivalism in a Nineteenth-Century City*. Studies in Evangelicalism 9. Metuchen, NJ: Scarecrow, 1989.

Ross, Kenneth R. "Calvinists in Controversy: John Kennedy, Horatius Bonar, and the Moody Mission of 1873–74." *Scottish Bulletin of Evangelical Theology* 9 (1991) 51–63.

Russell, C. Allyn. "Adoniram Judson Gordon: Nineteenth-Century Fundamentalist." *American Baptist Quarterly* 4 (1985) 61–89.

Sandeen, Ernest R. "Baptists and Millenarianism." *Foundations* 13 (1970) 18–25.

———. "Millennialism." In *The Rise of Adventism: Religion and Society in Mid-Nineteenth-Century America*, edited by Edwin S. Gaustad, 104–18. New York: Harper & Row, 1974.

———. *The Roots of Fundamentalism: British and American Millenarianism, 1800–1930*. Chicago: University of Chicago Press, 1970.

Sawin, John S. "The Fourfold Gospel." In *Birth of a Vision: Essays on the Ministry and Thought of Albert B. Simpson, Founder of the Christian and Missionary Alliance*, edited by David F. Hartzfeld and Charles Nienkirchen, 1–28. Beaverlodge, al: His Dominion, 1986.

Senft, Frederic H. "Introduction." In *The Fourfold Gospel* by Albert B. Simpson, 7–9. Camp Hill, PA: Christian Publications, 1984.

Shanks, T. J., editor. *A College of Colleges*. Chicago: Revell, 1887.

———, editor. *College Students at Northfield, or, A College of Colleges, no. 2. Containing addresses by D. L. Moody, J. Hudson Taylor . . . and others*. New York: Revell, 1888.

Shelley, Bruce. "A. J. Gordon and the Impact of Biblical Criticism." *Journal of the Evangelical Theological Society* 13 (1970) 109–18.

Simpson, Albert B. *Acts of the Apostles*. Christ in the Bible 16. New York: Alliance Press, 1904.

———. *Christ in the Tabernacle*. Originally titled *Christ in the Tabernacle*. Tabernacle Sermons 9. New York: Christian Alliance Publishing, 1888. Reprint, Camp Hill, PA: Christian Publications, 1985.

———. *The Christ Life*. New Edition with Select Poems. The Alliance Colportage Series. Harrisburg, PA: Christian Publications, 1925.

———. "Christ's Coming the Key to All Questions of the Age." *The Christian and Missionary Alliance* (9 March 1898) 228–29.

———. *The Coming One*. New York: Christian Alliance Publishing, 1912.

———. *The Cross of Christ*. New York. Christian Alliance Publishing, 1910. Reprint, Camp Hill, PA: Christian Publications, 1994.

———. *Discovery of Divine Healing*. New York: Alliance Press, 1903.

———. "Distinctive Teachings." *Word, Work, and World* (July 1887) 2.

———. *Divine Healing in the Atonement*. New York: Christian Alliance Publishing, 1890.

———. *Earnests of the Coming Age and Other Sermons*. New York: Christian Alliance Publishing, 1921.

———. "Editorial." *Alliance Weekly*, 8 February 1913, 289.

———. "Editorial." *Alliance Weekly*, 22 December 1917, 177.

———. "Editorial." *Christian Alliance and Foreign Missionary Weekly*, 24 January 1896, 84.

———. "Editorial." *Christian and Missionary Alliance*, 12 March 1897, 252.

———. "Editorial." *Christian and Missionary Alliance*, 3 June 1899, 8.

———. "Editorial." *Living Truths* (August 1905) 441–43.

———. "Editorial Paragraphs." *Word, Work, and World* (October 1886) 251–52.

———. *The Epistle to the Romans*. Christ in the Bible 17. Harrisburg, PA: Christian Publications, 1930.

———. *Evangelistic Addresses*. New York: Christian Alliance Publishing, 1926.

———. *Foundation Truths Respecting Sanctification*. New York: Christian Alliance Publishing, 1885.

———. *The Fourfold Gospel*. Camp Hill, PA: Christian Publications, 1984.

———. "Friday Meeting Talks." *Christian and Missionary Alliance Weekly*, October 13, 1900, 207.

———. *Friday Meeting Talks, or, Divine Prescriptions for the Sick and Suffering*. 2 vols. Nyack, NY: Christian Alliance Publishing, 1894–1899.

———. *The Fullness of Christ, or, Christian Life in the New Testament*. New York: Christian Alliance Publishing, 1890.

———. "Futurist and Praeterist." *The Christian Alliance and Foreign Missionary Weekly*, 20 April 1894, 416.

———. *The Gospel of Healing*. New York: Christian Alliance Publishing, 1915.

———. *The Gospel of John*. Christ in the Bible 15. New York, Christian Alliance Publishing, 1904.

———. *The Gospel of Matthew*. Christ in the Bible 13. Harrisburg, PA: Christian Publications, 1930.

———. "A Great Life Closed." *The Christian and Missionary Alliance*, 6 January 1900, 1.

———. *Heart Messages for Sabbaths at Home*. Nyack, NY: Christian Alliance Publishing, 1899.

———. "The Highest Christian Life." *Christian Alliance and Foreign Missionary Weekly*, 3 August 1894, 100–102.

———. "How I Was Led to Believe in Pre-millennialism." *Christian Alliance and Missionary Weekly*, 13 November 1891, 298–99.

———. *Inquiries and Answers*. New York: Word, Work, and World Publishing, 1887.

———. "Is the Christian Alliance an Evangelical Body?" *Christian Alliance* 29 (April 1892) 274.

———. *Isaiah*. 2Nd revised edition. Christ in the Bible 7. New York: Alliance Press, 1907.

———. *The King's Business*. New York: The Word, Work, and World Publishing, 1886.

———. *Kings and Prophets of Israel and Judah*. Christ in the Bible 6. New York: Alliance, 1903.

———. *A Larger Christian Life*. New York: Christian Alliance Publishing, 1890.

———. "Looking For and Hasting Forward." *The Christian and Missionary Alliance*, 15 June 1898, 557–58.

———. *The Lord for the Body: With Questions and Answers on Divine Healing*. New York: Christian Alliance Publishing, 1925.

———. "The Lord's Second Coming." *Word, Work, and World* (October 1886) 168–70.

———. *The Love Life of the Lord*. New York: Christian Alliance Publishing, 1895.

———. *Millennial Chimes: A Collection of Poems*. New York: Christian Alliance Publishing, 1894.

———. *Missionary Messages*. Camp Hill, PA: Christian Publications, 1925.

———. "The Missionary Standpoints of the Alliance." *Christian and Missionary Alliance*, 31 March 1900, 205.

———. "Missionary Wings." *The Christian and Missionary Alliance*, 8 August 1908, 315–16, 320.

———. "Motives to Missions." *The Christian and Missionary Alliance* (October 1899) 349.

———. "Mutual Responsibility." *The Christian Alliance and Foreign Missionary Weekly* (17 August 1894) 148–50.

———. "A New Missionary Alliance." *Word, Work, and World* (June 1887) 365–68.

———. [No title]. *The Gospel in All Lands* (February 1880) 60.

———. *The Old Faith and the New Gospels: Special Addresses on Christianity and Modern Thought*. New York: Alliance, 1911.

———. *Practical Christianity*. Brooklyn, NY: Christian Alliance Publishing, 1901.

———. *The Self Life and the Christ Life*. South Nyack, NY: Christian Alliance Publishing, 1897.

———. "Simpson Scrapbook, 1971." TMS (photocopy). Special Collections, Archibald-Thomson Library, Ambrose University College, Calgary, Alberta, Canada.

———. "A Story of Providence." *Living Truths* (March 1907) 150–64.

———. *The Story of the Christian and Missionary Alliance*. Nyack, NY: Christian and Missionary Alliance, 1900.

———. "That Blessed Hope." *Word, Work, and World* (May 1882) 166.

———. "Thy Kingdom Come." In *Hymns of the Christian Life*. Harrisburg, PA: Christian Publications, 1936.

———. "Timely Spiritual Watch Words." *Living Truths* (February 1906) 65.

———. *Wholly Sanctified*. Harrisburg, PA: Christian Publications, 1925.

Smith, David J. "Albert Benjamin Simpson: An Integrated Spirituality with Christ as the Centre." http://online.auc-nuc.ca/alliancestudies/dsmith/djs_spirituality. html

Smith, Timothy Lawrence. *Called unto Holiness: The Story of the Nazarenes*. Kansas City, MO: Nazarene Publishing House, 1962.

———. *Revivalism and Social Reform in Mid-Nineteenth-Century America*. New York: Abingdon, 1957.

Stein, Stephen J. "Editor's Introduction." In *Apocalyptic Writings*, edited by Stephen J. Stein, 1–94. The Works of Jonathan Edwards Series 5. New Haven: Yale University Press, 1977.

Stevenson, Herbert F., editor. *Keswick's Authentic Voice: Sixty-Five Dynamic Addresses Delivered at the Keswick Convention, 1875–1957*. Grand Rapids: Zondervan, 1959.

Stoesz, Samuel J. *Sanctification: An Alliance Distinctive*. Camp Hill, PA: Christian Publications, 1992.

———. *Understanding My Church: A Profile of the Christian and Missionary Alliance*. Revised edition. Camp Hill, PA: Christian Publications, 1983.

Stowe, Harriet Beecher, et al. *The Second Coming of Christ*. Chicago: Moody, n.d.

Sung, Kee Ho. "The Doctrine of the Second Advent of Jesus Christ in the Writings of Albert B. Simpson with Special Reference to His Premillennialism." PhD diss., Drew University, 1990.

Synan, Vinson. *In the Latter Days: The Outpouring of the Holy Spirit in the Twentieth Century*. Ann Arbor: Servant, 1984.

Thomas, George M. *Revivalism and Cultural Change: Christianity, Nation Building, and the Market in the Nineteenth-Century United States*. Chicago: University of Chicago Press, 1989.

Thompson, A. E. *The Life of A. B. Simpson*. New York: Christian Alliance Publishing, 1920.

Thompson, W. Ralph. "An Appraisal of the Keswick and Wesleyan Contemporary Positions." *Wesleyan Theological Journal* 1 (1966) 11–20.

Torrey, R. A. *Divine Healing: Does God Perform Miracles Today?* New York: Revell, 1924.

Tozer, A. W. *Wingspread*. Camp Hill, PA: Christian Publications, 1943.

Truesdale, Albert. "Reification of the Experience of Entire Sanctification in the American Holiness Movement." *Wesley Theological Journal* 31 (1996) 95–119.

Tucker, Ruth A. *From Jerusalem to Irian Jaya: A Biographical History of Christian Missions*. Grand Rapids: Zondervan, 1983.

Turnbull, W. M. "A Christian Educator." In *The Life of A. B. Simpson*, by A. E. Thompson, 214–23. New York: Christian Alliance Publishing, 1920.

———. "Introduction." In *Missionary Messages* by Albert B. Simpson, 6–7. Camp Hill, PA: Christian Publications, 1925.

Van De Walle, Bernie A. "How High of a Christian Life?: A. B. Simpson and the Classic Doctrine of Theosis." *Wesleyan Theological Journal* 43.2 (Fall 2008) 136–53.

Vaudry, Richard W. *The Free Church in Victorian Canada, 1844–1861*. Waterloo, ON: Wilfred Laurier University Press, 1989.

Waldvogel, Edith Lydia. "'The Overcoming Life:' A Study in the Reformed Evangelical Origins of Pentecostalism." PhD diss., Harvard University, 1977.

Warfield, Benjamin B. *Counterfeit Miracles*. 1918. Reprint, Carlisle, PA: Banner of Truth Trust, 1976.

———. *Perfectionism*. Vol. 2. 1931. Reprint, Grand Rapids: Baker, 1981.

———. *Selected Shorter Writings of Benjamin B. Warfield*. Vol. 1. Edited by John E. Meeter. Phillipsburg, NJ: Presbyterian and Reformed, 1970.

Weber, Eugen. *Apocalypses: Prophecies, Cults, and Millennial Beliefs through the Ages*. Toronto: Random House of Canada, 1999.

Weber, Timothy P. "Happily at the Edge of the Abyss: Popular Premillennialism in America." *Ex Auditu* 6 (1990) 87–100.

———. *Living in the Shadow of the Second Coming: American Premillennialism, 1875–1982*. Enlarged edition. Grand Rapids: Academie, 1983.

Wells, David F. "The Collision of Views on the Atonement." *Bibliotheca Sacra* 144 (1987) 363–76.

Wesley, John. "Minutes of Several Conversations between the Rev. Mr. Wesley and others, from the year 1744, to 1789." In *The Works of John Wesley*, 8:299–338. Kansas City: Nazarene Publishing House, 1960.

———. "A Plain Account of Christian Perfection as Believed and Taught by the Reverend Mr. John Wesley, from the year 1725, to the year 1777." In *The Works of John Wesley*, 11:366–446. Kansas City, MO: Nazarene Publishing House, 1960.

West, Nathaniel, editor. *Second Coming of Christ. Premillennial Essays of the Prophetic Conference, Held in the Church of the Holy Trinity, New York City*. Chicago: Revell, 1879.

White, Charles Edward. *The Beauty of Holiness: Phoebe Palmer as Theologian, Revivalist, Feminist, and Humanitarian*. Grand Rapids: Francis Asbury, 1986.

Wind, A. "The Protestant Missionary Movement from 1789–1963." In *Missiology: An Ecumenical Introduction*, edited by F. J. Verstraelen, A. Camps, L. A. Hoedemaker, and M. R. Spindler, 237–52. Grand Rapids: Eerdmans, 1995.

CPSIA information can be obtained at www.ICGtesting.com
Printed in the USA
BVOW06*0815070516

447188BV00010B/36/P